THE ESSAYS OF WARREN BUFFETT: LESSONS FOR CORPORATE AMERICA

CELEBRATING
50
20
· 50 Years of Berkshire Hathaway ·
20 Years of Buffett's Essays

THE ESSAYS OF WARREN BUFFETT: LESSONS FOR CORPORATE AMERICA

ESSAYS BY

WARREN E. BUFFETT

SELECTED, ARRANGED, AND INTRODUCED BY

LAWRENCE A. CUNNINGHAM

FOURTH EDITION

Library of Congress Cataloging-in-Publication Data

Cunningham, Lawrence A., 1962-
Buffett, Warren E., 1930-
    The Essays of Warren Buffett: Lessons for Corporate America /
selected, arranged, and introduced by Lawrence A. Cunningham—4th
ed.
    324 p. 26 cm.
    Includes previously copyrighted material. Reprinted with per-
mission. Includes bibliographical references and index.

    1. Corporations—United States—Finance. 2. Corporate gov-
ernance—United States.   3. Investments—United States.
4. Stocks—United States. 5. Consolidation and merger of corporations—United States. 6. Accounting—United States. I. Buffett,
Warren E. II. Cunningham, Lawrence A. III. Title.

    HG4061.B8372 2001
    (OCoLC) 38497313

ISBN: 978-1-61163-758-8

**Copies of this collection are available in larger quantities at special
discounts to use for teaching, training, promotions, premiums or other
purposes. For more information, please contact the editor and publisher, Lawrence A. Cunningham, at lacunningham@law.gwu.edu.**

"The speech I love is a simple, natural speech,

the same on paper as in the mouth;

a speech succulent and sinewy, brief and compressed,

not so much dainty and well-combed as vehement and brusque."

Michel de Montaigne
***The Essays of Montaigne* (1580)**

"The sincerity and marrow of the man reaches to his sentences.

I know not anywhere a book that seems less written.

Cut these words and they would bleed; they are vascular and alive."

Ralph Waldo Emerson
***Representative Man* (1850)**
(Referring to Montaigne and his *Essays*)

"Some books should be tasted, some devoured,

but only a few should be chewed and digested thoroughly."

Francis Bacon
***The Essays of Francis Bacon* (1696)**

TABLE OF CONTENTS

The year 2015 marks the fiftieth anniversary of Berkshire Hathaway under Warren Buffett's leadership, a milestone worth commemorating. The tenure sets a record for chief executive not only in duration but in value creation and philosophizing. This fourth edition of *The Essays of Warren Buffett: Lessons for Corporate America* celebrates its twentieth anniversary. As the book Buffett autographs most, its popularity and longevity attest to the widespread appetite for this unique compilation of Buffett's thoughts that is at once comprehensive, non-repetitive, and digestible.

The original edition of *The Essays of Warren Buffett* was the centerpiece of a symposium held two decades ago at the Benjamin N. Cardozo School of Law under the auspices of its Heyman Center on Corporate Governance. This gathering brought hundreds of students together for a two-day dissection of all the ideas in the compilation, featuring a series of vibrant debates among some 30 distinguished professors, investors, and managers, with Warren and Charles T. Munger, Berkshire's vice chairman, participating throughout from their seats in the front row.

In the two decades since initial publication, I have often taught *The Essays*, as this book has come to be known, in my classes and seminars at four different universities. The book is adopted by scores of professors at other schools for classes such as investment, finance and accounting. Investment firms have distributed copies to their professional employees and clients as part of training programs. I am grateful for the positive feedback from these students, teachers, and other users and delighted to know that the lessons are being taught.

As in previous editions of *The Essays*, this one retains the architecture and philosophy of the original edition but adds selections from Warren's most recent annual shareholder letters, including his fiftieth anniversary retrospective. All the letters are woven together into a fabric that reads as a complete and coherent narrative of a sound business and investment philosophy. As an aid to all readers, and to enable readers of the previous editions to see what is new in this one, a disposition table at the end of the book shows the various places in this collection where selections from each year's letter appear. Footnotes throughout indicate the year of the annual report from which essays are taken. To avoid interrupting the narrative flow, omissions of text within excerpts are not indicated by ellipses or other punctuation.

The new edition is called for not because anything has changed about the fundamentals of Warren's sound business and investment philosophy but because articulation of that philosophy is always delivered in the context of contemporary events and business conditions. So periodic updating is warranted to maintain its currency.

In preparing the previous editions, I was aided by numerous people, to whom I expressed gratitude in those editions, and I want to thank them again. Among those, I especially thank Warren Buffett. His generosity not only made the symposium possible but his participation enriched it manifold; his willingness to entrust the rearrangement and ongoing republication of his letters to me is a great honor. His partner, Charlie Munger, deserves explicit repeated thanks too, for not only did he participate in the 1996 symposium from the front row he also graciously chaired, on a moment's notice, one of the panels. He also granted me permission to reprint some of his letters in this collection as well, including his fiftieth anniversary retrospective.

At Berkshire's 2011 annual meeting, Charlie stressed to me how different Berkshire had become in the fifteen years since our symposium—and yet how much it remained the same. Back then, Berkshire looked more like a mutual fund, with 80 percent of its assets in minority common stock positions and 20 percent in wholly owned businesses; today, the ratio is reversed and Berkshire looks more like a conglomerate. Yet then and now, the company and its constituents are united by a core set of common values, values defined by the tone Warren set at the top and that animate *The Essays*. I thank the many thousands of devoted fans, followers, and friends who have been avid readers of *The Essays* over the past 20 years and look forward to continuing our journey.

Lawrence A. Cunningham
New York City
November 1, 2015

INTRODUCTION

Lawrence A. Cunningham

Experienced readers of Warren Buffett's letters to the shareholders of Berkshire Hathaway Inc. have gained an enormously valuable informal education. The letters distill in plain words all the basic principles of sound business practices. On selecting managers and investments, valuing businesses, and using financial information profitably, the writings are broad in scope, and long on wisdom. By arranging these writings as thematic essays, this collection presents a synthesis of the overall business and investment philosophy intended for dissemination to a wide general audience.

The central theme uniting Buffett's lucid essays is that the principles of fundamental business analysis, first formulated by his teachers Ben Graham and David Dodd, should guide investment practice. Linked to that theme are management principles that define the proper role of corporate managers as the stewards of invested capital, and the proper role of shareholders as the suppliers and owners of capital. Radiating from these main themes are practical and sensible lessons on the entire range of important business issues, from accounting to mergers to valuation.

Buffett has applied these traditional principles as chief executive officer of Berkshire Hathaway, a company with roots in a group of textile operations begun in the early 1800s. Buffett took the helm of Berkshire in 1965, when its book value per share was $19.46 and its intrinsic value per share far lower. Today, its book value per share is around $100,000 and its intrinsic value far higher. The growth rate in book value per share during that period is about 20% compounded annually.

Berkshire is now a holding company engaged in 80 distinct business lines. Berkshire's most important business is insurance, carried on through various companies including its 100% owned subsidiary, GEICO Corporation, among the largest auto insurers in the United States, and General Re Corporation, one of the largest reinsurers in the world. In 2010, Berkshire acquired Burlington Northern Santa Fe Railway Company, among the largest railroads in North America, and has long owned and operated large energy companies.

Some Berkshire subsidiaries are massive: ten would be included in the Fortune 500 if they were stand-alone companies. Its other interests are so vast that, as Buffett writes: "when you are looking at Berkshire, you are looking across corporate America."

3

Examples: food, clothing, building materials, tools, equipment, newspapers, books, transportation services and financial products. Berkshire also owns large equity interests in major corporations—including American Express, Coca-Cola, International Business Machines (IBM), and Wells Fargo—along with half the equity of Heinz and a valuable option to buy a sizeable stake in Bank of America.

Buffett and Berkshire Vice Chairman Charlie Munger built this sprawling enterprise by investing in businesses with excellent economic characteristics and run by outstanding managers. While they prefer negotiated acquisitions of 100% of such a business at a fair price, they take a "double-barreled approach" of buying on the open market less than 100% of some businesses when they can do so at a pro-rata price well below what it would take to buy 100%.

The double-barreled approach pays off handsomely. The value of marketable securities in Berkshire's portfolio, on a per share basis, increased from $4 in 1965 to more than $140,000 by 2015, a 19% compound annual gain. Per share operating earnings increased in the same period from just over $4 to nearly $11,000, a compound annual gain of about 20.6%. According to Buffett, these results follow not from any master plan but from focused investing—allocating capital by concentrating on businesses with outstanding economic characteristics and run by first-rate managers.

——————————————

Buffett views Berkshire as a partnership among him, Munger and other shareholders, and virtually all his net worth is in Berkshire stock. His economic goal is long-term—to maximize Berkshire's per share intrinsic value by owning all or part of a diversified group of businesses that generate cash and above-average returns. In achieving this goal, Buffett foregoes expansion for the sake of expansion and foregoes divestment of businesses so long as they generate some cash and have good management.

Berkshire retains and reinvests earnings when doing so delivers at least proportional increases in per share market value over time. It uses debt sparingly and sells equity only when it receives as much in value as it gives. Buffett penetrates accounting conventions, especially those that obscure real economic earnings.

These owner-related business principles, as Buffett calls them, are the organizing themes of the accompanying essays. As organized, the essays constitute an elegant and instructive manual on management, investment, finance, and accounting. Buffett's basic principles form the framework for a rich range of positions on the wide variety of issues that exist in all aspects of business. They go far beyond mere abstract platitudes. It is true that investors should focus on fundamentals, be patient, and exercise good judgment based on common sense. In Buffett's essays, these advisory tidbits are anchored in the more concrete principles by which Buffett lives and thrives.

CORPORATE GOVERNANCE

For Buffett, managers are stewards of shareholder capital. The best managers think like owners in making business decisions. They have shareholder interests at heart. But even first-rate managers will sometimes have interests that conflict with those of shareholders. How to ease those conflicts and to nurture managerial stewardship have been constant objectives of Buffett's long career and a prominent theme of his essays. The essays address some of the most important governance problems.

The first is the importance of forthrightness and candor in communications by managers to shareholders. Buffett tells it like it is, or at least as he sees it, and laments that he is in the minority. Berkshire's annual report is not glossy; Buffett prepares its contents using words and numbers people of average intelligence can understand; and all investors get the same information at the same time. Buffett and Berkshire avoid making predictions, a bad managerial habit that too often leads other managers to fudge their financial reports.

Besides the owner-orientation reflected in Buffett's disclosure practice and the owner-related business principles summarized above, the next management lesson is to dispense with formulas of managerial structure. Contrary to textbook rules on organizational behavior, mapping an abstract chain of command on to a particular business situation, according to Buffett, does little good. What matters is selecting people who are able, honest, and diligent. Having first-rate people on the team is more important than designing hierarchies and clarifying who reports to whom about what and at what times.

Special attention must be paid to selecting a chief executive officer (CEO) because of three major differences Buffett identifies between CEOs and other employees. First, standards for measuring a CEO's performance are inadequate or easy to manipulate, so a CEO's performance is harder to measure than that of most workers. Second, no one is senior to the CEO, so no senior person's performance can be measured either. Third, a board of directors cannot serve that senior role since relations between CEOs and boards are conventionally congenial.

Major reforms are often directed toward aligning management and shareholder interests or enhancing board oversight of CEO performance. Stock options for management were touted as one method; greater emphasis on board processes was another. Separating the identities and functions of the Chairman of the Board and the CEO or appointment of standing audit, nominating and compensation committees were also heralded as promising reforms. Perhaps the most pervasive prescription is to populate boards with independent directors. None of these innovations has solved governance problems, however, and some have exacerbated them.

The best solution, Buffett instructs, is to take great care in identifying CEOs who will perform capably regardless of weak structural restraints. In public companies, large institutional shareholders must exercise their power to oust CEOs that do not measure up to the demands of corporate stewardship. Outstanding CEOs do not need a lot of coaching from owners, although they can benefit from having a similarly outstanding board. Directors therefore must be chosen for their business savvy, their interest, and their owner-orientation. According to Buffett, one of the greatest problems among boards in corporate America is that members are selected for other reasons, such as adding diversity or prominence to a board—or, famously, independence.

Most reforms are painted with a broad brush, without noting the major differences among types of board situations that Buffett identifies. For example, director power is weakest in the case where there is a controlling shareholder who is also the manager. When disagreements arise between the directors and management, there is little a director can do other than to object and, in serious circumstances, resign. Director power is strongest at the other extreme, where there is a controlling shareholder who does not participate in management. The directors can take matters directly to the controlling shareholder when disagreement arises.

The most common situation, however, is a corporation without a controlling shareholder. This is where management problems are most acute, Buffett says. It would be helpful if directors could supply necessary discipline, but board congeniality usually prevents that. To maximize board effectiveness in this situation, Buffett believes the board should be small in size and composed mostly of outside directors. The strongest weapon a director can wield in these situations remains the threat to resign.

All these situations do share a common characteristic: the terrible manager is a lot easier to confront or remove than the mediocre manager. A chief problem in traditional governance structures was that in corporate America evaluation of chief executive officers was never conducted in regular meetings in the absence of that chief executive. Holding regular meetings without the chief executive to review his or her performance can produce a marked improvement in corporate governance.

The CEOs at Berkshire's various operating companies enjoy a unique position in corporate America. They are given a simple set of commands: to run their business as if (1) they are its sole owner, (2) it is the only asset they hold, and (3) they can never sell or merge it for fifty years. This enables Berkshire CEOs to manage with a long-term horizon ahead of them, something alien to the CEOs of public companies whose short-term oriented shareholders obsess with meeting the latest quarterly earnings estimate. Short-term results matter, of course, but the Berkshire approach avoids any pressure to achieve them at the expense of strengthening long-term competitive advantages.

If only short-term results mattered, many managerial decisions would be much easier, particularly those relating to businesses whose economic characteristics have eroded. Consider the time horizon trade-off Buffett faced in managing what he considers the worst investment he ever made, buying Berkshire in the first place. The economic characteristics of Berkshire's old textile business had begun to erode by the late 1970s. Buffett had hoped to devise a reversal of its misfortunes, noting how important Berkshire's textile business was to its employees and local communities in New England, and how able and understanding management and labor had been in addressing the economic difficulties. Buffett kept the ailing plant alive through 1985, but a financial reversal could not be achieved and Buffett eventually closed it. This balancing of short-term results with long-term prospects based on community trust is not easy, but it is intelligent. Kindred lessons carry over to other sectors in which Berkshire invests, such as the newspaper business in the internet age, and highly regulated industries, such as energy and railroads, in which Buffett sees an implicit social compact between private enterprise and regulatory overseers.

Sometimes management interests conflict with shareholder interests in subtle or easily disguised ways. Take corporate philanthropy, for example. At most major corporations, management allocates a portion of corporate profit to charitable concerns. The charities are chosen by management, for reasons often unrelated either to corporate interests or shareholder interests. Most state laws permit management to make these decisions, so long as aggregate annual donations are reasonable in amount, usually not greater than 10% of annual net profits.

Berkshire does things differently. It makes no contributions at the parent company level and allows its subsidiaries to follow philanthropic policies they had in effect before Berkshire acquired them. For two decades, moreover, Berkshire used an imaginative program through which its shareholders designated the charities to which Berkshire would donate and in what amounts. Nearly all shareholders participated, donating tens of millions of dollars annually to thousands of different charities. Political controversy over the abortion issue, however, interfered with this program. Political activists organized boycotts of Berkshire's products to protest particular charitable donations that were made, destroying this feature of Berkshire's "partnership" approach.

The plan to align management and shareholder interests by awarding executives stock options not only was oversold, but also subtly disguised a deeper division between those interests that the options created. Many corporations pay their managers stock options whose value increases simply by retention of earnings, rather than by superior deployment of capital. As Buffett explains, however, simply by retaining and reinvesting earnings, managers can report annual earnings increases without so much as lifting a finger to improve real returns on capital. Stock options thus often rob shareholders of wealth and allocate the booty to executives. Moreover, once granted, stock options are often irrevocable, unconditional, and benefit managers without regard to individual performance.

It is possible to use stock options to instill a managerial culture that encourages owner-like thinking, Buffett agrees. But the alignment will not be perfect. Shareholders are exposed to the downside risks of sub-optimal capital deployment in a way that an option holder is not. Buffett therefore cautions shareholders who are reading proxy statements about approving option plans to be aware of the asymmetry in this kind of alignment. Many shareholders rationally ignore proxy statements, but the abuse of stock options should be on the front-burner of shareholders, particularly institutional investors that periodically engage in promoting corporate governance improvements.

Buffett emphasizes that performance should be the basis for executive pay decisions. Executive performance should be measured by profitability, after profits are reduced by a charge for the capital employed in the relevant business or earnings retained by it. If stock options are used, they should be related to individual performance, rather than corporate performance, and priced based on business value. Better yet, as at Berkshire, stock options should simply not be part of an executive's compensation. After all, exceptional managers who earn cash bonuses based on the performance of their own business can simply buy stock if they want to; if they do, they "truly walk in the shoes of owners," Buffett says. And owners' interests are paramount on executive pay as with other corporate governance topics Buffett addresses, such as risk management, corporate compliance and financial reporting.

Corporate culture is among the most important yet least quantifiable factors in assessing a business. At Berkshire, culture runs deep. It begins with the tone at the top set at Omaha headquarters by the norms and values that animate this collection. Berkshire's culture also permeates the subsidiaries that call Berkshire home and the managers of the many and varied business units that comprise Berkshire today. Remarkably for a vast conglomerate comprised of a sprawling and diverse group of businesses, Berkshire's culture is uniform and enduring and, Buffett says, will help Berkshire prosper long after he and Munger leave the scene.

FINANCE AND INVESTING

The most revolutionary investing ideas of the past forty years were those called modern finance theory. This is an elaborate set of ideas that boil down to one simple and misleading practical implication: it is a waste of time to study individual investment opportunities in public securities. According to this view, you will do better by randomly selecting a group of stocks for a portfolio by throwing darts at the stock tables than by thinking about whether individual investment opportunities make sense.

One of modern finance theory's main tenets is modern portfolio theory. It says that you can eliminate the peculiar risk of any security by holding a diversified portfolio—that is, it formalizes the folk slogan "don't put all your eggs in one basket." The risk that is left over is the only risk for which investors will be compensated, the story goes.

This leftover risk can be measured by a simple mathematical term—called beta—that shows how volatile the security is compared to the market. Beta measures this volatility risk well for securities that trade on efficient markets, where information about publicly traded securities is swiftly and accurately incorporated into prices. In the modern finance story, efficient markets rule.

Reverence for these ideas was not limited to ivory tower academics, in colleges, universities, business schools, and law schools, but became standard dogma throughout financial America in the past forty years, from Wall Street to Main Street. Many professionals still believe that stock market prices always accurately reflect fundamental values, that the only risk that matters is the volatility of prices, and that the best way to manage that risk is to invest in a diversified group of stocks.

Being part of a distinguished line of investors stretching back to Graham and Dodd which debunks standard dogma by logic and experience, Buffett thinks most markets are not purely efficient and that equating volatility with risk is a gross distortion. Accordingly, Buffett worried that a whole generation of MBAs and JDs, under the influence of modern finance theory, was at risk of learning the wrong lessons and missing the important ones.

A particularly costly lesson of modern finance theory came from the proliferation of portfolio insurance—a computerized technique for readjusting a portfolio in declining markets. The promiscuous use of portfolio insurance helped precipitate the stock market crash of October 1987, as well as the market break of October 1989. It nevertheless had a silver lining: it shattered the modern finance story being told in business and law schools and faithfully being followed by many on Wall Street.

Ensuing market volatility could not be explained by modern finance theory, nor could mountainous other phenomena relating to the behavior of small capitalization stocks, high dividend-yield stocks, and stocks with low price-earnings ratios. The *piece de resistance* of market inefficiency was the technology and Internet stock bubble that blew up in the late 1990s and early 2000s, marked by stock price gyrations that spasmodically bounced between euphoria and gloom without the remotest nexus to business value. Growing numbers of skeptics emerged to say that beta does not really measure the investment risk that matters, and that capital markets are really not efficient enough to make beta meaningful anyway.

In stirring up the discussion, people started noticing Buffett's record of successful investing and calling for a return to the Graham-Dodd approach to investing and business. After all, for more than forty years Buffett has generated average annual returns of 20% or better, which double the market average. For more than twenty years before that, Ben Graham's Graham-Newman Corp. had done the same thing. As Buffett emphasizes, the stunning performances at Graham-Newman and at Berkshire deserve respect: the sample sizes were significant; they were conducted over an extensive time period, and were not skewed by a few fortunate experiences; no data-mining was involved; and the performances were longitudinal, not selected by hindsight.

Threatened by Buffett's performance, stubborn devotees of modern finance theory resorted to strange explanations for his success. Maybe he is just lucky—the monkey who typed out *Hamlet*—or maybe he has inside access to information that other investors do not. In dismissing Buffett, modern finance enthusiasts still insist that an investor's best strategy is to diversify based on betas or dart throwing, and constantly reconfigure one's portfolio of investments.

Buffett responds with a quip and some advice: the quip is that devotees of his investment philosophy should probably endow chaired professorships at colleges and universities to ensure the perpetual teaching of efficient market dogma; the advice is to ignore modern finance theory and other quasi-sophisticated views of the market and stick to investment knitting. That can best be done for many people through long-term investment in an index fund. Or it can be done by conducting hard-headed analyses of businesses within an investor's competence to evaluate. In that kind of thinking, the risk that matters is not beta or volatility, but the possibility of loss or injury from an investment.

Assessing that kind of investment risk requires thinking about a company's management, products, competitors, and debt levels. The inquiry is whether after-tax returns on an investment are at least equal to the purchasing power of the initial investment plus a fair rate of return. The primary relevant factors are the long-term economic characteristics of a business, the quality and integrity of its management, and future levels of taxation and inflation. Maybe these factors are vague, particularly compared with the seductive precision of beta, but the point is that judgments about such matters cannot be avoided, except to an investor's disadvantage.

Buffett points out the absurdity of beta by observing that "a stock that has dropped very sharply compared to the market . . . becomes 'riskier' at the lower price than it was at the higher price"—that is how beta measures risk. Equally unhelpful, beta cannot distinguish the risk inherent in "a single-product toy company selling pet rocks or hula hoops from another toy company whose sole product is Monopoly or Barbie." But ordinary investors can make those distinctions by thinking about consumer behavior and the way consumer products companies compete, and can also figure out when a huge stock-price drop signals a buying opportunity.

Contrary to modern finance theory, Buffett's investment knitting does not prescribe diversification. It may even call for concentration, if not of one's portfolio, then at least of its owner's mind. As to concentration of the portfolio, Buffett reminds us that Keynes, who was not only a brilliant economist but also an astute investor, believed that an investor should put fairly large sums into two or three businesses he knows something about and whose management is trustworthy. On that view, risk rises when investments and investment thinking are spread too thin. A strategy of financial and mental concentration may reduce risk by raising both the intensity of an investor's thinking about a business and the comfort level he must have with its fundamental characteristics before buying it.

The fashion of beta, according to Buffett, suffers from inattention to "a fundamental principle: It is better to be approximately right than precisely wrong." Long-term investment success depends not on studying betas and maintaining a diversified portfolio, but on recognizing that as an investor, one is the owner of a business. Reconfiguring a portfolio by buying and selling stocks to accommodate the desired beta-risk profile defeats long-term investment success. Such "flitting from flower to flower" imposes huge transaction costs in the forms of spreads, fees and commissions, not to mention taxes. Buffett jokes that calling someone who trades actively in the market an investor "is like calling someone who repeatedly engages in one-night stands a romantic." Investment knitting turns modern finance theory's folk wisdom on its head: instead of "don't put all your eggs in one basket," we get Mark Twain's advice from *Pudd'nhead Wilson*: "Put all your eggs in one basket—and watch that basket."

Buffett learned the art of investing from Ben Graham as a graduate student at Columbia Business School in the 1950s and later working at Graham-Newman. In a number of classic works, including *The Intelligent Investor*, Graham introduced some of the most profound investment wisdom in history. It rejects a prevalent but mistaken mind-set that equates price with value. On the contrary, Graham held that price is what you pay and value is what you get. These two things are rarely identical, but most people rarely notice any difference.

One of Graham's most profound contributions is a character who lives on Wall Street, Mr. Market. He is your hypothetical business partner who is daily willing to buy your interest in a business or sell you his at prevailing market prices. Mr. Market is moody, prone to manic swings from joy to despair. Sometimes he offers prices way higher than value; sometimes he offers prices way lower than value. The more manic-depressive he is, the greater the spread between price and value, and therefore the greater the investment opportunities he offers. Buffett reintroduces Mr. Market, emphasizing how valuable Graham's allegory of the overall market is for disciplined investment knitting—even though Mr. Market would be unrecognizable to modern finance theorists.

Another leading prudential legacy from Graham is his margin-of-safety principle. This principle holds that one should not make an investment in a security unless there is a sufficient basis for believing that the price being paid is substantially lower than the value being delivered. Buffett follows the principle devotedly, noting that Graham had said that if forced to distill the secret of sound investment into three words, they would be: margin of safety. Over forty years after first reading that, Buffett still thinks those are the right words. While modern finance theory enthusiasts cite market efficiency to deny there is a difference between price (what you pay) and value (what you get), Buffett and Graham regard it as all the difference in the world.

That difference also shows that the term "value investing" is a redundancy. All true investing must be based on an assessment of the relationship between price and value. Strategies that do not employ this comparison of price and value do not amount to investing at all, but to speculation—the hope that price will rise, rather than the conviction that the price being paid is lower than the value being obtained. Many professionals make another common mistake, Buffett notes, by distinguishing between "growth investing" and "value investing." Growth and value, Buffett says, are not distinct. They are integrally linked since growth must be treated as a component of value.

Nor does the phrase "relational investing" resonate with Buffett. The term became popular in the mid-1990s, describing a style of investing that is designed to reduce the costs of the separation of shareholder ownership from managerial control by emphasizing shareholder involvement and monitoring of management. Many people incorrectly identified Buffett and Berkshire as exemplars of this descriptive label. It is true that Buffett buys big blocks in a few companies and sticks around a long time. He also only invests in businesses run by people he trusts. But that is about as far as the similarity goes. If Buffett were pressed to use an adjective to describe his investment style, it would be something like "focused" or "intelligent" investing. Yet even these words ring redundant; the unadorned term *investor* best describes Buffett.

Other misuses of terms include blurring the difference between speculation and arbitrage as methods of sound cash management; the latter being very important for companies like Berkshire that generate substantial excess cash. Both speculation and arbitrage are ways to use excess cash rather than hold it in short-term cash equivalents such as commercial paper. Speculation describes the use of cash to bet on lots of corporate events based on rumors of unannounced coming transactions. Arbitrage, traditionally understood to mean exploiting different prices for the same thing on two different markets, for Buffett describes the use of cash to take short-term positions in a few opportunities that have been publicly announced. It exploits different prices for the same thing at different times. Deciding whether to employ cash this way requires evaluating four commonsense questions based on information rather than rumor: the probability of the event occurring, the time the funds will be tied up, the opportunity cost, and the downside if the event does not occur.

The circle of competence principle is the third leg of the Graham/Buffett stool of intelligent investing, along with Mr. Market and the margin of safety. This commonsense rule instructs investors to consider investments only concerning businesses they are capable of understanding with a modicum of effort. It is this commitment to stick with what he knows that enables Buffett to avoid the mistakes others repeatedly make, particularly those who feast on the fantasies of fast riches promised by technological fads and new era rhetoric that have recurrently infested speculative markets over the centuries.

In all investment thinking, one must guard against what Buffett calls the "institutional imperative." It is a pervasive force in which institutional dynamics produce resistance to change, absorption of available corporate funds, and reflexive approval of suboptimal CEO strategies by subordinates. Contrary to what is often taught in business and law schools, this powerful force often interferes with rational business decision-making. The ultimate result of the institutional imperative is a follow-the-pack mentality producing industry imitators, rather than industry leaders—what Buffett calls a lemming-like approach to business.

Every reader of this collection will savor, and want to share with family and friends, Buffett's compelling essays on the use of debt. Aptly dubbed "Life and Debt," these exquisitely explain both the temptation and perils of leverage in personal and corporate finance.

INVESTMENT ALTERNATIVES

All these investment principles are animated in Buffett's lively essays concerning investment opportunities. After explaining his preference for investing in productive assets, and defining what this means, a series of essays addresses a wide range of alternatives, starting with junk and zero-coupon bonds and preferred stock. Challenging both Wall Street and the academy, Buffett again draws on Graham's ideas to reject the "dagger thesis" advanced to defend junk bonds. The dagger thesis, using the metaphor of the intensified care an automobile driver would take facing a dagger mounted on the steering wheel, overemphasizes the disciplining effect that enormous amounts of debt in a capital structure exerts on management.

Buffett points to the large numbers of corporations that failed in the early 1990s recession under crushing debt burdens to dispute academic research showing that higher interest rates on junk bonds more than compensated for their higher default rates. He attributes this error to a flawed assumption recognizable to any first-year statistics student: that historical conditions prevalent during the study period would be identical in the future. They would not. Further illuminating the folly of junk bonds is an essay in this collection by Charlie Munger that discusses Michael Milken's approach to finance.

Wall Street tends to embrace ideas based on revenue-generating power, rather than on financial sense, a tendency that often perverts good ideas to bad ones. In a history of zero-coupon bonds, for example, Buffett shows that they can enable a purchaser to lock in a compound rate of return equal to a coupon rate that a normal bond paying periodic interest would not provide. Using zero-coupons thus for a time enabled a borrower to borrow more without need of additional free cash flow to pay the interest expense. Problems arose, however, when zero-coupon bonds started to be issued by weaker and weaker credits whose free cash flow could not sustain increasing debt obligations. Buffett laments, "as happens in Wall Street all too often, what the wise do in the beginning, fools do in the end."

Many culprits contributed to the financial crisis of 2008, among them the proliferation of derivative financial instruments, which Buffett's essays written several years earlier had warned about. Contemporary financial engineering has produced an explosion of complex instruments known as derivatives, because their fluctuating value is *derived* from movements in a contractually designated benchmark. Proponents believe that these devices are useful to manage risk—and Berkshire from time to time takes modest positions in derivatives contracts that Buffett judges as mis-priced. But while proponents also believe that derivatives tend to reduce overall *systemic* risk, Buffett presciently observed that they may have the opposite effect. They are hard to value, valuations can change rapidly and they create linkages and interdependencies among financial institutions. Buffett cautioned that the combination of these factors could mean that, should a single event cause challenges in one sector, that could spread rapidly to others with a domino effect bringing devastating systemic consequences. Such was the case with the crisis of 2008.

Buffett acknowledges that his view on derivative risks may be influenced by his aversion to any kind of mega-catastrophe risk that would jeopardize Berkshire's status as a fortress of financial strength. But this is no arm-chair opinion, for Buffett endured several years of direct experience in managing a derivatives dealership that came along with Berkshire's acquisition of the Gen Re reinsurance company. Buffett explains the unpleasant consequences of not dumping the business immediately but notes how it could not be sold and contained a maze of long term liabilities that took several painful years to unwind. Buffett offers extensive meditation on this experience so that others can learn from the Berkshire trials.

COMMON STOCK

Buffett recalls that on the day Berkshire listed on the New York Stock Exchange in 1988, he told Jimmy Maguire, the specialist in Berkshire stock, "I will consider you an enormous success if the next trade in this stock is about two years from now." While Buffett jokes that Maguire "didn't seem to get enthused about that," he emphasizes that his mind-set when he buys any stock is "if we aren't happy owning a piece of that business with the Exchange closed, we're not happy owning it with the Exchange open." While Berkshire and Buffett are investors for the long haul, too many others are temporary traders of common stock—whose actions pose high costs.

A significant portion of corporate earnings are dissipated through frictional costs associated with trading. Trading is the rearrangement of who owns what shares. The rearrangement entails paying commissions to brokers, fees to investment managers and cash to financial planners and business consultants who sell even more advice during this process. Of late, these frictional costs have escalated into whole industries that describe themselves variously as hedge funds and private equity firms. Buffett estimates that total costs may consume some 20% of the country's total annual corporate earnings.

Unlike many CEOs, who desire their company's stock to trade at the highest possible prices in the market, Buffett prefers Berkshire stock to trade at or around its intrinsic value—neither materially higher nor lower. Such linkage means that business results during one period will benefit the people who owned the company during that period. Maintaining the linkage requires a shareholder group with a collective long-term, business-oriented investment philosophy, rather than a short-term, market-oriented strategy.

Buffett notes Phil Fisher's suggestion that a company is like a restaurant, offering a menu that attracts people with particular tastes. Berkshire's long-term menu emphasizes that the costs of trading activity can impair long-term results. Indeed, Buffett estimates that the transaction costs of actively traded stocks—broker commissions and market-maker spreads—often amount to 10% or more of earnings. Avoiding or minimizing such costs is necessary for long-term investment success, and Berkshire's listing on the New York Stock Exchange helped contain those costs.

Corporate dividend policy is a major capital allocation issue, always of interest to investors but infrequently explained to them. Buffett's essays clarify this subject, emphasizing that "capital allocation is crucial to business and investment management." Since 1998, Berkshire's common stock has been priced in the market at above $50,000 per share and the company's book value, earnings, and intrinsic value have steadily increased well in excess of average annual rates. Yet the company has never effected a stock split, and has not paid a cash dividend in over three decades.

Apart from reflecting the long-term menu and minimization of transaction costs, Berkshire's dividend policy also reflects Buffett's conviction that a company's earnings payout versus retention decision should be based on a single test: each dollar of earnings should be retained if retention will increase market value by at least a like amount; otherwise it should be paid out. Earnings retention is justified only when "capital retained produces incremental earnings equal to, or above, those generally available to investors."

Like many of Buffett's simple rules, this one is often ignored by corporate managers, except of course when they make dividend decisions for their subsidiaries. Earnings are often retained for non-owner reasons, such as expanding the corporate empire or furnishing operational comfort for management.

Things are so different at Berkshire, Buffett said at the symposium, that under his test Berkshire "might distribute more than 100% of the earnings," to which Charlie Munger chimed in "You're damn right." That has not been necessary, however, for throughout Buffett's stewardship at Berkshire, opportunities for superior returns on capital have been discovered, and exploited.

Share repurchases of underpriced stock can be a value-enhancing way to allocate capital, though these are not always what they seem. In the 1980s and early 1990s, share buy-backs were uncommon and Buffett credited managers who recognized that the purchase of a share priced at $1 but with a value of $2 would rarely be inferior to any other use of corporate funds. Alas, as often happens, the imitators stepped in and now you frequently see companies paying $2 to buy back shares worth $1. These value-destroying share repurchases often are intended to prop up a sagging share price or to offset the simultaneous issuing of stock under stock options exercised at much lower prices.

Buffett lays out the rationale and terms under which Berkshire occasionally embarks on share repurchase programs: when the stock trades at a deep discount to intrinsic value. That makes the investment an easy case, of clear value to continuing holders, though Buffett has mixed feelings about repurchasing as Berkshire's selling shareholders cash in at a discount. The solution: clear disclosure to enable such selling holders to make an informed decision.

Stock splits are another common action in corporate America that Buffett points out disserve owner interests. Stock splits have three consequences: they increase transaction costs by promoting high share turnover; they attract shareholders with short-term, market-oriented views who unduly focus on stock market prices; and, as a result of both of those effects, they lead to prices that depart materially from intrinsic business value. With no offsetting benefits, splitting Berkshire's stock would be foolish. Not only that, Buffett adds, it would threaten to reverse five decades of hard work that has attracted to Berkshire a shareholder group comprised of more focused and long-term investors than probably any other major public corporation.

Two important consequences have followed from Berkshire's high stock price and its dividend policy. First, the extraordinarily high share price impaired the ability of Berkshire shareholders to effect gifts of their equity interest to family members or friends, though Buffett has offered a few sensible strategies like bargain sales to donees to deal with that. Second, Wall Street engineers tried to create securities that would purport to mimic Berkshire's performance and that would be sold to people lacking an understanding of Berkshire, its business, and its investment philosophy.

In response to these consequences, Berkshire effected a recapitalization by creating a new class of stock, called the Class B shares, and sold it to the public. The Class B shares have 1,500th the rights of the existing Class A shares, except with respect to voting rights they have 1/10,000th of those of the A shares. Accordingly, the Class B shares should (and do) trade somewhere in the vicinity of 1/1,500th of the market price of the Class A shares.

The Class A shares are convertible into Class B shares, giving Berkshire shareholders a do-it-yourself mechanism to effect a stock-split to facilitate gift giving and so on. More importantly, the Berkshire recapitalization would halt the marketing of Berkshire clones that contradict all the basic principles Buffett believes in. These clones—investment trusts that would buy and sell Berkshire shares according to demand for units in the trust—would have imposed costs on shareholders. If held by people who do not understand Berkshire's business or philosophy, they would have caused spikes in Berkshire's stock price, producing substantial deviations between price and value.

The Class B shares are designed to be attractive only to investors who share Buffett's philosophy of focused investing. For example, in connection with the offering of the Class B shares,
Buffett and Munger emphasized that Berkshire stock was, at that
time, not underpriced in the market. They said that neither of
them would buy the Class A shares at the market price nor the
Class B shares at the offering price. The message was simple: do
not buy these securities unless you are prepared to hold them for
the long term. The effort to attract only long-term investors to the
Class B shares appears to have worked: trading volume in the
shares after the offering was far below average for Big Board
stocks.

Some expressed surprise at Buffett and Munger's cautionary
statement, since most managers tell the market that newly-issued
equity in their companies is being offered at a very good price.
You should not be surprised by Buffett and Munger's disclosure,
however. A company that sells its stock at a price less than its
value is stealing from its existing shareholders. Quite plausibly,
Buffett considers that a crime.

MERGERS AND ACQUISITIONS

Berkshire's acquisition policy is the double-barreled approach:
buying portions or all of businesses with excellent economic characteristics and run by managers Buffett and Munger like, trust, and
admire. Contrary to common practice, Buffett argues that in buying all of a business, there is rarely any reason to pay a premium.

The rare cases involve businesses with franchise characteristics—those that can raise prices without impairing sales volume or
market share and only require incremental capital investment to
increase both. Even ordinary managers can operate franchise businesses to generate high returns on capital. The second category of
rare cases is where extraordinary managers exist who can achieve
the difficult feat of identifying underperforming businesses, and apply extraordinary talent to unlock hidden value.

These two categories are extremely limited, and certainly do
not explain the hundreds of high-premium takeovers that occur annually. Buffett attributes high-premium takeovers outside those
unusual categories to three motives of buying-managers: the thrill
of an acquisition, the thrill of enhanced size, and excessive optimism about synergies.

In paying for acquisitions, Berkshire issues stock only when it
receives as much in business value as it gives. This has become

increasingly difficult for Berkshire to do. This is the case because Berkshire has assembled the business equivalent of the art collection at the Louvre. Enhancing the value of the existing collection by adding a single new Botticelli is difficult enough, and even more so if you have to give up part of your Rembrandt collection to get it.

It has also been difficult for managers of other companies to follow this rule, but not so much because of the wonderful collection of businesses they have. Instead, Buffett notes that sellers in stock acquisitions measure the purchase price by the market price of the buyer's stock, not by its intrinsic value. If a buyer's stock is trading at a price equal to, say, half its intrinsic value, then a buyer who goes along with that measure gives twice as much in business value as it is getting. Its manager, usually rationalizing his or her actions by arguments about synergies or size, is elevating thrill or excessive optimism above shareholder interests.

Moreover, acquisitions paid for in stock are too often (almost always) described as "buyer buys seller" or "buyer acquires seller." Buffett suggests clearer thinking would follow from saying "buyer sells part of itself to acquire seller," or something of the sort. After all, that is what is happening; and it would enable one to evaluate what the buyer is giving up to make the acquisition.

Another abuse of shares-as-currency is the practice of greenmail, the repurchase of shares from an unwanted suitor at a premium price to fend off his acquisition overtures. While share repurchases available to all shareholders can be value enhancing, Buffett condemns this practice as simply another form of corporate robbery.

Nearly as reprehensible, a second Charlie Munger essay in this collection explains, were the cascades of leveraged buy-outs (LBOs) in the 1980s. Permissive laws made LBOs hugely profitable, Munger tells us, but the LBOs weakened corporations, put a heavy premium on cash generation to pay for enormous debt obligations, and raised the average cost of acquisitions.

Value-enhancing acquisitions are hard enough to find without the added burden of higher average costs for all of them. Indeed, most acquisitions are value-decreasing, Buffett says. Finding the best value-enhancing transactions requires concentrating on opportunity costs, measured principally against the alternative of buying small pieces of excellent businesses through stock market purchases. Such concentration is alien to the manager obsessed with synergies and size, but a vital part of Berkshire's double-barreled investment approach.

Berkshire has additional advantages in acquisitions: a high quality stock to pay with and a substantial amount of managerial autonomy to offer once a deal is done—both rare in an acquiring company, Buffett says. Buffett also puts his money where his mouth is, reminding prospective sellers that Berkshire has acquired many of its businesses from family or other closely-held groups, and inviting them to check with every previous seller about Berkshire's initial promises measured against its later actions. In short, Berkshire seeks to be the buyer of choice for attractive business sellers—a lesson so important that it explains why Buffett prefers to retain rather than sell even those acquired businesses that struggle against business headwinds.

VALUATION AND ACCOUNTING

Buffett's essays provide an entertaining and illuminating tutorial on understanding and using financial information. In dissecting significant aspects of generally accepted accounting principles (GAAP), Buffett shows both their importance and limits in understanding and valuing any business or investment. Buffett demystifies key topics that highlight the important differences between accounting earnings and economic earnings, between accounting goodwill and economic goodwill, and between accounting book value and intrinsic value. These are essential tools for any investor's or manager's valuation toolbox.

Aesop was to fables of the ancient world what Buffett is to business essays in ours. The essayist invokes the fabulist to show that valuation has been the same across the millennia—Aesop said "a bird in the hand is worth two in the bush" and Buffett extends the principle to dollars. Valuation is counting cash, not hopes or dreams, a lesson many should have learned amid the late 1990s tech rush bubble that burst when everyone finally realized there were few birds in the bushes. It is doubtful everyone learned the lesson, however, for it has been taught repeatedly since Aesop's time and yet, well, it has been taught repeatedly since Aesop's time.

A leading example of Buffett's specialized toolkit is intrinsic value, "the discounted value of the cash that can be taken out of a business during its remaining life." Though simple to state, calculating intrinsic value is neither easy nor objective. It depends on estimation of both future cash flows and interest rate movements.

But it is what ultimately matters about a business. Book value, in contrast, is easy to calculate, but of limited use. So too with market price, at least for most companies. Differences between intrinsic value and book value and market price may be hard to pin down. They can go either way, but there will almost certainly be differences.

Buffett emphasizes that useful financial statements must enable a user to answer three basic questions about a business: approximately how much a company is worth, its likely ability to meet its future obligations, and how good a job its managers are doing in operating the business. Buffett laments that GAAP conventions make these determinations difficult, and indeed almost any accounting system will be hard pressed to furnish completely accurate answers given the complexities of business. Acknowledging the monumental difficulty of inventing an accounting system superior to GAAP, Buffett articulates a range of concepts that go a longer way toward making financial information useful to investors and managers.

Consider a concept Buffett calls "look-through earnings." GAAP investment accounting calls for using the consolidation method for majority-owned equity, which means full reporting of all line items from the investee's financial statements on the parent's. For equity investments from 20% to 50%, GAAP calls for reporting the investor's proportionate share of earnings of the investee on its statements; for investments of less than 20%, GAAP provides that only dividends actually received by the investor be recorded, rather than any share of the investee's earnings. These accounting rules obscure a major factor in Berkshire's economic performance: the undistributed earnings of its investee companies are an enormous part of Berkshire's value, but would not be reported on its financial statements prepared using GAAP.

Recognizing that it is not the size of an equity investment that determines its value, but how the undistributed earnings are deployed, Buffett develops the concept of look-through earnings to gauge Berkshire's economic performance. Look-through earnings add to Berkshire's own net earnings the undistributed earnings in investee companies, less an incremental amount for taxes. Look-through earnings are not different from GAAP earnings for many businesses. But they are for Berkshire and probably are for many individual investors. Accordingly, individuals can adopt a similar approach for their own portfolios and try to design a portfolio that delivers the highest possible look-through earnings over the long term.

The difference between accounting goodwill and economic goodwill is well-known, but Buffett's lucidity makes the subject refreshing. Accounting goodwill is essentially the amount by which the purchase price of a business exceeds the fair value of the assets acquired (after deducting liabilities). It is recorded as an asset on the balance sheet and then amortized as an annual expense, usually over forty years. So the accounting goodwill assigned to that business decreases over time by the aggregate amount of that expense.

Economic goodwill is something else. It is the combination of intangible assets, like brand name recognition, that enable a business to produce earnings on tangible assets, like plant and equipment, in excess of average rates. The amount of economic goodwill is the capitalized value of that excess. Economic goodwill tends to increase over time, at least nominally in proportion to inflation for mediocre businesses, and more than that for businesses with solid economic or franchise characteristics. Indeed, businesses with more economic goodwill relative to tangible assets are hurt far less by inflation than businesses with less of that.

These differences between accounting goodwill and economic goodwill entail the following insights. First, the best guide to the value of a business's economic goodwill is what it can earn on unleveraged net tangible assets, excluding charges for amortization of goodwill. Therefore when a business acquires other businesses, and the acquisitions are reflected in an asset account called goodwill, analysis of that business should ignore the amortization charges. Second, since economic goodwill should be measured at its full economic cost, i.e., before amortization, evaluation of a possible business acquisition should be conducted without regard to those amortization charges as well.

Buffett emphasizes, however, that the same does not hold for depreciation charges—these should not be ignored because they are real economic costs. He makes this point in explaining why Berkshire always shows its shareholders the results of operations with respect to acquired businesses net of any purchase price adjustments GAAP requires.

It is common on Wall Street to value businesses using a calculation of cash flows equal to (a) operating earnings plus (b) depreciation expense and other non-cash charges. Buffett regards that calculation as incomplete. After taking (a) operating earnings and adding back (b) non-cash charges, Buffett argues that you must then subtract something else: *(c)* required reinvestment in the business. Buffett defines *(c)* as "the average amount of capitalized expenditures for plant and equipment, etc., that the business requires to fully maintain its long-term competitive position and its unit volume." Buffett calls the result of *(a)* + *(b)* − *(c)* "owner earnings."

When *(b)* and *(c)* differ, cash flow analysis and owner earnings analysis differ too. For most businesses, *(c)* usually exceeds *(b)*, so cash flow analysis usually overstates economic reality. In all cases where *(c)* differs from *(b)*, calculation of owner earnings enables one to appraise performance more accurately than would analysis of GAAP earnings, or cash flows affected by purchase price accounting adjustments. That is why Berkshire supplementally reports owner earnings for its acquired businesses, rather than rely solely on GAAP earnings figures, or cash flow figures.

Accounting Shenanigans

The ultimate point to understand about accounting is that it is a form. As a form, it can be manipulated. Buffett shows just how severe the manipulation can be with a satire written by Ben Graham in the 1930s. The advanced bookkeeping methods Graham presents enable his phantom US Steel to report "phenomenally enhanced" earnings without cash outlays or changes in operating conditions or sales. Except in its lampooning spirit, Graham's illustration of accounting chicanery is not all that different from what is often seen coming out of corporate America.

GAAP has enough trouble. Yet two groups of people make it worse: those who try to overcome GAAP requirements by stretching their accounting imagination, and those who deliberately employ GAAP to facilitate financial fraud. The former is especially hard to deal with, as Buffett suggests in illustrating how debate on accounting for stock options reveals the parochialism of many executives and accountants. For example, criticizing the view against treating stock options as expenses when granted, Buffett delivers this laconic argument: "If options aren't a form of compensation, what are they? If compensation isn't an expense, what is? And, if expenses shouldn't go into the calculation of earnings, where in the world should they go?" So far, he has gotten no answers.

The quest for integrity in financial reporting is endless, with new flavors of accounting machinations developed regularly and periodically sweeping the chief financial officer (CFO) suites of corporate America. The latest product to catch on is accounting for "restructurings," a label given to a whole range of maneuvers that enable managers to engage in age-old earnings management and smoothing techniques with greater felicity and deftness than ever before. Other examples concern estimates required when calculating pension liabilities and the timing of sales of assets that generate gains or losses to influence reported earnings. Investors beware.

One clear lesson from Buffett's discussions of financial information is that accounting has inherent limits, even though it is absolutely essential. Despite enormous managerial leeway in reporting earnings and potential abuse, financial information can be of great use to investors. Buffett uses it every day, and has allocated billions of dollars doing it. So it is possible to make important investment decisions on the basis of available financial information if one exercises knowledgeable judgment. That judgment may include making adjustments to determine look-through earnings, owner earnings and intrinsic value.

TAXATION

Bringing this collection full circle, the concluding essays note the obvious but often overlooked tax advantages of long-term investment. Linking life's two certainties, the final essay includes one of Buffett's many jokes about his personal longevity: if enjoying life promotes longevity, he is jeopardizing Methuselah's record (969 years). At the symposium featuring this collection, someone asked what effect Buffett's death would have on Berkshire stock. Another answered, "a negative effect." Without missing a beat, Buffett quipped: "It won't be as negative for the holders as it will be for me."

PROLOGUE: OWNER-RELATED BUSINESS PRINCIPLES[1]

In some ways, our shareholder group is a rather unusual one, and this affects our manner of reporting to you. For example, at the end of each year about 98% of the shares outstanding are held by people who also were shareholders at the beginning of the year. Therefore, in our annual report we build upon what we have told you in previous years instead of restating a lot of material. You get more useful information this way, and we don't get bored.

Furthermore, perhaps 90% of our shares are owned by investors for whom Berkshire is their largest security holding, very often far and away the largest. Many of these owners are willing to spend a significant amount of time with the annual report, and we attempt to provide them with the same information we would find useful if the roles were reversed.

In contrast, we include no narrative with our quarterly reports. Our owners and managers both have very long time-horizons in regard to this business, and it is difficult to say anything new or meaningful each quarter about events of long-term significance.

But when you do receive a communication from us, it will come from the fellow you are paying to run the business. Your Chairman has a firm belief that owners are entitled to hear directly from the CEO as to what is going on and how he evaluates the business, currently and prospectively. You would demand that in a private company; you should expect no less in a public company. A once-a-year report of stewardship should not be turned over to a staff specialist or public relations consultant who is unlikely to be in a position to talk frankly on a manager-to-owner basis.

We feel that you, as owners, are entitled to the same sort of reporting by your managers as we feel is owed to us at Berkshire Hathaway by managers of our business units. Obviously, the degree of detail must be different, particularly where information would be useful to a business competitor or the like. But the general scope, balance, and level of candor should be similar. We don't expect a public relations document when our operating managers tell us what is going on, and we don't feel you should receive such a document.

In large part, companies obtain the shareholder constituency that they seek and deserve. If they focus their thinking and communications on short-term results or short-term stock market con-

---

1 [1979; 1996 Owner's Manual—originally 1983, and annually beginning in 1988, with occasional modification.]

sequences they will, in large part, attract shareholders who focus on the same factors. And if they are cynical in their treatment of investors, eventually that cynicism is highly likely to be returned by the investment community.

Phil Fisher, a respected investor and author, once likened the policies of the corporation in attracting shareholders to those of a restaurant attracting potential customers. A restaurant could seek a given clientele—patrons of fast foods, elegant dining, Oriental food, etc.—and eventually obtain an appropriate group of devotees. If the job were expertly done, that clientele, pleased with the service, menu, and price level offered, would return consistently. But the restaurant could not change its character constantly and end up with a happy and stable clientele. If the business vacillated between French cuisine and take-out chicken, the result would be a revolving door of confused and dissatisfied customers.

So it is with corporations and the shareholder constituency they seek. You can't be all things to all men, simultaneously seeking different owners whose primary interests run from high current yield to long-term capital growth to stock market pyrotechnics, etc.

The reasoning of managements that seek large trading activity in their shares puzzles us. In effect, such managements are saying that they want a good many of the existing clientele continually to desert them in favor of new ones—because you can't add lots of new owners (with new expectations) without losing lots of former owners.

We much prefer owners who like our service and menu and who return year after year. It would be hard to find a better group to sit in the Berkshire Hathaway shareholder "seats" than those already occupying them. So we hope to continue to have a very low turnover among our owners, reflecting a constituency that understands our operation, approves of our policies, and shares our expectations. And we hope to deliver on those expectations.

1. *Although our form is corporate, our attitude is partnership. Charlie Munger and I think of our shareholders as owner-partners, and of ourselves as managing partners. (Because of the size of our shareholdings we are also, for better or worse, controlling partners.) We do not view the company itself as the ultimate owner of our business assets but instead view the company as a conduit through which our shareholders own the assets.*

Charlie and I hope that you do not think of yourself as merely owning a piece of paper whose price wiggles around daily and that is a candidate for sale when some economic or political event makes you nervous. We hope you instead visualize yourself as a part owner of a business that you expect to stay with indefinitely, much as you might if you owned a farm or apartment house in partnership with members of your family. For our part, we do not view Berkshire shareholders as faceless members of an ever-shifting crowd, but rather as co-venturers who have entrusted their funds to us for what may well turn out to be the remainder of their lives.

The evidence suggests that most Berkshire shareholders have indeed embraced this long-term partnership concept. The annual percentage turnover in Berkshire's shares is a fraction of that occurring in the stocks of other major American corporations, even when the shares I own are excluded from the calculation.

In effect, our shareholders behave in respect to their Berkshire stock much as Berkshire itself behaves in respect to companies in which it has an investment. As owners of, say, Coca-Cola or American Express shares, we think of Berkshire as being a non-managing partner in two extraordinary businesses, in which we measure our success by the long-term progress of the companies rather than by the month-to-month movements of their stocks. In fact, we would not care in the least if several years went by in which there was no trading, or quotation of prices, in the stocks of those companies. If we have good long-term expectations, short-term price changes are meaningless for us except to the extent they offer us an opportunity to increase our ownership at an attractive price.

2. *In line with Berkshire's owner-orientation, most of our directors have a major portion of their net worth invested in the company. We eat our own cooking.*

Charlie's family has the majority of its net worth in Berkshire shares; I have more than 99%. In addition, many of my relatives—my sisters and cousins, for example—keep a huge portion of their net worth in Berkshire stock.

Charlie and I feel totally comfortable with this eggs-in-one-basket situation because Berkshire itself owns a wide variety of truly extraordinary businesses. Indeed, we believe that Berkshire is close to being unique in the quality and diversity of the businesses in which it owns either a controlling interest or a minority interest of significance.

Charlie and I cannot promise you results. But we can guarantee that your financial fortunes will move in lockstep with ours for whatever period of time you elect to be our partner. We have no interest in large salaries or options or other means of gaining an "edge" over you. We want to make money only when our partners do and in exactly the same proportion. Moreover, when I do something dumb, I want you to be able to derive some solace from the fact that my financial suffering is proportional to yours.

3.   *Our long-term economic goal (subject to some qualifications mentioned later) is to maximize Berkshire's average annual rate of gain in intrinsic business value on a per-share basis. We do not measure the economic significance or performance of Berkshire by its size; we measure by per-share progress. We are certain that the rate of per-share progress will diminish in the future—a greatly enlarged capital base will see to that. But we will be disappointed if our rate does not exceed that of the average large American corporation.*

4.   *Our preference would be to reach our goal by directly owning a diversified group of businesses that generate cash and consistently earn above-average returns on capital. Our second choice is to own parts of similar businesses, attained primarily through purchases of marketable common stocks by our insurance subsidiaries. The price and availability of businesses and the need for insurance capital determine any given year's capital allocation.*

In recent years, we have made a number of acquisitions. Though there will be dry years, we expect to make many more in the decades to come, and our hope is that they will be large. If these purchases approach the quality of those we have made in the past, Berkshire will be well served.

The challenge for us is to generate ideas as rapidly as we generate cash. In this respect, a depressed stock market is likely to present us with significant advantages. For one thing, it tends to reduce the prices at which entire companies become available for purchase. Second, a depressed market makes it easier for our insurance companies to buy small pieces of wonderful businesses—including additional pieces of businesses we already own—at attractive prices. And third, some of those same wonderful businesses, such as Coca-Cola, are consistent buyers of their own shares, which means that they, and we, gain from the cheaper prices at which they can buy.

Overall, Berkshire and its long-term shareholders benefit from a sinking stock market much as a regular purchaser of food benefits from declining food prices. So when the market plummets—as it will from time to time—neither panic nor mourn. It's good news for Berkshire.

5. *Because of our two-pronged approach to business owner-ship and because of the limitations of conventional accounting, con-solidated reported earnings may reveal relatively little about our true economic performance. Charlie and I, both as owners and manag-ers, virtually ignore such consolidated numbers. However, we will also report to you the earnings of each major business we control, numbers we consider of great importance. These figures, along with other information we will supply about the individual businesses, should generally aid you in making judgments about them.*

To state things simply, we try to give you in the annual report the numbers and other information that really matter. Charlie and I pay a great deal of attention to how well our businesses are doing, and we also work to understand the environment in which each business is operating. For example, is one of our businesses en-joying an industry tailwind or is it facing a headwind? Charlie and I need to know exactly which situation prevails and to adjust our expectations accordingly. We will also pass along our conclusions to you.

Over time, the large majority of our businesses have exceeded our expectations. But sometimes we have disappointments, and we will try to be as candid in informing you about those as we are in describing the happier experiences. When we use unconventional measures to chart our progress, we will try to explain these con-cepts and why we regard them as important. In other words, we believe in telling you how we think so that you can evaluate not only Berkshire's businesses but also assess our approach to man-agement and capital allocation.

6. *Accounting consequences do not influence our operating or capital-allocation decisions. When acquisition costs are similar, we much prefer to purchase $2 of earnings that is not reportable by us under standard accounting principles than to purchase $1 of earn-ings that is reportable. This is precisely the choice that often faces us since entire businesses (whose earnings will be fully reportable) fre-quently sell for double the pro-rata price of small portions (whose earnings will be largely unreportable). In aggregate and over time, we expect the unreported earnings to be fully reflected in our intrin-sic business value through capital gains.*

We have found over time that the undistributed earnings of our investees, in aggregate, have been as fully as beneficial to Berkshire as if they had been distributed to us (and therefore had been included in the earnings we officially report). This pleasant result has occurred because most of our investees are engaged in truly outstanding businesses that can often employ incremental capital to great advantage, either by putting it to work in their businesses or by repurchasing their shares. Obviously, every capital decision that our investees have made has not benefitted us as shareholders, but overall we have garnered far more than a dollar of value for each dollar they have retained. We consequently regard look-through earnings as realistically portraying our yearly gain from operations.

7. *We use debt sparingly and, when we do borrow, we attempt to structure our loans on a long-term fixed-rate basis. We will reject interesting opportunities rather than over-leverage our balance sheet. This conservatism has penalized our results but it is the only behavior that leaves us comfortable, considering our fiduciary obligations to policyholders, lenders and the many equity holders who have committed unusually large portions of their net worth to our care. (As one of the Indianapolis "500" winners said: "To finish first, you must first finish.")*

The financial calculus that Charlie and I employ would never permit our trading a good night's sleep for a shot at a few extra percentage points of return. I've never believed in risking what my family and friends have and need in order to pursue what they don't have and don't need.

Besides, Berkshire has access to two low-cost, non-perilous sources of leverage that allow us to safely own far more assets than our equity capital alone would permit: deferred taxes and "float," the funds of others that our insurance business holds because it receives premiums before needing to pay out losses. Both of these funding sources have grown rapidly and now total about $146 billion.

Better yet, this funding to date has often been cost-free. Deferred tax liabilities bear no interest. And as long as we can break even in our insurance underwriting, the cost of the float developed from that operation is zero. Neither item, of course, is equity; these are real liabilities. But they are liabilities without covenants or due dates attached to them. In effect, they give us the benefit of debt—an ability to have more assets working for us—but saddle us with none of its drawbacks.

Of course, there is no guarantee that we can obtain our float in the future at no cost. But we feel our chances of attaining that goal are as good as those of anyone in the insurance business. Not only have we reached the goal in the past (despite a number of important mistakes by your Chairman), our 1996 acquisition of GEICO materially improved our prospects for getting there in the future.

[Since 2011], we expect additional borrowings to be concentrated in our utilities and railroad businesses, loans that are non-recourse to Berkshire. Here, we will favor long-term, fixed-rate loans.

8. *A managerial "wish list" will not be filled at shareholder expense. We will not diversify by purchasing entire businesses at control prices that ignore long-term economic consequences to our shareholders. We will only do with your money what we would do with our own, weighing fully the values you can obtain by diversifying your own portfolios through direct purchases in the stock market.*

Charlie and I are interested only in acquisitions that we believe will raise the *per-share* intrinsic value of Berskhire's stock. The size of our paychecks or our offices will never be related to the size of Berkshire's balance sheet.

9. *We feel noble intentions should be checked periodically against results. We test the wisdom of retaining earnings by assessing whether retention, over time, delivers shareholders at least $1 of market value for each $1 retained. To date, this test has been met. We will continue to apply it on a five-year rolling basis. As our net worth grows, it is more difficult to use retained earnings wisely.*

I should have written the "five-year rolling basis" sentence differently, an error I didn't realize until I received a question about this subject at the 2009 annual meeting.

When the stock market has declined sharply over a five-year stretch, our market-price premium to book value has sometimes shrunk. And when that happens, we fail the test as I improperly formulated it. In fact, we fell far short as early as 1971-75, well before I wrote this principle in 1983.

The five-year test should be: (1) during the period did our book-value gain exceed the performance of the S&P; and (2) did our stock consistently sell at a premium to book, meaning that every $1 of retained earnings was always worth more than $1? If these tests are met, retaining earnings has made sense.

10. *We will issue common stock only when we receive as much in business value as we give. This rule applies to all forms of issuance—not only mergers or public stock offerings, but stock-for-debt swaps, stock options, and convertible securities as well. We will not sell small portions of your company—and that is what the issu-*

ance of shares amounts to—on a basis inconsistent with the value of the entire enterprise.

When we sold the Class B shares in 1996, we stated that Berkshire stock was not undervalued—and some people found that shocking. That reaction was not well-founded. Shock should have registered instead had we issued shares when our stock *was* undervalued. Managements that say or imply during a public offering that their stock is undervalued are usually being economical with the truth or uneconomical with their existing shareholders' money: Owners unfairly lose if their managers deliberately sell assets for 80¢ that in fact are worth $1. We didn't commit that kind of crime in our offering of Class B shares and we never will. (We did *not*, however, say at the time of the sale that our stock was overvalued, though many media have reported that we did.)

11. *You should be fully aware of one attitude Charlie and I share that hurts our financial performance: Regardless of price, we have no interest at all in selling any good businesses that Berkshire owns. We are also very reluctant to sell sub-par businesses as long as we expect them to generate at least some cash and as long as we feel good about their managers and labor relations. We hope not to repeat the capital-allocation mistakes that led us into such sub-par businesses. And we react with great caution to suggestions that our poor businesses can be restored to satisfactory profitability by major capital expenditures. (The projections will be dazzling and the advocates sincere, but, in the end, major additional investment in a terrible industry usually is about as rewarding as struggling in quicksand.) Nevertheless, gin rummy managerial behavior (discard your least promising business at each turn) is not our style. We would rather have our overall results penalized a bit than engage in that kind of behavior.*

We continue to avoid gin rummy behavior. True, we closed our textile business in the mid-1980s after 20 years of struggling with it, but only because we felt it was doomed to run never-ending operating losses. We have not, however, given thought to selling operations that would command very fancy prices nor have we dumped our laggards, though we focus hard on curing the problems that cause them to lag.

12. *We will be candid in our reporting to you, emphasizing the pluses and minuses important in appraising business value. Our guideline is to tell you the business facts that we would want to know if our positions were reversed. We owe you no less. Moreover, as a company with a major communications business, it would be inex-*

cusable for us to apply lesser standards of accuracy, balance and incisiveness when reporting on ourselves than we would expect our news people to apply when reporting on others. We also believe candor benefits us as managers: The CEO who misleads others in public may eventually mislead himself in private.

At Berkshire you will find no "big bath" accounting maneuvers or restructurings nor any "smoothing" of quarterly or annual results. We will always tell you how many strokes we have taken on each hole and never play around with the scorecard. When the numbers are a very rough "guesstimate," as they necessarily must be in insurance reserving, we will try to be both consistent and conservative in our approach.

We will be communicating with you in several ways. Through the annual report, I try to give all shareholders as much value-defining information as can be conveyed in a document kept to reasonable length. We also try to convey a liberal quantity of condensed but important information in the quarterly reports we post on the internet, though I don't write those (one recital a year is enough). Still another important occasion for communication is our Annual Meeting, at which Charlie and I are delighted to spend five hours or more answering questions about Berkshire. But there is one way we *can't* communicate: on a one-on-one basis. That isn't feasible given Berkshire's many thousands of owners.

In all of our communications, we try to make sure that no single shareholder gets an edge: We do not follow the usual practice of giving earnings "guidance" or other information of value to analysts or large shareholders. Our goal is to have all of our owners updated at the same time.

13.   *Despite our policy of candor we will discuss our activities in marketable securities only to the extent legally required. Good investment ideas are rare, valuable and subject to competitive appropriation just as good product or business acquisition ideas are. Therefore we normally will not talk about our investment ideas. This ban extends even to securities we have sold (because we may purchase them again) and to stocks we are incorrectly rumored to be buying. If we deny those reports but say "no comment" on other occasions, the no-comments become confirmation.*

Though we continue to be unwilling to talk about specific stocks, we freely discuss our business and investment philosophy. I benefitted enormously from the intellectual generosity of Ben Graham, the greatest teacher in the history of finance, and I believe it appropriate to pass along what I learned from him, even if that creates new and able investment competitors for Berkshire just as Ben's teachings did for him.

14. *To the extent possible, we would like each Berkshire shareholder to record a gain or loss in market value during his period of ownership that is proportional to the gain or loss in per-share intrinsic value recorded by the company during that holding period. For this to come about, the relationship between the intrinsic value and the market price of a Berkshire share would need to remain constant, and by our preferences at 1-to-1. As that implies, we would rather see Berkshire's stock price at a **fair** level than a **high** level. Obviously, Charlie and I can't control Berkshire's price. But by our policies and communications, we can encourage informed, rational behavior by owners that, in turn, will tend to produce a stock price that is also rational. Our it's-as-bad-to-be-overvalued-as-to-be-undervalued approach may disappoint some shareholders. We believe, however, that it affords Berkshire the best prospect of attracting long-term investors who seek to profit from the progress of the company rather than from the investment mistakes of their partners.*

15. *We regularly compare the gain in Berkshire's per-share book value to the performance of the S&P 500. Over time, we hope to outpace this yardstick. Otherwise, why do our investors need us? The measurement, however, has certain shortcomings. Moreover, it now is less meaningful on a year-to-year basis than was formerly the case. That is because our equity holdings, whose value tends to move with the S&P 500, are a far smaller portion of our net worth than they were in earlier years. Additionally, gains in the S&P stocks are counted in full in calculating that index, whereas gains in Berkshire's equity holdings are counted at 65% because of the federal tax we incur. We, therefore, expect to outperform the S&P in lackluster years for the stock market and underperform when the market has a strong year.*

I. Corporate Governance

Many annual meetings are a waste of time, both for shareholders and for management. Sometimes that is true because management is reluctant to open up on matters of business substance. More often a non-productive session is the fault of shareholder participants who are more concerned about their own moment on stage than they are about the affairs of the corporation. What should be a forum for business discussion becomes a forum for theatrics, spleen-venting and advocacy of issues. (The deal is irresistible: for the price of one share you get to tell a captive audience your ideas as to how the world should be run.) Under such circumstances, the quality of the meeting often deteriorates from year to year as the antics of those interested in themselves discourage attendance by those interested in the business.

Berkshire's meetings are a different story. The number of shareholders attending grows a bit each year and we have yet to experience a silly question or an ego-inspired commentary.[2] Instead, we get a wide variety of thoughtful questions about the business. Because the annual meeting is the time and place for these, Charlie and I are happy to answer them all, no matter how long it takes. (We cannot, however, respond to written or phoned questions at other times of the year; one-person-at-a-time reporting is a poor use of management time in a company with [thousands of] shareholders.) The only business matters that are off limits at the annual meeting are those about which candor might cost our company real money. Our activities in securities would be the main example.[3]

A. *Full and Fair Disclosure*[4]

At Berkshire, full reporting means giving you the information that we would wish you to give to us if our positions were reversed. What Charlie and I would want under that circumstance would be all the important facts about current operations as well as the CEO's frank view of the long-term economic characteristics of the business. We would expect both a lot of financial details and a discussion of any significant data we would need to interpret what was presented.

---

2 [Subsequent letters sometimes report on the turnout at prior annual meetings. The turnout went from 12 at the 1975 meeting to approximately 7,500 at the 1997 meeting; to over 15,000 in the early 2000s; 35,000 in 2008; and 40,000 in 2015.]

3 [Introductory essay, 1984.]

4 [Divided by hash lines: 2000; 2002.]

When Charlie and I read reports, we have no interest in pictures of personnel, plants or products. References to EBITDA make us shudder—does management think the tooth fairy pays for capital expenditures?[5] We're very suspicious of accounting methodology that is vague or unclear, since too often that means management wishes to hide something. And we don't want to read messages that a public relations department or consultant has turned out. Instead, we expect a company's CEO to explain in his or her own words what's happening.

For us, fair reporting means getting information to our 300,000 "partners" simultaneously, or as close to that mark as possible. We therefore put our annual and quarterly financials on the Internet between the close of the market on a Friday and the following morning. By our doing that, shareholders and other interested investors have timely access to these important releases and also have a reasonable amount of time to digest the information they include before the markets open on Monday.

We applaud the work that Arthur Levitt, Jr., until recently Chairman of the SEC, has done in cracking down on the corporate practice of "selective disclosure" that had spread like cancer in recent years. Indeed, it had become virtually standard practice for major corporations to "guide" analysts or large holders to earnings expectations that were intended either to be on the nose or a tiny bit below what the company truly expected to earn. Through the selectively dispersed hints, winks and nods that companies engaged in, speculatively-minded institutions and advisors were given an information edge over investment-oriented individuals. This was corrupt behavior, unfortunately embraced by both Wall Street and corporate America.

Thanks to Chairman Levitt, whose general efforts on behalf of investors were both tireless and effective, corporations are now required to treat all of their owners equally. The fact that this reform came about because of coercion rather than conscience should be a matter of shame for CEOs and their investor relations departments.

One further thought while I'm on my soapbox: Charlie and I think it is both deceptive and dangerous for CEOs to predict growth rates for their companies. They are, of course, frequently egged on to do so by both analysts and their own investor relations

---

5 [*See* the essay Owner Earnings and the Cash Flow Fallacy in Part VI.E.]

departments. They should resist, however, because too often these predictions lead to trouble.

It's fine for a CEO to have his own internal goals and, in our view, it's even appropriate for the CEO to publicly express some hopes about the future, if these expectations are accompanied by sensible caveats. But for a major corporation to predict that its per-share earnings will grow over the long term at, say, 15% annually is to court trouble.

That's true because a growth rate of that magnitude can only be maintained by a very small percentage of large businesses. Here's a test: Examine the record of, say, the 200 highest earning companies from 1970 to 1980 and tabulate how many have increased per-share earnings by 15% annually since those dates. You will find that only a handful have. I would wager you a very significant sum that fewer than 10 of the 200 most profitable companies in 2000 will attain 15% annual growth in earnings-per-share over the next 20 years.

The problem arising from lofty predictions is not just that they spread unwarranted optimism. Even more troublesome is the fact that they corrode CEO behavior. Over the years, Charlie and I have observed many instances in which CEOs engaged in uneconomic operating maneuvers so that they could meet earnings targets they had announced. Worse still, after exhausting all that operating acrobatics would do, they sometimes played a wide variety of accounting games to "make the numbers." These accounting shenanigans have a way of snowballing: Once a company moves earnings from one period to another, operating shortfalls that occur thereafter require it to engage in further accounting maneuvers that must be even more "heroic." These can turn fudging into fraud. (More money, it has been noted, has been stolen with the point of a pen than at the point of a gun.)

Charlie and I tend to be leery of companies run by CEOs who woo investors with fancy predictions. A few of these managers will prove prophetic—but others will turn out to be congenital optimists, or even charlatans. Unfortunately, it's not easy for investors to know in advance which species they are dealing with.

––––––––––––––––

Three suggestions for investors: First, beware of companies displaying weak accounting. If a company still does not expense options, or if its pension assumptions are fanciful, watch out. When managements take the low road in aspects that are visible, it is likely they are following a similar path behind the scenes. There is seldom just one cockroach in the kitchen.

Trumpeting EBITDA (earnings before interest, taxes, depreciation and amortization) is a particularly pernicious practice. Doing so implies that depreciation is not truly an expense, given that it is a "non-cash" charge. That's nonsense. In truth, depreciation is a particularly unattractive expense because the cash outlay it represents is paid up front, before the asset acquired has delivered any benefits to the business. Imagine, if you will, that at the beginning of this year a company paid all of its employees for the next ten years of their service (in the way they would lay out cash for a fixed asset to be useful for ten years). In the following nine years, compensation would be a "non-cash" expense—a reduction of a prepaid compensation asset established this year. Would anyone care to argue that the recording of the expense in years two through ten would be simply a bookkeeping formality?

Second, unintelligible footnotes usually indicate untrustworthy management. If you can't understand a footnote or other managerial explanation, it's usually because the CEO doesn't want you to. Enron's descriptions of certain transactions *still* baffle me.

Finally, be suspicious of companies that trumpet earnings projections and growth expectations. Businesses seldom operate in a tranquil, no-surprise environment, and earnings simply don't advance smoothly (except, of course, in the offering books of investment bankers).

Charlie and I not only don't know today what our businesses will earn *next year*—we don't even know what they will earn *next quarter*. We are suspicious of those CEOs who regularly claim they do know the future—and we become downright incredulous if they consistently reach their declared targets. Managers that always promise to "make the numbers" will at some point be tempted to *make up* the numbers.

B. *Boards and Managers*[6]

[The performance of CEOs of investee companies], which we have observed at close range, contrasts vividly with that of many CEOs, which we have fortunately observed from a safe distance. Sometimes these CEOs clearly do not belong in their jobs; their positions, nevertheless, are usually secure. The supreme irony of

---

6 [Divided by hash lines: 1988; 1993; 2002; 2004; 1986; 1998; 2005.]

business management is that it is far easier for an inadequate CEO to keep his job than it is for an inadequate subordinate.

If a secretary, say, is hired for a job that requires typing ability of at least 80 words a minute and turns out to be capable of only 50 words a minute, she will lose her job in no time. There is a logical standard for this job; performance is easily measured; and if you can't make the grade, you're out. Similarly, if new sales people fail to generate sufficient business quickly enough, they will be let go. Excuses will not be accepted as a substitute for orders.

However, a CEO who doesn't perform is frequently carried indefinitely. One reason is that performance standards for his job seldom exist. When they do, they are often fuzzy or they may be waived or explained away, even when the performance shortfalls are major and repeated. At too many companies, the boss shoots the arrow of managerial performance and then hastily paints the bullseye around the spot where it lands.

Another important, but seldom recognized, distinction between the boss and the foot soldier is that the CEO has no immediate superior whose performance is itself getting measured. The sales manager who retains a bunch of lemons in his sales force will soon be in hot water himself. It is in his immediate self-interest to promptly weed out his hiring mistakes. Otherwise, he himself may be weeded out. An office manager who has hired inept secretaries faces the same imperative.

But the CEO's boss is a Board of Directors that seldom measures itself and is infrequently held to account for substandard corporate performance. If the Board makes a mistake in hiring, and perpetuates that mistake, so what? Even if the company is taken over because of the mistake, the deal will probably bestow substantial benefits on the outgoing Board members. (The bigger they are, the softer they fall.)

Finally, relations between the Board and the CEO are expected to be congenial. At board meetings, criticism of the CEO's performance is often viewed as the social equivalent of belching. No such inhibitions restrain the office manager from critically evaluating the substandard typist.

These points should not be interpreted as a blanket condemnation of CEOs or Boards of Directors: Most are able and hardworking, and a number are truly outstanding. But the management failings that Charlie and I have seen make us thankful that we are linked with the managers of our permanent holdings. They love their businesses, they think like owners, and they exude integrity and ability.

———————

At our annual meetings, someone usually asks "What happens to this place if you get hit by a truck?" I'm glad they are still asking the question in this form. It won't be too long before the query becomes: "What happens to this place if you *don't* get hit by a truck?"

Such questions, in any event, raise a reason for me to discuss corporate governance, a hot topic during the past year. In general, I believe that directors have stiffened their spines recently and that shareholders are now being treated somewhat more like true owners than was the case not long ago. Commentators on corporate governance, however, seldom make any distinction among three fundamentally different manager/owner situations that exist in publicly-held companies. Though the legal responsibility of directors is identical throughout, their ability to effect change differs in each of the cases. Attention usually falls on the first case, because it prevails on the corporate scene. Since Berkshire falls into the second category, however, and will someday fall into the third, we will discuss all three variations.

The first, and by far most common, board situation is one in which a corporation has no controlling shareholder. In that case, I believe directors should behave as if there is a single absentee owner, whose long-term interest they should try to further in all proper ways. Unfortunately, "long-term" gives directors a lot of wiggle room. If they lack either integrity or the ability to think independently, directors can do great violence to shareholders while still claiming to be acting in their long-term interest. But assume the board is functioning well and must deal with a management that is mediocre or worse. Directors then have the responsibility for changing that management, just as an intelligent owner would do if he were present. And if able but greedy managers over-reach and try to dip too deeply into the shareholders' pockets, directors must slap their hands.

In this plain-vanilla case, a director who sees something he doesn't like should attempt to persuade the other directors of his view. If he is successful, the board will have the muscle to make the appropriate change. Suppose, though, that the unhappy director can't get other directors to agree with him. He should then feel free to make his views known to the absentee owners. Directors seldom do that, of course. The temperament of many directors would in fact be incompatible with critical behavior of that sort. But I see nothing improper in such actions, assuming the issues are serious. Naturally, the complaining director can expect a vigorous rebuttal from the unpersuaded directors, a prospect that should discourage the dissenter from pursuing trivial or non-rational causes.

For the boards just discussed, I believe the directors ought to be relatively few in number—say, ten or less—and ought to come mostly from the outside. The outside board members should establish standards for the CEO's performance and should also periodically meet, without his being present, to evaluate his performance against those standards.

The requisites for board membership should be business savvy, interest in the job, and owner-orientation. Too often, directors are selected simply because they are prominent or add diversity to the board. That practice is a mistake. Furthermore, mistakes in selecting directors are particularly serious because appointments are so hard to undo: The pleasant but vacuous director need never worry about job security.

The second case is that existing at Berkshire, where the controlling owner is also the manager. At some companies, this arrangement is facilitated by the existence of two classes of stock endowed with disproportionate voting power. In these situations, it's obvious that the board does not act as an agent between owners and management and that the directors cannot effect change except through persuasion. Therefore, if the owner/manager is mediocre or worse—or is over-reaching—there is little a director can do about it except object. If the directors having no connections to the owner/manager make a unified argument, it may well have some effect. More likely it will not.

If change does not come, and the matter is sufficiently serious, the outside directors should resign. Their resignation will signal their doubts about management, and it will emphasize that no outsider is in a position to correct the owner/manager's shortcomings.

The third governance case occurs when there is a controlling owner who is not involved in management. This case, examples of which are Hershey Foods and Dow Jones, puts the outside directors in a potentially useful position. If they become unhappy with either the competence or integrity of the manager, they can go directly to the owner (who may also be on the board) and report their dissatisfaction. This situation is ideal for an outside director, since he need make his case only to a single, presumably interested owner, who can forthwith effect change if the argument is persuasive. Even so, the dissatisfied director has only that single course of action. If he remains unsatisfied about a critical matter, he has no choice but to resign.

Logically, the third case should be the most effective in insuring first-class management. In the second case the owner is not going to fire himself, and in the first case, directors often find it very difficult to deal with mediocrity or mild over-reaching. Unless the unhappy directors can win over a majority of the board—an awkward social and logistical task, particularly if management's behavior is merely odious, not egregious—their hands are effectively tied. In practice, directors trapped in situations of this kind usually convince themselves that by staying around they can do at least some good. Meanwhile, management proceeds unfettered.

In the third case, the owner is neither judging himself nor burdened with the problem of garnering a majority. He can also insure that outside directors are selected who will bring useful qualities to the board. These directors, in turn, will know that the good advice they give will reach the right ears, rather than being stifled by a recalcitrant management. If the controlling owner is intelligent and self-confident, he will make decisions in respect to management that are meritocratic and pro-shareholder. Moreover—and this is critically important—he can readily correct any mistake he makes.

At Berkshire we operate in the second mode now and will for as long as I remain functional. My health, let me add, is excellent. For better or worse, you are likely to have me as an owner/manager for some time. All in all, we're prepared for "the truck."

Both the ability and fidelity of managers have long needed monitoring. Indeed, nearly 2,000 years ago, Jesus Christ addressed this subject, speaking (Luke 16:2) approvingly of "a certain rich man" who told his manager, "Give an account of thy stewardship; for thou mayest no longer be steward."

Accountability and stewardship withered in the last decade, becoming qualities deemed of little importance by those caught up in the Great Bubble. As stock prices went up, the behavioral norms of managers went down. By the late '90s, as a result, CEOs who traveled the high road did not encounter heavy traffic.

Most CEOs, it should be noted, are men and women you would be happy to have as trustees for your children's assets or as next-door neighbors. Too many of these people, however, have in recent years behaved badly at the office, fudging numbers and drawing obscene pay for mediocre business achievements.

Why have intelligent and decent directors failed so miserably? The answer lies not in inadequate laws—it's always been clear that directors are obligated to represent the interests of shareholders— but rather in what I'd call "boardroom atmosphere."

It's almost impossible, for example, in a boardroom populated by well-mannered people, to raise the question of whether the CEO should be replaced. It's equally awkward to question a proposed acquisition that has been endorsed by the CEO, particularly when his inside staff and outside advisors are present and unanimously support his decision. (They wouldn't be in the room if they didn't.) Finally, when the compensation committee—armed, as always, with support from a high-paid consultant—reports on a mega-grant of options to the CEO, it would be like belching at the dinner table for a director to suggest that the committee reconsider.

These "social" difficulties argue for outside directors regularly meeting without the CEO—a reform that is being instituted and that I enthusiastically endorse. I doubt, however, that most of the other new governance rules and recommendations will provide benefits commensurate with the monetary and other costs they impose.

The current cry is for "independent" directors. It is certainly true that it is desirable to have directors who think and speak independently—but they must also be business-savvy, interested and shareholder oriented [as noted in the previous essay].

Over a span of 40 years, I have been on 19 public-company boards (excluding Berkshire's) and have interacted with perhaps 250 directors. Most of them were "independent" as defined by today's rules. But the great majority of these directors lacked at least one of the three qualities I value. As a result, their contribution to shareholder well-being was minimal at best and, too often, negative.

These people, decent and intelligent though they were, simply did not know enough about business and/or care enough about shareholders to question foolish acquisitions or egregious compensation. My own behavior, I must ruefully add, frequently fell short as well: Too often I was silent when management made proposals that I judged to be counter to the interests of shareholders. In those cases, collegiality trumped independence.

So that we may further see the failings of "independence," let's look at a 62-year case study covering thousands of companies. Since 1940, federal law has mandated that a large proportion of the directors of investment companies (most of these mutual funds) be independent. The requirement was originally 40% and now it is 50%. In any case, the typical fund has long operated with a majority of directors who qualify as independent.

These directors and the entire board have many perfunctory duties, but in actuality have only two important responsibilities: obtaining the best possible investment manager and negotiating with that manager for the lowest possible fee. When you are seeking investment help yourself, those two goals are the only ones that count, and directors acting for other investors should have exactly the same priorities. Yet when it comes to independent directors pursuing either goal, their record has been absolutely pathetic.

Many thousands of investment-company boards meet annually to carry out the vital job of selecting who will manage the savings of the millions of owners they represent. Year after year the directors of Fund A select manager A, Fund B directors select manager B, etc. . . . in a zombie-like process that makes a mockery of stewardship. Very occasionally, a board will revolt. But for the most part, a monkey will type out a Shakespeare play before an "independent" mutual-fund director will suggest that his fund look at other managers, even if the incumbent manager has persistently delivered substandard performance. When they are handling their own money, of course, directors will look to alternative advisors— but it never enters their minds to do so when they are acting as fiduciaries for others.

The hypocrisy permeating the system is vividly exposed when a fund management company—call it "A"—is sold for a huge sum to Manager "B". Now the "independent" directors experience a "counter-revelation" and decide that Manager B is the best that can be found—even though B was available (and ignored) in previous years. Not so incidentally, B also could formerly have been hired at a far lower rate than is possible now that it has bought Manager A. That's because B has laid out a fortune to acquire A, and B must now recoup that cost through fees paid by the A shareholders who were "delivered" as part of the deal. (For a terrific discussion of the mutual fund business, read John Bogle's *Common Sense on Mutual Funds*.)

Investment company directors have failed as well in negotiating management fees. If you or I were empowered, I can assure you that we could easily negotiate materially lower management fees with the incumbent managers of most mutual funds. And, believe me, if directors were promised a portion of any fee savings they realized, the skies would be filled with falling fees. Under the current system, though, reductions mean nothing to "independent" directors while meaning everything to managers. So guess who wins?

Having the right money manager, of course, is far more important to a fund than reducing the manager's fee. Both tasks are nonetheless the job of directors. And in stepping up to these all-important responsibilities, tens of thousands of "independent" directors, over more than six decades, have failed miserably. (They've succeeded, however, in taking care of themselves; their fees from serving on multiple boards of a single "family" of funds often run well into six figures.)

When the manager cares deeply and the directors don't, what's needed is a powerful countervailing force—and that's the missing element in today's corporate governance. Getting rid of mediocre CEOs and eliminating overreaching by the able ones requires action by owners—big owners. The logistics aren't that tough: The ownership of stock has grown increasingly concentrated in recent decades, and today it would be easy for institutional managers to exert their will on problem situations. Twenty, or even fewer, of the largest institutions, acting together, could effectively reform corporate governance at a given company, simply by withholding their votes for directors who were tolerating odious behavior. In my view, this kind of concerted action is the only way that corporate stewardship can be meaningfully improved.

Several institutional shareholders and their advisors decided I lacked "independence" in my role as a director of Coca-Cola. One group wanted me removed from the board and another simply wanted me booted from the audit committee.

My first impulse was to secretly fund the group behind the second idea. Why anyone would wish to be on an audit committee is beyond me. But since directors must be assigned to one committee or another, and since no CEO wants me on his compensation committee, it's often been my lot to get an audit committee assignment. As it turned out, the institutions that opposed me failed and I was re-elected to the audit job. (I fought off the urge to ask for a recount.)

Some institutions questioned my "independence" because, among other things, McLane and Dairy Queen buy lots of Coke products. (Do they want us to favor Pepsi?) But independence is defined in Webster's as "not subject to control by others." I'm puzzled how anyone could conclude that our Coke purchases would "control" my decision-making when the counterweight is the well-being of $8 billion of Coke stock held by Berkshire. Assuming I'm even marginally rational, elementary arithmetic should make it clear that my heart and mind belong to the owners of Coke, not to its management.

I can't resist mentioning that Jesus understood the calibration of independence far more clearly than do the protesting institutions. In Matthew 6:21 He observed: "For where your treasure is, there will your heart be also." Even to an institutional investor, $8 billion should qualify as "treasure" that dwarfs any profits Berkshire might earn on its routine transactions with Coke.

Measured by the biblical standard, the Berkshire board is a model: (a) every director is a member of a family owning at least $4 million of stock; (b) none of these shares were acquired from Berkshire via options or grants; (c) no directors receive committee, consulting or board fees from the company that are more than a tiny portion of their annual income; and (d) although we have a standard corporate indemnity arrangement, we carry no liability insurance for directors. At Berkshire, board members travel the same road as shareholders.

Charlie and I have seen much behavior confirming the Bible's "treasure" point. In our view, based on our considerable boardroom experience, the least independent directors are likely to be those who receive an important fraction of their annual income from the fees they receive for board service (and who hope as well to be recommended for election to other boards and thereby to boost their income further). Yet these are the very board members most often classed as "independent."

Most directors of this type are decent people and do a first-class job. But they wouldn't be human if they weren't tempted to thwart actions that would threaten their livelihood. Some may go on to succumb to such temptations.

Let's look at an example based upon circumstantial evidence. I have first-hand knowledge of a recent acquisition proposal (not from Berkshire) that was favored by management, blessed by the company's investment banker and slated to go forward at a price above the level at which the stock had sold for some years (or now sells for). In addition, a number of directors favored the transaction and wanted it proposed to shareholders.

Several of their brethren, however, each of whom received board and committee fees totaling about $100,000 annually, scuttled the proposal, which meant that shareholders never learned of this multi-billion offer. Non-management directors owned little stock except for shares they had received from the company. Their open-market purchases in recent years had meanwhile been nominal, even though the stock had sold far below the acquisition price proposed. In other words, these directors didn't want the shareholders to be offered X even though they had consistently declined the opportunity to buy stock for their own account at a fraction of X.

I don't know which directors opposed letting shareholders see the offer. But I do know that $100,000 is an important portion of the annual income of some of those deemed "independent," clearly meeting the Matthew 6:21 definition of "treasure." If the deal had gone through, these fees would have ended.

Neither the shareholders nor I will ever know what motivated the dissenters. Indeed they themselves will not likely know, given that self-interest inevitably blurs introspection. We do know one thing, though: At the same meeting at which the deal was rejected, the board voted itself a significant increase in directors' fees.

Charlie and I really have only two jobs. One is to attract and keep outstanding managers to run our various operations.[7] This hasn't been all that difficult. Usually the managers came with the companies we bought, having demonstrated their talents throughout careers that spanned a wide variety of business circumstances. They were managerial stars long before they knew us, and our main contribution has been to not get in their way. This approach seems elementary: if my job were to manage a golf team—and if Jack Nicklaus or Arnold Palmer were willing to play for me— neither would get a lot of directives from me about how to swing.

Some of our key managers are independently wealthy (we hope they all become so), but that poses no threat to their continued interest: they work because they love what they do and relish the thrill of outstanding performance. They unfailingly think like owners (the highest compliment we can pay a manager) and find all aspects of their business absorbing.

---

[7] [The other is capital allocation, discussed in Parts II and VI.]

(Our prototype for occupational fervor is the Catholic tailor who used his small savings of many years to finance a pilgrimage to the Vatican. When he returned, his parish held a special meeting to get his first-hand account of the Pope. "Tell us," said the eager faithful, "just what sort of fellow is he?" Our hero wasted no words: "He's a forty-four medium.")

Charlie and I know that the right players will make almost any team manager look good. We subscribe to the philosophy of Ogilvy & Mather's founding genius, David Ogilvy: "If each of us hires people who are smaller than we are, we shall become a company of dwarfs. But, if each of us hires people who are bigger than we are, we shall become a company of giants."

A by-product of our managerial style is the ability it gives us to easily expand Berkshire's activities. We've read management treatises that specify exactly how many people should report to any one executive, but they make little sense to us. When you have able managers of high character running businesses about which they are passionate, you can have a dozen or more reporting to you and still have time for an afternoon nap. Conversely, if you have even one person reporting to you who is deceitful, inept or uninterested, you will find yourself with more than you can handle. Charlie and I could work with double the number of managers we now have, so long as they had the rare qualities of the present ones.

We intend to continue our practice of working only with people whom we like and admire. This policy not only maximizes our chances for good results, it also ensures us an extraordinarily good time. On the other hand, working with people who cause your stomach to churn seems much like marrying for money—probably a bad idea under any circumstances, but absolute madness if you are already rich.

———————

At Berkshire we feel that telling outstanding CEOs, such as Tony [Nicely of GEICO], how to run their companies would be the height of foolishness. Most of our managers wouldn't work for us if they got a lot of backseat driving. (Generally, they don't have to work for *anyone*, since 75% or so are independently wealthy.) Besides, they are the Mark McGwires of the business world and need no advice from us as to how to hold the bat or when to swing.

Nevertheless, Berkshire's ownership may make even the best of managers more effective. First, we eliminate all of the ritualistic and nonproductive activities that normally go with the job of CEO. Our managers are totally in charge of their personal schedules.

Second, we give each a simple mission: Just run your business as if: (1) you own 100% of it; (2) it is the only asset in the world that you and your family have or will ever have; and (3) you can't sell or merge it for at least a century. As a corollary, we tell them they should not let any of their decisions be affected even slightly by accounting considerations. We want our managers to think about what counts, not how it will be counted.

Very few CEOs of public companies operate under a similar mandate, mainly because they have owners who focus on short-term prospects and reported earnings. Berkshire, however, has a shareholder base—which it will have for decades to come—that has the longest investment horizon to be found in the public-company universe. Indeed, a majority of our shares are held by investors who expect to die still holding them. We can therefore ask our CEOs to manage for maximum long-term value, rather than for next quarter's earnings. We certainly don't ignore the current results of our businesses—in most cases, they are of great importance—but we *never* want them to be achieved at the expense of our building ever-greater competitive strengths.

I believe the GEICO story demonstrates the benefits of Berkshire's approach. Charlie and I haven't taught Tony a thing—and never will—but we *have* created an environment that allows him to apply all of his talents to what's important. He does not have to devote his time or energy to board meetings, press interviews, presentations by investment bankers or talks with financial analysts. Furthermore, he need never spend a moment thinking about financing, credit ratings or "Street" expectations for earnings per share. Because of our ownership structure, he also knows that this operational framework will endure for decades to come. In this environment of freedom, both Tony and his company can convert their almost limitless potential into matching achievements.

———————————

Every day, in countless ways, the competitive position of each of our businesses grows either weaker or stronger. If we are delighting customers, eliminating unnecessary costs and improving our products and services, we gain strength. But if we treat customers with indifference or tolerate bloat, our businesses will wither. On a daily basis, the effects of our actions are imperceptible; cumulatively, though, their consequences are enormous.

When our long-term competitive position improves as a result of these almost unnoticeable actions, we describe the phenomenon as "widening the moat." And doing that is essential if we are to have the kind of business we want a decade or two from now. We always, of course, hope to earn more money in the short-term. But when short-term and long-term conflict, widening the moat *must* take precedence.

If a management makes bad decisions in order to hit short-term earnings targets, and consequently gets behind the eight-ball in terms of costs, customer satisfaction or brand strength, no amount of subsequent brilliance will overcome the damage that has been inflicted. Take a look at the dilemmas of managers in the auto and airline industries today as they struggle with the huge problems handed them by their predecessors. Charlie is fond of quoting Ben Franklin's "An ounce of prevention is worth a pound of cure." But sometimes no amount of cure will overcome the mistakes of the past.

C.   *The Anxieties of Business Change*[8]

In July we decided to close our textile operation, and by yearend this unpleasant job was largely completed. The history of this business is instructive.

When Buffett Partnership, Ltd., an investment partnership of which I was general partner, bought control of Berkshire Hathaway [in 1965], it had an accounting net worth of $22 million, all devoted to the textile business. The company's intrinsic business value, however, was considerably less because the textile assets were unable to earn returns commensurate with their accounting value. Indeed, during the previous nine years (the period in which Berkshire and Hathaway operated as a merged company) aggregate sales of $530 million had produced an aggregate loss of $10 million. Profits had been reported from time to time but the net effect was always one step forward, two steps back.

At the time we made our purchase, southern textile plants—largely non-union—were believed to have an important competitive advantage. Most northern textile operations had closed and many people thought we would liquidate our business as well.

We felt, however, that the business would be run much better by a long-time employee whom we immediately selected to be president, Ken Chace. In this respect we were 100% correct: Ken and his recent successor, Garry Morrison, have been excellent managers, every bit the equal of managers at our more profitable businesses.

---

[8] [1985; 2006.]

In early 1967 cash generated by the textile operation was used to fund our entry into insurance via the purchase of National Indemnity Company. Some of the money came from earnings and some from reduced investment in textile inventories, receivables, and fixed assets. This pullback proved wise: although much improved by Ken's management, the textile business never became a good earner, not even in cyclical upturns.

Further diversification for Berkshire followed, and gradually the textile operation's depressing effect on our overall return diminished as the business became a progressively smaller portion of the corporation. We remained in the business for reasons that I stated in the 1978 annual report (and summarized at other times also): "(1) our textile businesses are very important employers in their communities, (2) management has been straightforward in reporting on problems and energetic in attacking them, (3) labor has been cooperative and understanding in facing our common problems, and (4) the business should average modest cash returns relative to investment." I further said, "As long as these conditions prevail—and we expect that they will—we intend to continue to support our textile business despite more attractive alternative uses for capital."

It turned out that I was very wrong about (4). Though 1979 was moderately profitable, the business thereafter consumed major amounts of cash. By mid-1985 it became clear, even to me, that this condition was almost sure to continue. Could we have found a buyer who would continue operations, I would have certainly preferred to sell the business rather than liquidate it, even if that meant somewhat lower proceeds for us. But the economics that were finally obvious to me were also obvious to others, and interest was nil.

I won't close down businesses of sub-normal profitability merely to add a fraction of a point to our corporate rate of return. However, I also feel it inappropriate for even an exceptionally profitable company to fund an operation once it appears to have unending losses in prospect. Adam Smith would disagree with my first proposition, and Karl Marx would disagree with my second; the middle ground is the only position that leaves me comfortable.

I should reemphasize that Ken and Garry have been resourceful, energetic and imaginative in attempting to make our textile operation a success. Trying to achieve sustainable profitability, they reworked product lines, machinery configurations and distribution arrangements. We also made a major acquisition, Waumbec Mills, with the expectation of important synergy (a term widely used in business to explain an acquisition that otherwise makes no sense). But in the end nothing worked and I should be faulted for not quitting sooner. A recent *Business Week* article stated that 250 textile mills have closed since 1980. Their owners were not privy to any information that was unknown to me; they simply processed it more objectively. I ignored Comte's advice—"the intellect should be the servant of the heart, but not its slave"—and believed what I preferred to believe.

The domestic textile industry operates in a commodity business, competing in a world market in which substantial excess capacity exists. Much of the trouble we experienced was attributable, both directly and indirectly, to competition from foreign countries whose workers are paid a small fraction of the U.S. minimum wage. But that in no way means that our labor force deserves any blame for our closing. In fact, in comparison with employees of American industry generally, our workers were poorly paid, as has been the case throughout the textile business. In contract negotiations, union leaders and members were sensitive to our disadvantageous cost position and did not push for unrealistic wage increases or unproductive work practices. To the contrary, they tried just as hard as we did to keep us competitive. Even during our liquidation period they performed superbly. (Ironically, we would have been better off financially if our union had behaved unreasonably some years ago; we then would have recognized the impossible future that we faced, promptly closed down, and avoided significant future losses.)

Over the years, we had the option of making large capital expenditures in the textile operation that would have allowed us to somewhat reduce variable costs. Each proposal to do so looked like an immediate winner. Measured by standard return-on-investment tests, in fact, these proposals usually promised greater economic benefits than would have resulted from comparable expenditures in our highly-profitable candy and newspaper businesses.

But the promised benefits from these textile investments were illusory. Many of our competitors, both domestic and foreign, were stepping up to the same kind of expenditures and, once enough companies did so, their reduced costs became the baseline for reduced prices industrywide. Viewed individually, each company's capital investment decision appeared cost-effective and rational; viewed collectively, the decisions neutralized each other and were irrational (just as happens when each person watching a parade decides he can see a little better if he stands on tiptoes). After each round of investment, all the players had more money in the game and returns remained anemic.

Thus, we faced a miserable choice: huge capital investment would have helped to keep our textile business alive, but would have left us with terrible returns on ever-growing amounts of capital. After the investment, moreover, the foreign competition would still have retained a major, continuing advantage in labor costs. A refusal to invest, however, would make us increasingly non-competitive, even measured against domestic textile manufacturers. I always thought myself in the position described by Woody Allen in one of his movies: "More than any other time in history, mankind faces a crossroads. One path leads to despair and utter hopelessness, the other to total extinction. Let us pray we have the wisdom to choose correctly."

For an understanding of how the to-invest-or-not-to-invest dilemma plays out in a commodity business, it is instructive to look at Burlington Industries, by far the largest U.S. textile company both 21 years ago and now. In 1964 Burlington had sales of $1.2 billion against our $50 million. It had strengths in both distribution and production that we could never hope to match and also, of course, had an earnings record far superior to ours. Its stock sold at 60 at the end of 1964; ours was 13.

Burlington made a decision to stick to the textile business, and in 1985 had sales of about $2.8 billion. During the 1964-85 period, the company made capital expenditures of about $3 billion, far more than any other U.S. textile company and more than $200-per-share on that $60 stock. A very large part of the expenditures, I am sure, was devoted to cost improvement and expansion. Given Burlington's basic commitment to stay in textiles, I would also surmise that the company's capital decisions were quite rational.

Nevertheless, Burlington has lost sales volume in real dollars and has far lower returns on sales and equity now than 20 years ago. Split 2-for-1 in 1965, the stock now sells at 34—on an adjusted basis, just a little over its $60 price in 1964. Meanwhile, the CPI has more than tripled. Therefore, each share commands about one-third the purchasing power it did at the end of 1964. Regular dividends have been paid but they, too, have shrunk significantly in purchasing power.

This devastating outcome for the shareholders indicates what can happen when much brain power and energy are applied to a faulty premise. The situation is suggestive of Samuel Johnson's horse: "A horse that can count to ten is a remarkable horse—not a remarkable mathematician." Likewise, a textile company that allocates capital brilliantly within its industry is a remarkable textile company—but not a remarkable business.

My conclusion from my own experiences and from much observation of other businesses is that a good managerial record (measured by economic returns) is far more a function of what business boat you get into than it is of how effectively you row (though intelligence and effort help considerably, of course, in any business, good or bad). Should you find yourself in a chronically-leaking boat, energy devoted to changing vessels is likely to be more productive than energy devoted to patching leaks.

Not all of our businesses are destined to increase profits. When an industry's underlying economics are crumbling, talented management may slow the rate of decline. Eventually, though, eroding fundamentals will overwhelm managerial brilliance. (As a wise friend told me long ago, "If you want to get a reputation as a good businessman, be sure to get into a good business.") And fundamentals are definitely eroding in the newspaper industry, a trend that has caused the profits of our Buffalo News to decline. The skid will almost certainly continue.

When Charlie and I were young, the newspaper business was as easy a way to make huge returns as existed in America. As one not-too-bright publisher famously said, "I owe my fortune to two great American institutions: monopoly and nepotism." No paper in a one-paper city, however bad the product or however inept the management, could avoid gushing profits.

The industry's staggering returns could be simply explained. For most of the 20th Century, newspapers were the primary source of information for the American public. Whether the subject was sports, finance, or politics, newspapers reigned supreme. Just as important, their ads were the easiest way to find job opportunities or to learn the price of groceries at your town's supermarkets.

The great majority of families therefore felt the need for a paper every day, but understandably most didn't wish to pay for two. Advertisers preferred the paper with the most circulation, and readers tended to want the paper with the most ads and news pages. This circularity led to a law of the newspaper jungle: Survival of the Fattest.

Thus, when two or more papers existed in a major city (which was almost universally the case a century ago), the one that pulled ahead usually emerged as the stand-alone winner. After competition disappeared, the paper's pricing power in both advertising and circulation was unleashed. Typically, rates for both advertisers and readers would be raised annually—and the profits rolled in. For owners this was economic heaven. (Interestingly, though papers regularly—and often in a disapproving way—reported on the profitability of, say, the auto or steel industries, they never enlightened readers about their own Midas-like situation. Hmmm . . .)

As long ago as my 1991 letter to shareholders, I nonetheless asserted that this insulated world was changing, writing that "the media businesses . . . will prove considerably less marvelous than I, the industry, or lenders thought would be the case only a few years ago." Some publishers took umbrage at both this remark and other warnings from me that followed. Newspaper properties, moreover, continued to sell as if they were indestructible slot machines. In fact, many intelligent newspaper executives who regularly chronicled and analyzed important worldwide events were either blind or indifferent to what was going on under their noses.

Now, however, almost all newspaper owners realize that they are constantly losing ground in the battle for eyeballs. Simply put, if cable and satellite broadcasting, as well as the internet, had come along first, newspapers as we know them probably would never have existed. In Berkshire's world, Stan Lipsey does a terrific job running the Buffalo News, and I am enormously proud of its editor, Margaret Sullivan. The News' penetration of its market is the highest among that of this country's large newspapers. We also do better financially than most metropolitan newspapers, even though Buffalo's population and business trends are not good.

Nevertheless, this operation faces unrelenting pressures that will cause profit margins to slide. True, we have the leading online news operation in Buffalo, and it will continue to attract more viewers and ads. However, the economic potential of a newspaper internet site—given the many alternative sources of information and entertainment that are free and only a click away—is at best a small fraction of that existing in the past for a print newspaper facing no competition.

For a local resident, ownership of a city's paper, like ownership of a sports team, still produces instant prominence. With it typically comes power and influence. These are ruboffs that appeal to many people with money. Beyond that, civic-minded, wealthy

individuals may feel that local ownership will serve their community well. That's why Peter Kiewit bought the Omaha paper more
than 40 years ago.

We are likely therefore to see non-economic individual buyers
of newspapers emerge, just as we have seen such buyers acquire
major sports franchises. Aspiring press lords should be careful,
however: There's no rule that says a newspaper's revenues can't
fall below its expenses and that losses can't mushroom. Fixed costs
are high in the newspaper business, and that's bad news when unit
volume heads south. As the importance of newspapers diminishes,
moreover, the "psychic" value of possessing one will wane,
whereas owning a sports franchise will likely retain its cachet.

Unless we face an irreversible cash drain, we will stick with the
News, just as we've said that we would. Charlie and I love newspapers—we each read five a day—and believe that a free and energetic press is a key ingredient for maintaining a great democracy.
We hope that some combination of print and online will ward off
economic doomsday for newspapers, and we will work hard in Buffalo to develop a sustainable business model. I think we will be
successful. But the days of lush profits from our newspaper are
over.

D. *Social Compacts*[9]

We have two very large businesses, BNSF [Burlington Northern Santa Fe Railroad Corporation] and Mid-American Energy
[later renamed Berkshire Hathaway Energy], with important common characteristics that distinguish them from our many others. A
key characteristic of both companies is the huge investment they
have in very long-lived, regulated assets, with these funded by large
amounts of long-term debt that is *not* guaranteed by Berkshire.
Our credit is not needed: Both businesses have earning power that,
even under very adverse business conditions, amply covers their
interest requirements.

Both companies are heavily regulated, and both will have a
never-ending need to make major investments in plant and equipment. Both also need to provide efficient, customer-satisfying service to earn the respect of their communities and regulators. In
return, both need to be assured that they will be allowed to earn
reasonable earnings on future capital investments.

---

9 [2010 with variations in subsequent years; 2009]

[R]ailroads are [vital] to our country's future. Rail moves 42% of America's inter-city freight, measured by ton-miles, and BNSF moves more than any other railroad—about 28% of the industry total. A little math will tell you that more than 11% of *all* inter-city ton-miles of freight in the U.S. is transported by BNSF. Given the shift of population to the West, our share may well inch higher.

All of this adds up to a huge responsibility. We are a major and essential part of the American economy's circulatory system, obliged to constantly maintain and improve our 23,000 miles of track along with its ancillary bridges, tunnels, engines and cars. In carrying out this job, we must anticipate society's needs, not merely react to them. Fulfilling our societal obligation, we will regularly spend far more than our depreciation, with this excess amounting to $2 billion in 2011. I'm confident we will earn appropriate returns on our huge incremental investments. Wise regulation and wise investment are two sides of the same coin.

At MidAmerican, we participate in a similar "social compact." We are expected to put up ever increasing sums to satisfy the future needs of our customers. If we meanwhile operate reliably and efficiently, we know that we will obtain a fair return on these investments.

MidAmerican supplies 2.4 million customers in the U.S. with electricity, operating as the largest supplier in Iowa, Wyoming and Utah and as an important provider in other states as well. Our pipelines transport 8% of the country's natural gas. Obviously, many millions of Americans depend on us every day.

MidAmerican has delivered outstanding results for both its owners (Berkshire's interest is 89.8%) and its customers. Shortly after MidAmerican purchased Northern Natural Gas pipeline in 2002, that company's performance as a pipeline was rated dead last, 43 out of 43, by the leading authority in the field. In the most recent report published, Northern Natural was ranked second. The top spot was held by our other pipeline, Kern River.

In its electric business, MidAmerican has a comparable record. Iowa rates have not increased since we purchased our operation there in 1999. During the same period, the other major electric utility in the state has raised prices more than 70% and now has rates far above ours. In certain metropolitan areas in which the two utilities operate side by side, electric bills of our customers run far below those of their neighbors. I am told that comparable houses sell at higher prices in these cities if they are located in our service area.

MidAmerican will have 2,909 megawatts of wind generation in operation by the end of 2011, more than any other regulated electric utility in the country. The total amount that MidAmerican has invested or committed to wind is a staggering $5.4 billion. We can make this sort of investment because MidAmerican retains *all* of its earnings, unlike other utilities that generally pay out most of what they earn.

MidAmerican has consistently kept its end of the bargain with society and, to society's credit, it has reciprocated: With few exceptions, our regulators have promptly allowed us to earn a fair return on the ever increasing sums of capital we must invest. Going forward, we will do whatever it takes to serve our territories in the manner they expect. We believe that, in turn, we will be allowed the return we deserve on the funds we invest.

We see a "social compact" existing between the public and our railroad business, just as is the case with our utilities. If either side shirks its obligations, both sides will inevitably suffer. Therefore, both parties to the compact should—and we believe will—understand the benefit of behaving in a way that encourages good behavior by the other. It is inconceivable that our country will realize anything close to its full economic potential without its possessing first-class electricity and railroad systems. We will do our part to see that they exist.

E. *An Owner-Based Approach to Corporate Charity*[10]

A recent survey reported that about 50% of major American companies match charitable contributions made by directors (sometimes by a factor of three to one). In effect, these representatives of the owners direct funds to their favorite charities, and never consult the owners as to their charitable preferences. (I wonder how they would feel if the process were reversed and shareholders could invade the directors' pockets for charities favored by the shareholders.) When A takes money from B to give to C and A is a legislator, the process is called taxation. But when A is an officer or director of a corporation, it is called philanthropy. We continue to believe that contributions, aside from those with quite clear direct benefits to the company, should reflect the charitable preferences of owners rather than those of officers and directors.

---

[10] [Divided by hash lines: 1987; 1981 (reprinted 1988); 1981; 1990-93; 1993; 2003.]

On September 30, 1981 Berkshire received a tax ruling from the U.S. Treasury Department that, in most years, should produce a significant benefit for charities of your choice.

Each Berkshire shareholder—on a basis proportional to the number of shares of Berkshire that he owns—will be able to designate recipients of charitable contributions by our company. You'll name the charity; Berkshire will write the check. The ruling states that there will be no personal tax consequences to our shareholders from making such designations.

Thus, our owners now can exercise a perquisite that, although routinely exercised by the owners in closely-held businesses, is almost exclusively exercised by the managers in more widely-held businesses.

In a widely-held corporation the executives ordinarily arrange all charitable donations, with no input at all from shareholders, in two main categories:

(1) Donations considered to benefit the corporation directly in an amount roughly commensurate with the cost of the donation; and

(2) Donations considered to benefit the corporation indirectly through hard-to-measure, long-delayed feedback effects of various kinds.

I and other Berkshire executives have arranged in the past, as we will arrange in the future, all charitable donations in the first category. However, the aggregate level of giving in such category has been quite low, and very likely will remain quite low, because not many gifts can be shown to produce roughly commensurate direct benefits to Berkshire.

In the second category, Berkshire's charitable gifts have been virtually nil, because I am not comfortable with ordinary corporate practice and had no better practice to substitute. What bothers me about ordinary corporate practice is the way gifts tend to be made based more on who does the asking and how corporate peers are responding than on an objective evaluation of the donee's activities. Conventionality often overpowers rationality.

A common result is the use of the stockholder's money to implement the charitable inclinations of the corporate manager, who usually is heavily influenced by specific social pressures on him. Frequently there is an added incongruity; many corporate managers deplore governmental allocation of the taxpayer's dollar but embrace enthusiastically their own allocation of the shareholder's dollar.

For Berkshire, a different model seems appropriate. Just as I wouldn't want you to implement your personal judgments by writing checks on my bank account for charities of your choice, I feel it inappropriate to write checks on your corporate "bank account" for charities of my choice. Your charitable preferences are as good as mine and, for both you and me, funds available to foster charitable interests in a tax-deductible manner reside largely at the corporate level rather than in our own hands.

Under such circumstances, I believe Berkshire should imitate more closely-held companies, not larger public companies. If you and I each own 50% of a corporation, our charitable decision making would be simple. Charities very directly related to the operations of the business would have first claim on our available charitable funds. Any balance available after the "operations-related" contributions would be divided among various charitable interests of the two of us, on a basis roughly proportional to our ownership interest. If the manager of our company had some suggestions, we would listen carefully—but the final decision would be ours. Despite our corporate form, in this aspect of the business we probably would behave as if we were a partnership.

Wherever feasible, I believe in maintaining such a partnership frame of mind, even though we operate through a large, fairly widely-held corporation. Our Treasury ruling will allow such partnership-like behavior in this area.

I am pleased that Berkshire donations can become owner-directed. It is ironic, but understandable, that a large and growing number of major corporations have charitable policies pursuant to which they will match gifts made by their employees (and—[as noted above]—many even match gifts made by directors) but none, to my knowledge, has a plan matching charitable gifts by owners. I say "understandable" because much of the stock of many large corporations is owned on a "revolving door" basis by institutions that have short-term investment horizons, and that lack a long-term owner's perspective.

Our own shareholders are a different breed. [A]t the end of each year, more than 98% of our shares are owned by people who were shareholders at the beginning of the year. This long-term commitment to the business reflects an owner mentality which, as your manager, I intend to acknowledge in all feasible ways. The designated contributions policy is an example of that intent.

Our new program enabling shareholders to designate the recipients of corporate charitable contributions was greeted with extraordinary enthusiasm. Of 932,206 shares eligible for participation (shares where the name of the actual owner appeared on our stockholder record), 95.6% responded. Even excluding Buffett-related shares, the response topped 90%.

In addition, more than 3% of our shareholders voluntarily wrote letters or notes, all but one approving of the program. Both the level of participation and of commentary surpass any shareholder response we have witnessed, even when such response has been intensively solicited by corporate staff and highly-paid professional proxy organizations. In contrast, your extraordinary level of response occurred without even the nudge of a company-provided return envelope. This self-propelled behavior speaks well for the program, and speaks well for our shareholders.

Apparently the owners of our corporation like both possessing and exercising the ability to determine where gifts of their funds shall be made. The "father-knows-best" school of corporate governance will be surprised to find that none of our shareholders sent in a designation sheet with instructions that the officers of Berkshire—in their superior wisdom, of course—make the decision on charitable funds applicable to his shares. Nor did anyone suggest that his share of our charitable funds be used to match contributions made by our corporate directors to charities of the directors' choice (a popular, proliferating and non-publicized policy at many large corporations).

All told, $1,783,655 of shareholder-designed contributions were distributed to about 675 charities. In addition, Berkshire and subsidiaries continue to make certain contributions pursuant to local level decisions made by our operating managers.

There will be some years, perhaps two or three out of ten, when contributions by Berkshire will produce substandard tax deductions—or none at all. In those years we will not effect our shareholder-designated charitable program. In all other years we expect to inform you about October 10th of the amount per share that you may designate. A reply form will accompany the notice, and you will be given about three weeks to respond with your designation.

The designated-contributions idea, along with many other ideas that have turned out well for us, was conceived by Charlie Munger, Vice Chairman of Berkshire. Irrespective of titles, Charlie and I work as partners in managing all controlled companies.

To almost a sinful degree, we enjoy our work as managing partners. And we enjoy having you as our financial partners.

In addition to the shareholder-designated contributions that Berkshire distributes, managers of our operating businesses make contributions, including merchandise, averaging [between $1.5 million and $2.5 million] annually. These contributions support local charities, such as The United Way, and produce roughly commensurate benefits for our businesses.

However, neither our operating managers nor officers of the parent company use Berkshire funds to make contributions to broad national programs or charitable activities of special personal interest to them, except to the extent they do so as shareholders. If your employees, including your CEO, wish to give to their alma maters or other institutions to which they feel a personal attachment, we believe they should use their own money, not yours.

Let me add that our program is easy to administer. Last fall, for two months, we borrowed one person from National Indemnity to help us implement the instructions that came from our 7,500 registered shareholders. I'd guess that the average corporate program in which employee gifts are matched incurs far greater administrative costs. Indeed, our entire corporate overhead is less than half the size of our charitable contributions. (Charlie, however, insists that I tell you that $1.4 million of our $4.9 million overhead is attributable to our corporate jet, The Indefensible.)[11]

---

[11] [Typesetting in original] [The 1986 letter contained the following:]

We bought a corporate jet last year. [Typesetting in original] What you have heard about such planes is true: they are very expensive and a luxury in situations like ours where little travel to out-of-the-way places is required. And planes not only cost a lot to operate, they cost a lot just to look at. Pre-tax, cost of capital plus depreciation on a new $15 million plane probably runs $3 million annually. On our own plane, bought for $850,000 used, such costs run close to $200,000 annually.

Cognizant of such figures, your Chairman, unfortunately, has in the past made a number of rather intemperate remarks about corporate jets. Accordingly, prior to our purchase, I was forced into my Galileo mode. I promptly experienced the necessary "counter-revelation" and travel is now considerably easier—and considerably costlier—than in the past. Whether Berkshire will get its money's worth from the plane is an open question, but I will work at achieving some business triumph that I can (no matter how dubiously) attribute to it. I'm afraid Ben Franklin had my number. Said he: "So convenient a thing it is to be a reasonable creature, since it enables one to find or make a reason for everything one has a mind to do."

[The 1989 letter contained the following:]

Last summer we sold the corporate jet that we purchased for $850,000 three years ago and bought another used jet for $6.7 million. [Noting an amusing anecdote of Carl Sagan

Below is a list showing the largest categories to which our shareholders have steered their contributions.

(a) 347 churches and synagogues received 569 gifts

(b) 238 colleges and universities received 670 gifts

(c) 244 K-12 schools (about two-thirds secular, one-third religious) received 525 gifts

(d) 288 institutions dedicated to art, culture or the humanities received 447 gifts

(e) 180 religious social-service organizations (split about equally between Christian and Jewish) received 411 gifts

(f) 445 secular social-service organizations (about 40% youth-related) received 759 gifts

(g) 153 hospitals received 261 gifts

(h) 186 health-related organizations (American Heart Association, American Cancer Society, etc.) received 320 gifts

Three things about this list seem particularly interesting to me. First, to some degree it indicates what people choose to give money to when they are acting of their own accord, free of pressure from solicitors or emotional appeals from charities. Second, the contributions programs of publicly-held companies almost never allow gifts to churches and synagogues, yet clearly these institutions are what many shareholders would like to support. Third, the gifts made by our shareholders display conflicting philosophies: 130 gifts were directed to organizations that believe in making abortions readily available for women and 30 gifts were directed to organizations (other than churches) that discourage or are opposed to abortion.

Last year I told you that I was thinking of raising the amount that Berkshire shareholders can give under our designated-contri-

---

about obstacles that impede exponential growth of bacteria—referred to in the Epilogue below, some readers] will understandably panic: If our net worth continues to increase at current rates, and the cost of replacing planes also continues to rise at the now-established rate of 100% compounded annually, it will not be long before Berkshire's entire net worth is consumed by its jet.

Charlie doesn't like it when I equate the jet with bacteria; he feels it's degrading to the bacteria. His idea of traveling in style is an air-conditioned bus, a luxury he steps up to only when bargain fares are in effect. My own attitude toward the jet can be summarized by the prayer attributed, apocryphally I'm sure, to St. Augustine as he contemplated leaving a life of secular pleasures to become a priest. Battling the conflict between intellect and glands, he pled: "Help me, Oh Lord, to become chaste—but not yet."

Naming the plane has not been easy. I initially suggested "The Charles T. Munger." Charlie countered with "The Aberration." We finally settled on "The Indefensible."

[The 1998 letter indicates that Buffett sold the Berkshire plane and now does all his flying with Berkshire's flight services businesses.]

butions program and asked for your comments. We received a few well-written letters opposing the entire idea, on the grounds that it was our job to run the business and not our job to force shareholders into making charitable gifts. Most of the shareholders responding, however, noted the tax efficiency of the plan and urged us to increase the designated amount. Several shareholders who have given stock to their children or grandchildren told me that they consider the program a particularly good way to get youngsters thinking at an early age about the subject of giving. These people, in other words, perceive the program to be an educational, as well as philanthropic, tool. The bottom line is that we did raise the amount in 1993, from $8 per share to $10.

We reluctantly terminated the [shareholder-designated contribution] program in 2003 because of controversy over the abortion issue. Over the years numerous organizations on both sides of this issue had been designated by our shareholders to receive contributions. As a result, we regularly received some objections to the gifts designated for pro-choice operations. A few of these came from people and organizations that proceeded to boycott products of our subsidiaries.

In 2003, many independent associates of The Pampered Chef began to feel the boycotts. This development meant that people who trusted us—but who were neither employees of ours nor had a voice in Berkshire decision-making—suffered serious losses of income.

For our shareholders, there was some modest tax efficiency in Berkshire doing the giving rather than their making their gifts directly. Additionally, the program was consistent with our "partnership" approach. But these advantages paled when they were measured against damage done loyal associates who had with great personal effort built businesses of their own. Indeed, Charlie and I see nothing charitable in harming decent, hard-working people just so we and other shareholders can gain some minor tax efficiencies.

Berkshire now makes no contributions at the parent company level. Our various subsidiaries follow philanthropic policies consistent with their practices prior to their acquisition by Berkshire, except that any personal contributions that former owners had earlier made from their corporate pocketbook are now funded by them personally.[12]

F. A Principled Approach to Executive Pay[13]

When returns on capital are ordinary, an earn-more-by-putting-up-more record is no great managerial achievement. You can get the same result personally while operating from your rocking chair. Just quadruple the capital you commit to a savings account and you will quadruple your earnings. You would hardly expect hosannas for that particular accomplishment. Yet, retirement announcements regularly sing the praises of CEOs who have, say, quadrupled earnings of their widget company during their reign—with no one examining whether this gain was attributable simply to many years of retained earnings and the workings of compound interest.

If the widget company consistently earned a superior return on capital throughout the period, or if capital employed only doubled during the CEO's reign, the praise for him may be well deserved. But if return on capital was lackluster and capital employed increased in pace with earnings, applause should be withheld. A savings account in which interest was reinvested would achieve the same year-by-year increase in earnings—and, at only 8% interest, would quadruple its annual earnings in 18 years.

The power of this simple math is often ignored by companies to the detriment of their shareholders. Many corporate compensation plans reward managers handsomely for earnings increases produced solely, or in large part, by retained earnings—i.e., earnings withheld from owners. For example, ten-year, fixed-price stock options are granted routinely, often by companies whose dividends are only a small percentage of earnings.

An example will illustrate the inequities possible under such circumstances. Let's suppose that you had a $100,000 savings account earning 8% interest and "managed" by a trustee who could decide each year what portion of the interest you were to be paid in cash. Interest not paid out would be "retained earnings" added to the savings account to compound. And let's suppose that your trustee, in his superior wisdom, set the "pay-out ratio" at one-quarter of the annual earnings.

Under these assumptions, your account would be worth $179,084 at the end of ten years. Additionally, your annual earnings would have increased about 70% from $8,000 to $13,515 under this inspired management. And, finally, your "dividends" would have increased commensurately, rising regularly from $2,000 in the first year to $3,378 in the tenth year. Each year, when your manager's public relations firm prepared his annual report to you, all of the charts would have had lines marching skyward.

Now, just for fun, let's push our scenario one notch further and give your trustee-manager a ten-year fixed-price option on part of your "business" (i.e., your savings account) based on its fair value in the first year. With such an option, your manager would reap a substantial profit at your expense—just from having held on to most of your earnings. If he were both Machiavellian and a bit of a mathematician, your manager might also have cut the pay-out ratio once he was firmly entrenched.

This scenario is not as farfetched as you might think. Many stock options in the corporate world have worked in exactly that fashion: they have gained in value simply because management retained earnings, not because it did well with the capital in its hands.

Managers actually apply a double standard to options. Leaving aside warrants (which deliver the issuing corporation immediate and substantial compensation), I believe it is fair to say that nowhere in the business world are ten-year, fixed-price options on all or a portion of a business granted to outsiders. Ten months, in fact, would be regarded as extreme. It would be particularly unthinkable for managers to grant a long-term option on a business that was regularly adding to its capital. Any outsider wanting to secure such an option would be required to pay fully for capital added during the option period.

The unwillingness of managers to do-unto-outsiders, however, is not matched by an unwillingness to do-unto-themselves. (Negotiating with one's self seldom produces a barroom brawl.) Managers regularly engineer ten-year, fixed-price options for themselves and associates that, first, totally ignore the fact that retained earnings automatically build value and, second, ignore the carrying cost of capital. As a result, these managers end up profiting much as they would have had they had an option on that savings account that was automatically building up in value.

Of course, stock options often go to talented, value-adding managers and sometimes deliver them rewards that are perfectly appropriate. (Indeed, managers who are really exceptional almost always get far less than they should.) But when the result is equitable, it is accidental. Once granted, the option is blind to individual performance. Because it is irrevocable and unconditional (so long as a manager stays in the company), the sluggard receives rewards from his options precisely as does the star. A managerial Rip Van Winkle, ready to doze for ten years, could not wish for a better "incentive" system.

(I can't resist commenting on one long-term option given an "outsider": that granted the U.S. Government on Chrysler shares as partial consideration for the government's guarantee of some life-saving loans. When these options worked out well for the government, Chrysler sought to modify the payoff, arguing that the rewards to the government were both far greater than intended and outsize[d] in relation to its contribution to Chrysler's recovery. The company's anguish over what it saw as an imbalance between payoff and performance made national news. That anguish may well be unique: to my knowledge, no managers—anywhere—have been similarly offended by unwarranted payoffs arising from options granted to themselves or their colleagues.)

Ironically, the rhetoric about options frequently describes them as desirable because they put managers and owners in the same financial boat. In reality, the boats are far different. No owner has ever escaped the burden of capital costs, whereas a holder of a fixed-price option bears no capital costs at all. An owner must weigh upside potential against downside risk; an option holder has no downside. In fact, the business project in which you would wish to have an option frequently is a project in which you would reject ownership. (I'll be happy to accept a lottery ticket as a gift—but I'll never buy one.)

In dividend policy also, the option holders' interests are best served by a policy that may ill serve the owner. Think back to the savings account example. The trustee, holding his option, would benefit from a no-dividend policy. Conversely, the owner of the account should lean to a total payout so that he can prevent the option-holding manager from sharing in the account's retained earnings.[14]

---

14 [*See* the essay Dividend Policy and Share Repurchases in Part IV.C.]

Despite their shortcomings, options can be appropriate under some circumstances. My criticism relates to their indiscriminate use and, in that connection, I would like to emphasize three points:

First, stock options are inevitably tied to the overall performance of a corporation. Logically, therefore, they should be awarded only to those managers with overall responsibility. Managers with limited areas of responsibility should have incentives that pay off in relation to results under their control. The .350 hitter expects, and also deserves, a big payoff for his performance—even if he plays for a cellar-dwelling team. And the .150 hitter should get no reward—even if he plays for a pennant winner. Only those with overall responsibility for the team should have their rewards tied to its results.

Second, options should be structured carefully. Absent special factors, they should have built into them a retained-earnings or carrying-cost factor. Equally important, they should be priced realistically. When managers are faced with offers for their companies, they unfailingly point out how unrealistic market prices can be as an index of real value. But why, then, should these same depressed prices be the valuations at which managers sell portions of their businesses to themselves? (They may go further: officers and directors sometimes consult the Tax Code to determine the *lowest* prices at which they can, in effect, sell part of the business to insiders. While they're at it, they often elect plans that produce the *worst* tax result for the company.) Except in highly unusual cases, owners are not well served by the sale of part of their business at a bargain price—whether the sale is to outsiders or to insiders. The obvious conclusion: options should be priced at true business value.

Third, I want to emphasize that some managers whom I admire enormously—and whose operating records are far better than mine—disagree with me regarding fixed-price options. They have built corporate cultures that work, and fixed-price options have been a tool that helped them. By their leadership and example, and by the use of options as incentives, these managers have taught their colleagues to think like owners. Such a culture is rare and when it exists should perhaps be left intact—despite inefficiencies and inequities that may infest the option program. "If it ain't broke, don't fix it" is preferable to "purity at any price".

Take, for instance, ten year, fixed-price options (and who wouldn't?). If Fred Futile, CEO of Stagnant, Inc., receives a bundle of these—let's say enough to give him an option on 1% of the company—his self-interest is clear: He should skip dividends entirely and instead use all of the company's earnings to repurchase stock.

Let's assume that under Fred's leadership Stagnant lives up to its name. In each of the ten years after the option grant, it earns $1 billion on $10 billion of net worth, which initially comes to $10 per share on the 100 million shares then outstanding. Fred eschews dividends and regularly uses all earnings to repurchase shares. If the stock constantly sells at ten times earnings per share, it will have appreciated 158% by the end of the option period. That's because repurchases would reduce the number of shares to 38.7 million by that time, and earnings per share would thereby increase to $25.80. Simply by withholding earnings from owners, Fred gets very rich, making a cool $158 million, despite the business itself improving not at all. Astonishingly, Fred could have made more than $100 million if Stagnant's earnings had *declined* by 20% during the ten-year period.

Fred can also get a splendid result for himself by paying no dividends and deploying the earnings he withholds from shareholders into a variety of disappointing projects and acquisitions. Even if these initiatives deliver a paltry 5% return, Fred will still make a bundle. Specifically— with Stagnant's p/e ratio remaining unchanged at ten—Fred's option will deliver him $63 million. Meanwhile, his shareholders will wonder what happened to the "alignment of interests" that was supposed to occur when Fred was issued options.

A "normal" dividend policy, of course—one-third of earnings paid out, for example—produces less extreme results but still can provide lush rewards for managers who achieve nothing.

CEOs understand this math and know that every dime paid out in dividends reduces the value of all outstanding options. I've never, however, seen this manager-owner conflict referenced in proxy materials that request approval of a fixed-priced option plan. Though CEOs invariably preach *internally* that capital comes at a cost, they somehow forget to tell shareholders that fixed-price options give them capital that is free.

It doesn't have to be this way: It's child's play for a board to design options that give effect to the automatic build-up in value that occurs when earnings are retained. But—surprise, surprise—options of that kind are almost never issued. Indeed, the very thought of options with strike prices that are adjusted for retained earnings seems foreign to compensation "experts," who are nevertheless encyclopedic about every management-friendly plan that exists. ("Whose bread I eat, his song I sing.")

Getting fired can produce a particularly bountiful payday for a CEO. Indeed, he can "earn" more in that single day, while cleaning out his desk, than an American worker earns in a lifetime of cleaning toilets. Forget the old maxim about nothing succeeding like success: Today, in the executive suite, the all too-prevalent rule is that nothing succeeds like *failure*.

———————

At Berkshire, however, we use an incentive-compensation system that rewards key managers for meeting targets in their own bailiwicks. If See's does well, that does not produce incentive compensation at the News—nor vice versa. Neither do we look at the price of Berkshire stock when we write bonus checks. We believe good unit performance should be rewarded whether Berkshire stock rises, falls, or stays even. Similarly, we think average performance should earn no special rewards even if our stock should soar. "Performance", furthermore, is defined in different ways depending upon the underlying economics of the business: in some our managers enjoy tailwinds not of their own making, in others they fight unavoidable headwinds.

The rewards that go with this system can be large. At our various business units, top managers sometimes receive incentive bonuses of five times their base salary, or more, and it would appear possible that one manager's bonus could top $2 million in 1986. (I hope so.) We do not put a cap on bonuses, and the potential for rewards is not hierarchical. The manager of a relatively small unit can earn far more than the manager of a larger unit if results indicate he should. We believe, further, that such factors as seniority and age should not affect incentive compensation (though they sometimes influence basic compensation.) A 20 year-old who can hit .300 is as valuable to us as a 40 year-old performing as well.

Obviously, all Berkshire managers can use their bonus money (or other funds, including borrowed money) to buy our stock in the market. Many have done just that—and some now have large holdings. By accepting both the risks and the carrying cost that go with outright purchases, these managers truly walk in the shoes of owners.

———————

At Berkshire, we try to be as logical about compensation as about capital allocation. For example, we compensate Ralph Schey based upon the results of Scott Fetzer rather than those of Berkshire. What could make more sense, since he's responsible for one operation but not the other? A cash bonus or a stock option tied to the fortunes of Berkshire would provide totally capricious rewards to Ralph. He could, for example, be hitting home runs at Scott Fetzer while Charlie and I rang up mistakes at Berkshire, thereby negating his efforts many times over. Conversely, why should option profits or bonuses be heaped upon Ralph if good things are occurring in other parts of Berkshire but Scott Fetzer is lagging?

In setting compensation, we like to hold out the promise of large carrots, but make sure their delivery is tied directly to results in the area that a manager controls. When capital invested in an operation is significant, we also both charge managers a high rate for incremental capital they employ and credit them at an equally high rate for capital they release.

The product of this money's-not-free approach is definitely visible at Scott Fetzer. If Ralph can employ incremental funds at good returns, it pays him to do so: His bonus increases when earnings on additional capital exceed a meaningful hurdle charge. But our bonus calculation is symmetrical: If incremental investment yields sub-standard returns, the shortfall is costly to Ralph as well as to Berkshire. The consequence of this two-way arrangement is that it pays Ralph—and pays him well—to send to Omaha any cash he can't advantageously use in his business.

It has become fashionable at public companies to describe almost every compensation plan as aligning the interests of management with those of shareholders. In our book, alignment means being a partner in both directions, not just on the upside. Many "alignment" plans flunk this basic test, being artful forms of "heads I win, tails you lose."

A common form of misalignment occurs in the typical stock option arrangement, which does not periodically increase the option price to compensate for the fact that retained earnings are building up the wealth of the company. Indeed, the combination of a ten-year option, a low dividend payout, and compound interest can provide lush gains to a manager who has done no more than tread water in his job. A cynic might even note that when payments to owners are held down, the profit to the option-holding manager increases. I have yet to see this vital point spelled out in a proxy statement asking shareholders to approve an option plan.

I can't resist mentioning that our compensation arrangement with Ralph Schey was worked out in about five minutes, immediately upon our purchase of Scott Fetzer and without the "help" of lawyers or compensation consultants. This arrangement embodies a few very simple ideas—not the kind of terms favored by consultants who cannot easily send a large bill unless they have established that you have a large problem (and one, of course, that requires an annual review). Our agreement with Ralph has never been changed. It made sense to him and to me in 1986, and it makes sense now. Our compensation arrangements with the managers of all our other units are similarly simple, though the terms of each agreement vary to fit the economic characteristics of the business at issue, the existence in some cases of partial ownership of the unit by managers, etc.

In all instances, we pursue rationality. Arrangements that pay off in capricious ways, unrelated to a manager's personal accomplishments, may well be welcomed by certain managers. Who, after all, refuses a free lottery ticket? But such arrangements are wasteful to the company and cause the manager to lose focus on what should be his real areas of concern. Additionally, irrational behavior at the parent may well encourage imitative behavior at subsidiaries.

At Berkshire, only Charlie and I have the managerial responsibility for the entire business. Therefore, we are the only parties who should logically be compensated on the basis of what the enterprise does as a whole. Even so, that is not a compensation arrangement we desire. We have carefully designed both the company and our jobs so that we do things we enjoy with people we like. Equally important, we are forced to do very few boring or unpleasant tasks. We are the beneficiaries as well of the abundant array of material and psychic perks that flow to the heads of corporations. Under such idyllic conditions, we don't expect shareholders to ante up loads of compensation for which we have no possible need.

Indeed, if we were not paid at all, Charlie and I would be delighted with the cushy jobs we hold. At bottom, we subscribe to Ronald Reagan's creed: "It's probably true that hard work never killed anyone, but I figure why take the chance."

――――――――――――

We made a sizable acquisition in 1991—the H.H. Brown Shoe Co., the leading North American manufacturer of work shoes and boots, and it has a history of earning unusually fine margins on sales and assets. Shoes are a tough business—of the billion pairs purchased in the United States each year, about 85% are imported—and most manufacturers in the industry do poorly. The wide range of styles and sizes that producers offer causes inventories to be heavy; substantial capital is also tied up in receivables.

A distinguishing characteristic of H.H. Brown is one of the most unusual compensation systems I've encountered—but one that warms my heart: A number of key managers are paid an annual salary of $7,800, to which is added a designated percentage of the profits of the company after these are reduced by a charge for capital employed. These managers therefore truly stand in the shoes of owners. In contrast, most managers talk the talk but don't walk the walk, choosing instead to employ compensation systems that are long on carrots but short on sticks (and that almost invariably treat equity capital as if it were cost-free). The arrangement at Brown, in any case, has served both the company and its managers exceptionally well, which should be no surprise: Managers eager to bet heavily on their abilities usually have plenty of ability to bet on.

It's understandable how [CEO] pay got out of hand. When management hires employees, or when companies bargain with a vendor, the intensity of interest is equal on both sides of the table. One party's gain is the other party's loss, and the money involved has real meaning to both. The result is an honest-to-God negotiation.

But when CEOs (or their representatives) have met with compensation committees, too often one side—the CEO's—has cared far more than the other about what bargain is struck. A CEO, for example, will always regard the difference between receiving options for 100,000 shares or for 500,000 as monumental. To a comp committee, however, the difference may seem unimportant—particularly if, as has been the case at most companies, neither grant will have any effect on reported earnings. Under these conditions, the negotiation often has a "play-money" quality.

Overreaching by CEOs greatly accelerated in the 1990s as compensation packages gained by the most avaricious—a title for which there was vigorous competition—were promptly replicated elsewhere. The couriers for this epidemic of greed were usually consultants and human relations departments, which had no trouble perceiving who buttered their bread. As one compensation consultant commented: "There are two classes of clients you don't want to offend—actual and potential."

In recent years compensation committees too often have been tail-wagging puppy dogs meekly following recommendations by consultants, a breed not known for allegiance to the faceless shareholders who pay their fees. (If you can't tell whose side someone is on, they are *not* on yours.) True, each committee is required by the SEC to state its reasoning about pay in the proxy. But the words are usually boilerplate written by the company's lawyers or its human-relations department.

This costly charade should cease. Directors should not serve on compensation committees unless they are *themselves* capable of negotiating on behalf of owners. They should explain both how they think about pay and how they measure performance. Dealing with shareholders' money, moreover, they should behave as they would were it their own.

In the 1890s, Samuel Gompers described the goal of organized labor as "More!" In the 1990s, America's CEOs adopted his battle cry. The upshot is that CEOs have often amassed riches while their shareholders have experienced financial disasters.

Directors should stop such piracy. There's nothing wrong with paying well for truly exceptional business performance. But, for anything short of that, it's time for directors to shout "Less!" It would be a travesty if the bloated pay of recent years became a baseline for future compensation. Compensation committees should go back to the drawing boards.

G.   *Risk, Reputation and Oversight*[15]

Charlie and I believe that a CEO must not delegate risk control. It's simply too important. At Berkshire, [for example], I both initiate and monitor *every* derivatives contract on our books, with the exception of operations-related contracts at a few of our subsidiaries, such as MidAmerican, and the minor runoff contracts at General Re. If Berkshire ever gets in trouble, it will be *my* fault. It will not be because of misjudgments made by a Risk Committee or Chief Risk Officer.

In my view a board of directors of a huge financial institution is *derelict* if it does not insist that its CEO bear full responsibility for risk control. If he's incapable of handling that job, he should look for other employment. And if he fails at it—with the government thereupon required to step in with funds or guarantees—the financial consequences for him and his board should be severe.

---

15 [2009; appendix to 2010 annual report; 2002.]

It has not been shareholders who have botched the operations of some of our country's largest financial institutions. Yet they have borne the burden, with 90% or more of the value of their holdings wiped out in most cases of failure. Collectively, they have lost more than $500 billion in just the four largest financial fiascos of the last two years. To say these *owners* have been "bailed-out" is to make a mockery of the term.

The CEOs and directors of the failed companies, however, have largely gone unscathed. Their fortunes may have been diminished by the disasters they oversaw, but they still live in grand style. It is the behavior of these CEOs and directors that needs to be changed: If their institutions and the country are harmed by their recklessness, they should pay a heavy price—one not reimbursable by the companies they've damaged nor by insurance. CEOs and, in many cases, directors have long benefitted from oversized financial carrots; some *meaningful* sticks now need to be part of their employment picture as well.

———————

[The 2010 annual report included the following dated July 26, 2010 to Berkshire's managers.] This is my biennial letter to reemphasize Berkshire's top priority [which] is that all of us continue to zealously guard Berkshire's reputation. We can't be perfect but we can try to be. As I've said in these memos for more than 25 years: "We can afford to lose money—even a lot of money. But we can't afford to lose reputation—even a shred of reputation." We *must* continue to measure every act against not only what is legal but also what we would be happy to have written about on the front page of a national newspaper in an article written by an unfriendly but intelligent reporter.

Sometimes your associates will say "Everybody else is doing it." This rationale is almost always a bad one if it is the main justification for a business action. It is totally unacceptable when evaluating a moral decision. Whenever somebody offers that phrase as a rationale, in effect they are saying that they can't come up with a *good* reason. If anyone gives this explanation, tell them to try using it with a reporter or a judge and see how far it gets them.

If you see anything whose propriety or legality causes you to hesitate, be sure to give me a call. However, it's very likely that if a given course of action evokes such hesitation, it's too close to the line and should be abandoned. There's plenty of money to be made in the center of the court. If it's questionable whether some action is close to the line, just assume it is outside and forget it.

As a corollary, let me know promptly if there's any significant bad news. I can handle bad news but I don't like to deal with it after it has festered for awhile. A reluctance to face up immediately to bad news is what turned a problem at Salomon from one that could have easily been disposed of into one that almost caused the demise of a firm with 8,000 employees.

Somebody is doing something today at Berkshire that you and I would be unhappy about if we knew of it. That's inevitable: We now employ more than 250,000 people and the chances of that number getting through the day without any bad behavior occurring is nil. But we can have a huge effect in minimizing such activities by jumping on anything immediately when there is the slightest odor of impropriety. Your attitude on such matters, expressed by behavior as well as words, will be the most important factor in how the culture of your business develops. Culture, more than rule books, determines how an organization behaves.

In other respects, talk to me about what is going on as little or as much as you wish. Each of you does a first-class job of running your operation with your own individual style and you don't need me to help. The only items you need to clear with me are any changes in post-retirement benefits and any unusually large capital expenditures or acquisitions.

Audit committees can't audit. Only a company's outside auditor can determine whether the earnings that a management purports to have made are suspect. Reforms that ignore this reality and that instead focus on the structure and charter of the audit committee will accomplish little. The key job of the audit committee is simply to get the auditors to divulge what they know.

To do this job, the committee must make sure that the auditors worry more about misleading its members than about offending management. In recent years auditors have not felt that way. They have instead generally viewed the CEO, rather than the shareholders or directors, as their client. That has been a natural result of day-to-day working relationships and also of the auditors' understanding that, no matter what the book says, the CEO and CFO pay their fees and determine whether they are retained for both auditing and other work.

[Rules in 2002's Sarbanes-Oxley Act requiring board audit committees to oversee auditors and set their pay] won't materially change this reality. What *will* break this cozy relationship is audit committees unequivocally putting auditors on the spot, making them understand they will become liable for major monetary penalties if they don't come forth with what they know or suspect.

In my opinion, audit committees can accomplish this goal by asking four questions of auditors, the answers to which should be recorded and reported to shareholders. These questions are:

1. If the auditor were solely responsible for preparation of the company's financial statements, would they have in any way been prepared differently from the manner selected by management? This question should cover both material and nonmaterial differences. If the auditor would have done something differently, both management's argument and the auditor's response should be disclosed. The audit committee should then evaluate the facts.

2. If the auditor were an investor, would he have received—in plain English—the information essential to his understanding the company's financial performance during the reporting period?

3. Is the company following the same internal audit procedure that would be followed if the auditor himself were CEO? If not, what are the differences and why?

4. Is the auditor aware of any actions—either accounting or operational—that have had the purpose and effect of moving revenues or expenses from one reporting period to another?

If the audit committee asks these questions, its composition—the focus of most reforms—is of minor importance. In addition, the procedure will save time and expense. When auditors are put on the spot, they will do their duty. If they are not put on the spot . . . well, we have seen the results of that.

The primary advantage of our four questions is that they will act as a prophylactic. Once the auditors know that the audit committee will require them to affirmatively endorse, rather than merely acquiesce to, management's actions, they will resist misdoings early in the process, well before specious figures become embedded in the company's books. Fear of the plaintiff's bar will see to that.

H.   *Corporate Culture*[16]

Our flexibility in respect to capital allocation has accounted for much of our progress to date. We have been able to take money we earn from, say, See's Candies or Business Wire (two of our best-run businesses, but also two offering limited reinvestment opportunities) and use it as part of the stake we needed to buy BNSF.

---

[16] [2010.]

[Another] advantage is the hard-to-duplicate culture that permeates Berkshire. And in businesses, culture counts.

To start with, the directors who represent you think and act like owners. This same owner-orientation prevails among our managers. In many cases, these are people who have sought out Berkshire as an acquirer for a business that they and their families have long owned. They came to us with an owner's mindset, and we provide an environment that encourages them to retain it. Having managers who love their businesses is no small advantage.

Cultures self-propagate. Bureaucratic procedures beget more bureaucracy, and imperial corporate palaces induce imperious behavior. (As one wag put it, "You know you're no longer CEO when you get in the back seat of your car and it doesn't move.") At Berkshire's "World Headquarters" our annual rent is $270,212. Moreover, the home-office investment in furniture, art, Coke dispenser, lunch room, high-tech equipment—you name it—totals $301,363. As long as Charlie and I treat your money as if it were our own, Berkshire's managers are likely to be careful with it as well.

Our compensation programs, our annual meeting and even our annual reports are all designed with an eye to reinforcing the Berkshire culture, and making it one that will repel and expel managers of a different bent. This culture grows stronger every year, and it will remain intact long after Charlie and I have left the scene.

II. Finance and Investing

We bought [substantial Washington Post Company ("WPC")] holdings in mid-1973 at a price of not more than one-fourth of the then per-share business value of the enterprise. Calculating the price/value ratio required no unusual insights. Most security analysts, media brokers, and media executives would have estimated WPC's intrinsic business value at $400 to $500 million just as we did. And its $100 million stock market valuation was published daily for all to see. Our advantage, rather, was attitude: we had learned from Ben Graham that the key to successful investing was the purchase of shares in good businesses when market prices were at a large discount from underlying business values.

Most institutional investors in the early 1970s, on the other hand, regarded business value as of only minor relevance when they were deciding the prices at which they would buy or sell. This now seems hard to believe. However, these institutions were then under the spell of academics at prestigious business schools who were preaching a newly-fashioned theory: the stock market was totally efficient, and therefore calculations of business value—and even thought, itself—were of no importance in investment activities. (We are enormously indebted to those academics: what could be more advantageous in an intellectual contest—whether it be bridge, chess, or stock selection—than to have opponents who have been taught that thinking is a waste of energy?)[17]

A. *Farms, Real Estate and Stock*[18]

From 1973 to 1981, the Midwest experienced an explosion in farm prices, caused by a widespread belief that runaway inflation was coming and fueled by the lending policies of small rural banks. Then the bubble burst, bringing price declines of 50% or more that devastated both leveraged farmers and their lenders. Five times as many Iowa and Nebraska banks failed in that bubble's aftermath than [the] Great Recession [of 2008-09].

In 1986, I purchased a 400-acre farm, located 50 miles north of Omaha, from the FDIC. It cost me $280,000, considerably less than what a failed bank had lent against the farm a few years earlier. I knew nothing about operating a farm. But I have a son who loves farming and I learned from him both how many bushels of corn and soybeans the farm would produce and what the operating ex-

---

[17] [Introductory essay, 1985.]
[18] [2013.]

81

penses would be. From these estimates, I calculated the normalized return from the farm to then be about 10%. I also thought it was likely that productivity would improve over time and that crop prices would move higher as well. Both expectations proved out.

I needed no unusual knowledge or intelligence to conclude that the investment had no downside and potentially had substantial upside. There would, of course, be the occasional bad crop and prices would sometimes disappoint. But so what? There would be some unusually good years as well, and I would never be under any pressure to sell the property. Now, [three decades] later, the farm has tripled its earnings and is worth five times or more what I paid. I still know nothing about farming and recently made just my second visit to the farm.

In 1993, I made another small investment. Larry Silverstein, Salomon's landlord when I was the company's CEO, told me about a New York retail property adjacent to NYU that the Resolution Trust Corp. was selling. Again, a bubble had popped—this one involving commercial real estate—and the RTC had been created to dispose of the assets of failed savings institutions whose optimistic lending practices had fueled the folly.

Here, too, the analysis was simple. As had been the case with the farm, the unleveraged current yield from the property was about 10%. But the property had been under-managed by the RTC, and its income would increase when several vacant stores were leased. Even more important, the largest tenant—who occupied around 20% of the project's space—was paying rent of about $5 per foot, whereas other tenants averaged $70. The expiration of this bargain lease in nine years was certain to provide a major boost to earnings. The property's location was also superb: NYU wasn't going anywhere.

I joined a small group, including Larry and my friend Fred Rose, that purchased the parcel. Fred was an experienced, high-grade real estate investor who, with his family, would manage the property. And manage it they did. As old leases expired, earnings tripled. Annual distributions now exceed 35% of our original equity investment. Moreover, our original mortgage was refinanced in 1996 and again in 1999, moves that allowed several special distributions totaling more than 150% of what we had invested. I've yet to view the property.

Income from both the farm and the NYU real estate will probably increase in the decades to come. Though the gains won't be dramatic, the two investments will be solid and satisfactory holdings for my lifetime and, subsequently, for my children and grandchildren. I tell these tales to illustrate certain fundamentals of investing:

• You don't need to be an expert in order to achieve satisfactory investment returns. But if you aren't, you must recognize your limitations and follow a course certain to work reasonably well. Keep things simple and don't swing for the fences. When promised quick profits, respond with a quick "no."

• Focus on the future productivity of the asset you are considering. If you don't feel comfortable making a rough estimate of the asset's future earnings, just forget it and move on. No one has the ability to evaluate every investment possibility. But omniscience isn't necessary; you only need to understand the actions you undertake.

• If you instead focus on the prospective price change of a contemplated purchase, you are speculating. There is nothing improper about that. I know, however, that I am unable to speculate successfully, and I am skeptical of those who claim sustained success at doing so. Half of all coin-flippers will win their first toss; *none* of those winners has an expectation of profit if he continues to play the game. And the fact that a given asset has appreciated in the recent past is *never* a reason to buy it.

• With my two small investments, I thought *only* of what the properties would produce and cared not at all about their daily valuations. Games are won by players who focus on the playing field—not by those whose eyes are glued to the scoreboard. If you can enjoy Saturdays and Sundays without looking at stock prices, give it a try on weekdays.

• Forming macro opinions or listening to the macro or market predictions of others is a waste of time. Indeed, it is dangerous because it may blur your vision of the facts that are truly important. (When I hear TV commentators glibly opine on what the market will do next, I am reminded of Mickey Mantle's scathing comment: "You don't know how easy this game is until you get into that broadcasting booth.")

• My two purchases were made in 1986 and 1993. What the economy, interest rates, or the stock market might do in the years immediately following—1987 and 1994—was of no importance to me in making those investments. I can't remember what the headlines or pundits were saying at the time. Whatever the chatter, corn would keep growing in Nebraska and students would flock to NYU.

There is one major difference between my two small invest-ments and an investment in stocks. Stocks provide you minute-to-minute valuations for your holdings whereas I have yet to see a quotation for either my farm or the New York real estate.

It should be an enormous advantage for investors in stocks to have those wildly fluctuating valuations placed on their holdings—and for some investors, it is. After all, if a moody fellow with a farm bordering my property yelled out a price every day to me at which he would either buy my farm or sell me his—and those prices varied widely over short periods of time depending on his mental state—how in the world could I be other than benefited by his erratic behavior? If his daily shout-out was ridiculously low, and I had some spare cash, I would buy his farm. If the number he yelled was absurdly high, I could either sell to him or just go on farming.

Owners of stocks, however, too often let the capricious and often irrational behavior of their fellow owners cause them to be-have irrationally as well. Because there is so much chatter about markets, the economy, interest rates, price behavior of stocks, etc., some investors believe it is important to listen to pundits—and, worse yet, important to consider acting upon their comments.

Those people who can sit quietly for decades when they own a farm or apartment house too often become frenetic when they are exposed to a stream of stock quotations and accompanying com-mentators delivering an implied message of "Don't just sit there, *do* something." For these investors, liquidity is transformed from the unqualified benefit it should be to a curse.

A "flash crash" or some other extreme market fluctuation can't hurt an investor any more than an erratic and mouthy neigh-bor can hurt my farm investment. Indeed, tumbling markets can be helpful to the true investor if he has cash available when prices get far out of line with values. A climate of fear is your *friend* when investing; a euphoric world is your enemy.

During the extraordinary financial panic that occurred late in 2008, I never gave a thought to selling my farm or New York real estate, even though a severe recession was clearly brewing. And, if I had owned 100% of a solid business with good long-term pros-pects, it would have been foolish for me to even consider dumping it. So why would I have sold my stocks that were small participa-tions in wonderful businesses? True, any one of them might eventu-ally disappoint, but as a group they were certain to do well. Could anyone really believe the earth was going to swallow up the incredible productive assets and unlimited human ingenuity existing in America?

When Charlie and I buy stocks—which we think of as small portions of businesses—our analysis is very similar to that which we use in buying entire businesses. We first have to decide whether we can sensibly estimate an earnings range for five years out, or more. If the answer is yes, we will buy the stock (or business) if it sells at a reasonable price in relation to the bottom boundary of our estimate. If, however, we lack the ability to estimate future earnings—which is usually the case—we simply move on to other prospects. In the 54 years we have worked together, we have *never* foregone an attractive purchase because of the macro or political environment, or the views of other people. In fact, these subjects never come up when we make decisions.

B. *Mr. Market*[19]

Whenever Charlie and I buy common stocks for Berkshire's insurance companies (leaving aside arbitrage purchases, discussed [in the next essay]) we approach the transaction as if we were buying into a private business. We look at the economic prospects of the business, the people in charge of running it, and the price we must pay. We do not have in mind any time or price for sale. Indeed, we are willing to hold a stock indefinitely so long as we expect the business to increase in intrinsic value at a satisfactory rate. When investing, we view ourselves as business analysts—not as market analysts, not as macroeconomic analysts, and not even as security analysts.

Our approach makes an active trading market useful, since it periodically presents us with mouth-watering opportunities. But by no means is it essential: a prolonged suspension of trading in the securities we hold would not bother us any more than does the lack of daily quotations on World Book or Fechheimer. Eventually, our economic fate will be determined by the economic fate of the business we own, whether our ownership is partial or total.

Ben Graham, my friend and teacher, long ago described the mental attitude toward market fluctuations that I believe to be most conducive to investment success. He said that you should imagine market quotations as coming from a remarkably accommodating fellow named Mr. Market who is your partner in a private

---

[19] [Divided by hash lines: 1987; 1997.]

business. Without fail, Mr. Market appears daily and names a price at which he will either buy your interest or sell you his.

Even though the business that the two of you own may have economic characteristics that are stable, Mr. Market's quotations will be anything but. For, sad to say, the poor fellow has incurable emotional problems. At times he feels euphoric and can see only the favorable factors affecting the business. When in that mood, he names a very high buy-sell price because he fears that you will snap up his interest and rob him of imminent gains. At other times he is depressed and can see nothing but trouble ahead for both the business and the world. On these occasions he will name a very low price, since he is terrified that you will unload your interest on him.

Mr. Market has another endearing characteristic: He doesn't mind being ignored. If his quotation is uninteresting to you today, he will be back with a new one tomorrow. Transactions are strictly at your option. Under these conditions, the more manic-depressive his behavior, the better for you.

But, like Cinderella at the ball, you must heed one warning or everything will turn into pumpkins and mice: Mr. Market is there to serve you, not to guide you. It is his pocketbook, not his wisdom, that you will find useful. If he shows up some day in a particularly foolish mood, you are free to either ignore him or to take advantage of him, but it will be disastrous if you fall under his influence. Indeed, if you aren't certain that you understand and can value your business far better than Mr. Market you don't belong in the game. As they say in poker, "If you've been in the game 30 minutes and you don't know who the patsy is, *you're* the patsy."

Ben's Mr. Market allegory may seem out-of-date in today's investment world, in which most professionals and academicians talk of efficient markets, dynamic hedging and betas. Their interest in such matters is understandable, since techniques shrouded in mystery clearly have value to the purveyor of investment advice. After all, what witch doctor has ever achieved fame and fortune by simply advising "Take two aspirins"?

The value of market esoterica to the consumer of investment advice is a different story. In my opinion, investment success will not be produced by arcane formulae, computer programs or signals flashed by the price behavior of stocks and markets. Rather an investor will succeed by coupling good business judgment with an ability to insulate his thoughts and behavior from the super-contagious emotions that swirl about the marketplace. In my own efforts to stay insulated, I have found it highly useful to keep Ben's Mr. Market concept firmly in mind.

Following Ben's teachings, Charlie and I let our marketable equities tell us by their operating results—not by their daily, or even yearly, price quotations—whether our investments are successful. The market may ignore business success for a while, but eventually will confirm it. As Ben said: "In the short run, the market is a voting machine but in the long run it is a weighing machine." The speed at which a business's success is recognized, furthermore, is not that important as long as the company's intrinsic value is increasing at a satisfactory rate. In fact, delayed recognition can be an advantage: It may give us the chance to buy more of a good thing at a bargain price.

Sometimes, of course, the market may judge a business to be more valuable than the underlying facts would indicate it is. In such a case, we will sell our holdings. Sometimes, also, we will sell a security that is fairly valued or even undervalued because we require funds for a still more undervalued investment or one we believe we understand better.

We need to emphasize, however, that we do not sell holdings just because they have appreciated or because we have held them for a long time. (Of Wall Street maxims the most foolish may be "You can't go broke taking a profit.") We are quite content to hold any security indefinitely, so long as the prospective return on equity capital of the underlying business is satisfactory, management is competent and honest, and the market does not overvalue the business.

However, our insurance companies own some marketable common stocks that we would not sell even though they became far overpriced in the market. In effect, we view these investments exactly like our successful controlled businesses—a permanent part of Berkshire rather than merchandise to be disposed of once Mr. Market offers us a sufficiently high price. To that, I will add one qualifier: These stocks are held by our insurance companies and we would, if absolutely necessary, sell portions of our holdings to pay extraordinary insurance losses. We intend, however, to manage our affairs so that sales are never required.

A determination to have and to hold, which Charlie and I share, obviously involves a mixture of personal and financial considerations. To some, our stand may seem highly eccentric. (Charlie and I have long followed David Ogilvy's advice: "Develop your eccentricities while you are young. That way, when you get old, people won't think you're going ga-ga.") Certainly, in the transaction-fixated Wall Street of recent years, our posture must seem odd: To many in that arena, both companies and stocks are seen only as raw material for trades.

Our attitude, however, fits our personalities and the way we want to live our lives. Churchill once said, "You shape your houses and then they shape you." We know the manner in which we wish to be shaped. For that reason, we would rather achieve a return of X while associating with people whom we strongly like and admire than realize 110% of X by exchanging these relationships for uninteresting or unpleasant ones.

A short quiz: If you plan to eat hamburgers throughout your life and are not a cattle producer, should you wish for higher or lower prices for beef? Likewise, if you are going to buy a car from time to time but are not an auto manufacturer, should you prefer higher or lower car prices? These questions, of course, answer themselves.

But now for the final exam: If you expect to be a net saver during the next five years, should you hope for a higher or lower stock market during that period? Many investors get this one wrong. Even though they are going to be net buyers of stocks for many years to come, they are elated when stock prices rise and depressed when they fall. In effect, they rejoice because prices have risen for the "hamburgers" they will soon be buying. This reaction makes no sense. Only those who will be sellers of equities in the near future should be happy at seeing stocks rise. Prospective purchasers should much prefer sinking prices.

For shareholders of Berkshire who do not expect to sell, the choice is even clearer. To begin with, our owners are automatically saving even if they spend every dime they personally earn: Berkshire "saves" for them by retaining all earnings, thereafter using these savings to purchase businesses and securities. Clearly, the more cheaply we make these buys, the more profitable our owners' indirect savings program will be.

Furthermore, through Berkshire you own major positions in companies that consistently repurchase their shares. The benefits that these programs supply us grow as prices fall: When stock prices are low, the funds that an investee spends on repurchases increase our ownership of that company by a greater amount than is the case when prices are higher. For example, the repurchases that Coca-Cola and Wells Fargo made in past years at very low prices benefitted Berkshire far more than do today's repurchases, made at loftier prices.

[Since at the end of every year, almost all Berkshire shares are held by the same investors who owned them at the start of the year, Berkshire shareholders are] savers. They should therefore rejoice when markets decline and allow both us and our investees to deploy funds more advantageously.

So smile when you read a headline that says "Investors lose as market falls." Edit it in your mind to "Disinvestors lose as market falls—but investors gain." Though writers often forget this truism, there is a buyer for every seller and what hurts one necessarily helps the other. (As they say in golf matches: "Every putt makes *someone* happy.")

We gained enormously from the low prices placed on many equities and businesses in the 1970s and 1980s. Markets that then were hostile to investment transients were friendly to those taking up permanent residence. In recent years, the actions we took in those decades have been validated, but we have found few new opportunities. In its role as a corporate "saver," Berkshire continually looks for ways to sensibly deploy capital, but it may be some time before we find opportunities that get us truly excited.

C. *Arbitrage*[20]

[O]ur insurance subsidiaries sometimes engage in arbitrage as an alternative to holding short-term cash equivalents. We prefer, of course, to make major long-term commitments, but we often have more cash than good ideas. At such times, arbitrage sometimes promises much greater returns than Treasury Bills and, equally important, cools any temptation we may have to relax our standards for long-term investments. (Charlie's signoff after we've talked about an arbitrage commitment is usually: "Okay, at least it will keep you out of bars.")

During 1988 we made unusually large profits from arbitrage, measured both by absolute dollars and rate of return. Our pre-tax gain was about $78 million on average invested funds of about $147 million.

This level of activity makes some detailed discussion of arbitrage and our approach to it appropriate. Once, the word applied only to the simultaneous purchase and sale of securities or foreign exchange in two different markets. The goal was to exploit tiny

---

[20] [Divided by hash lines: 1988; 1989.]

price differentials that might exist between, say, Royal Dutch stock trading in guilders in Amsterdam, pounds in London, and dollars in New York. Some people might call this scalping: it won't surprise you that practitioners opted for the French term, arbitrage.

Since World War I the definition of arbitrage—or "risk arbitrage," as it is now sometimes called—has expanded to include the pursuit of profits from an announced corporate event such as sale of the company, merger, recapitalization, reorganization, liquidation, self-tender, etc. In most cases the arbitrageur expects to profit regardless of the behavior of the stock market. The major risk he usually faces instead is that the announced event won't happen.

Some offbeat opportunities occasionally arise in the arbitrage field. I participated in one of these when I was 24 and working in New York for Graham-Newman Corp. Rockwood & Co., a Brooklyn-based chocolate products company of limited profitability, had adopted LIFO inventory valuation in 1941 when cocoa was selling for 5 cents per pound. In 1954 a temporary shortage of cocoa caused the price to soar to over 60 cents. Consequently Rockwood wished to unload its valuable inventory—quickly, before the price dropped. But if the cocoa had simply been sold off, the company would have owed close to a 50% tax on the proceeds.

The 1954 Tax Code came to the rescue. It contained an arcane provision that eliminated the tax otherwise due on LIFO profits if inventory was distributed to shareholders as part of a plan reducing the scope of a corporation's business. Rockwood decided to terminate one of its businesses, the sale of cocoa butter, and said 13 million pounds of its cocoa bean inventory was attributable to that activity. Accordingly, the company offered to repurchase its stock in exchange for the cocoa beans it no longer needed, paying 80 pounds of beans for each share.

For several weeks I busily bought shares, sold beans, and made periodic stops at Schroeder Trust to exchange stock certificates for warehouse receipts. The profits were good and my only expense was subway tokens.

The architect of Rockwood's restructuring was an unknown, but brilliant Chicagoan, Jay Pritzker, then 32. If you're familiar with Jay's subsequent record, you won't be surprised to hear the action worked out rather well for Rockwood's continuing shareholders also. From shortly before the tender until shortly after it, Rockwood stock appreciated from 15 to 100, even though the company was experiencing large operating losses. Sometimes there is more to stock valuation than price-earnings ratios.

In recent years, most arbitrage operations have involved take-overs, friendly and unfriendly. With acquisition fever rampant, with anti-trust challenges almost non-existent, and with bids often ratcheting upward, arbitrageurs have prospered mightily. They have not needed special talents to do well; the trick, à la Peter Sellers in the movie, has simply been "Being There." In Wall Street the old proverb has been reworded: "Give a man a fish and you feed him for a day. Teach him how to arbitrage and you feed him forever." (If, however, he studied at the Ivan Boesky School of Arbitrage, it may be a state institution that supplies his meals.)

To evaluate arbitrage situations you must answer four questions: (1) How likely is it that the promised event will indeed occur? (2) How long will your money be tied up? (3) What chance is there that something still better will transpire—a competing take-over bid, for example? and (4) What will happen if the event does not take place because of anti-trust action, financing glitches, etc.?

Arcata Corp., one of our more serendipitous arbitrage experiences, illustrates the twists and turns of the business. On September 28, 1981 the directors of Arcata agreed in principle to sell the company to Kohlberg Kravis Roberts & Co. (KKR), then and now a major leveraged-buyout firm. Arcata was in the printing and forest products businesses and had one other thing going for it: In 1978 the U.S. Government had taken title to 10,700 acres of Arcata timber, primarily old-growth redwood, to expand Redwood National Park. The government had paid $97.9 million, in several installments, for this acreage, a sum Arcata was contesting as grossly inadequate. The parties also disputed the interest rate that should apply to the period between the taking of the property and final payment for it. The enabling legislation stipulated 6% simple interest; Arcata argued for a much higher and compounded rate.

Buying a company with a highly-speculative, large-sized claim in litigation creates a negotiating problem, whether the claim is on behalf of or against the company. To solve this problem, KKR offered $37.00 per Arcata share plus two-thirds of any additional amounts paid by the government for the redwood lands.

Appraising this arbitrage opportunity, we had to ask ourselves whether KKR would consummate the transaction since, among other things, its offer was contingent upon its obtaining "satisfactory financing." A clause of this kind is always dangerous for the seller: It offers an easy exit for a suitor whose ardor fades between proposal and marriage. However, we were not particularly worried about this possibility because KKR's past record for closing had been good.

We also had to ask ourselves what would happen if the KKR deal did fall through, and here we also felt reasonably comfortable: Arcata's management and directors had been shopping the company for some time and were clearly determined to sell. If KKR went away, Arcata would likely find another buyer, though of course, the price might be lower.

Finally, we had to ask ourselves what the redwood claim might be worth. Your Chairman, who can't tell an elm from an oak, had no trouble with that one: He coolly evaluated the claim at somewhere between zero and a whole lot.

We started buying Arcata stock, then around $33.50, on September 30 and in eight weeks purchased about 400,000 shares, or 5% of the company. The initial announcement said that the $37.00 would be paid in January, 1982. Therefore, if everything had gone perfectly, we would have achieved an annual rate of return of about 40%—not counting the redwood claim, which would have been frosting.

All did not go perfectly. In December it was announced that the closing would be delayed a bit. Nevertheless, a definitive agreement was signed on January 4. Encouraged, we raised our stake, buying at around $38.00 per share and increasing our holdings to 655,000 shares, or over 7% of the company. Our willingness to pay up—even though the closing had been postponed—reflected our leaning toward "a whole lot" rather than "zero" for the redwoods.

Then, on February 25 the lenders said they were taking a "second look" at financing terms "in view of the severely depressed housing industry and its impact on Arcata's outlook." The stockholders' meeting was postponed again, to April. An Arcata spokesman said he "did not think the fate of the acquisition itself was imperiled." When arbitrageurs hear such reassurances, their minds flash to the old saying: "He lied like a finance minister on the eve of devaluation."

On March 12 KKR said its earlier deal wouldn't work, first cutting its offer to $33.50, then two days later raising it to $35.00. On March 15, however, the directors turned this bid down and accepted another group's offer of $37.50 plus one-half of any redwood recovery. The shareholders okayed the deal, and the $37.50 was paid on June 4.

We received $24.6 million versus our cost of $22.9 million; our average holding period was close to six months. Considering the trouble this transaction encountered, our 15% annual rate of return—excluding any value for the redwood claim—was more than satisfactory.

But the best was yet to come. The trial judge appointed two commissions, one to look at the timber's value, the other to consider the interest rate questions. In January 1987, the first commission said the redwoods were worth $275.7 million and the second commission recommended a compounded, blended rate of return working out to about 14%.

In August 1987 the judge upheld these conclusions, which meant a net amount of about $600 million would be due Arcata. The government then appealed. In 1988, though, before this appeal was heard, the claim was settled for $519 million. Consequently, we received an additional $29.48 per share, or about $19.3 million. We will get another $800,000 or so in 1989.

Berkshire's arbitrage activities differ from those of many arbitrageurs. First, we participate in only a few, and usually very large, transactions each year. Most practitioners buy into a great many deals—perhaps 50 or more per year. With that many irons in the fire, they must spend most of their time monitoring both the progress of deals and the market movements of the related stocks. This is not how Charlie nor I wish to spend our lives. (What's the sense in getting rich just to stare at a ticker tape all day?)

Because we diversify so little, one particularly profitable or unprofitable transaction will affect our yearly result from arbitrage far more than it will the typical arbitrage operation. So far, Berkshire has not had a really bad experience. But we will—and when it happens we'll report the gory details to you.

The other way we differ from some arbitrage operations is that we participate only in transactions that have been publicly announced. We do not trade on rumors or try to guess takeover candidates. We just read the newspapers, think about a few of the big propositions, and go by our own sense of probabilities.

At yearend, our only major arbitrage position was 3,342,000 shares of RJR Nabisco with a cost of $281.8 million and a market value of $304.5 million. In January we increased our holdings to roughly four million shares and in February we eliminated our position. About three million shares were accepted when we tendered our holdings to KKR, which acquired RJR, and the returned shares were promptly sold in the market. Our pre-tax profit was a better-than-expected $64 million.

Earlier, another familiar face turned up in the RJR bidding contest: Jay Pritzker, who was part of a First Boston group that made a tax-oriented offer. To quote Yogi Berra; "It was déjà vu all over again."

During most of the time when we normally would have been purchasers of RJR, our activities in the stock were restricted because of Salomon's participation in a bidding group. Customarily, Charlie and I, though we are directors of Salomon, are walled off from information about its merger and acquisition work. We have asked that it be that way: The information would do us no good and could, in fact, occasionally inhibit Berkshire's arbitrage operations.

However, the unusually large commitment that Salomon proposed to make in the RJR deal required that all directors be fully informed and involved. Therefore, Berkshire's purchases of RJR were made at only two times: first, in the few days immediately following management's announcement of buyout plans, before Salomon became involved; and considerably later, after the RJR board made its decision in favor of KKR. Because we could not buy at other times, our directorships cost Berkshire significant money.

Considering Berkshire's good results in 1988, you might expect us to pile into arbitrage during 1989. Instead, we expect to be on the sidelines.

One pleasant reason is that our cash holdings are down—because our position in equities that we expect to hold for a very long time is substantially up. As regular readers of this report know, our new commitments are not based on a judgment about short-term prospects for the stock market. Rather, they reflect an opinion about long-term business prospects for specific companies. We do not have, never have had, and never will have an opinion about where the stock market, interest rates, or business activity will be a year from now.

Even if we had a lot of cash we probably would do little in arbitrage in 1989. Some extraordinary excesses have developed in the takeover field. As Dorothy says: "Toto, I have a feeling we're not in Kansas any more."

We have no idea how long the excesses will last, nor do we know what will change the attitudes of government, lender and buyer that fuel them. But we do know that the less the prudence with which others conduct their affairs, the greater the prudence with which we should conduct our own affairs. We have no desire to arbitrage transactions that reflect the unbridled—and, in our view, often unwarranted—optimism of both buyers and lenders. In our activities, we will heed the wisdom of Herb Stein: "If something can't go on forever, it will end."

We told you last year that we expected to do little in arbitrage during 1989, and that's the way it turned out. Arbitrage positions are a substitute for short-term cash equivalents, and during part of the year we held relatively low levels of cash. In the rest of the year we had a fairly good-sized cash position and even so chose not to engage in arbitrage. The main reason was corporate transactions that made no economic sense to us; arbitraging such deals comes too close to playing the greater-fool game. (As Wall Streeter Ray DeVoe says: "Fools rush in where angels fear to trade.") We will engage in arbitrage from time to time—sometimes on a large scale—but only when we like the odds.

D. *Debunking Standard Dogma*[21]

The preceding discussion about arbitrage makes a small discussion of "efficient market theory" (EMT) also seem relevant. This doctrine became highly fashionable—indeed, almost holy scripture—in academic circles during the 1970s. Essentially, it said that analyzing stocks was useless because all public information about them was appropriately reflected in their prices. In other words, the market always knew everything. As a corollary, the professors who taught EMT said that someone throwing darts at the stock tables could select a stock portfolio having prospects just as good as one selected by the brightest, most hard-working security analyst. Amazingly, EMT was embraced not only by academics, but by many investment professionals and corporate managers as well. Observing correctly that the market was *frequently* efficient, they went on to conclude incorrectly that it was *always* efficient. The difference between these propositions is night and day.

In my opinion, the continuous 63-year arbitrage experience of Graham-Newman Corp., Buffett Partnership, and Berkshire illustrates just how foolish EMT is. (There's plenty of other evidence, also.) While at Graham-Newman, I made a study of its earnings from arbitrage during the entire 1926-1956 lifespan of the com-

---

21 [Divided by hash lines: 1988; 1993; 1991; 1987.]

pany. Unleveraged returns averaged 20% per year. Starting in 1956, I applied Ben Graham's arbitrage principles, first at Buffett Partnership and then Berkshire. Though I've not made an exact calculation, I have done enough work to know that the 1956-1988 returns averaged well over 20%. (Of course, I operated in an environment far more favorable than Ben's; he had 1929-1932 to contend with.)

All of the conditions are present that are required for a fair test of portfolio performance: (1) the three organizations traded hundreds of different securities while building this 63-year record; (2) the results are not skewed by a few fortunate experiences; (3) we did not have to dig for obscure facts or develop keen insights about products or managements—we simply acted on highly-publicized events; and (4) our arbitrage positions were a clearly identified universe—they have not been selected by hindsight.

Over the 63 years, the general market delivered just under a 10% annual return, including dividends. That means $1,000 would have grown to $405,000 if all income had been reinvested. A 20% rate of return, however, would have produced $97 million. That strikes us a statistically-significant differential that might, conceivably, arouse one's curiosity.

Yet proponents of the theory have never seemed interested in discordant evidence of this type. True, they don't talk quite as much about their theory today as they used to. But no one, to my knowledge, has ever said he was wrong, no matter how many thousands of students he has sent forth misinstructed. EMT, moreover, continues to be an integral part of the investment curriculum at major business schools. Apparently, a reluctance to recant, and thereby to demystify the priesthood, is not limited to theologians.

Naturally the disservice done students and gullible investment professionals who have swallowed EMT has been an extraordinary service to us and other followers of Graham. In any sort of a contest—financial, mental, or physical—it's an enormous advantage to have opponents who have been taught that it's useless to even try. From a selfish point of view, Grahamites should probably endow chairs to ensure the perpetual teaching of EMT.

All this said, a warning is appropriate. Arbitrage has looked easy recently. But this is not a form of investing that guarantees profits of 20% a year or, for that matter, profits of any kind. As noted, the market is reasonably efficient much of the time: For every arbitrage opportunity we seized in that 63-year period, many more were foregone because they seemed properly-priced.

An investor cannot obtain superior profits from stocks by simply committing to a specific investment category or style. He can earn them only by carefully evaluating facts and continuously exercising discipline. Investing in arbitrage situations, per se, is no better a strategy than selecting a portfolio by throwing darts.

[W]hen we own portions of outstanding businesses with outstanding managements, our favorite holding period is forever. We are just the opposite of those who hurry to sell and book profits when companies perform well but who tenaciously hang on to businesses that disappoint. Peter Lynch aptly likens such behavior to cutting the flowers and watering the weeds.

––––––––––––––

[W]e continue to think that it is usually foolish to part with an interest in a business that is both understandable and durably wonderful. Business interests of that kind are simply too hard to replace.

Interestingly, corporate managers have no trouble understanding that point when they are focusing on a business they operate: A parent company that owns a subsidiary with superb long-term economics is not likely to sell that entity regardless of price. "Why," the CEO would ask, "should I part with my crown jewel?" Yet that same CEO, when it comes to running his personal investment portfolio, will offhandedly—and even impetuously—move from business to business when presented with no more than superficial arguments by his broker for doing so. The worst of these is perhaps, "You can't go broke taking a profit." Can you imagine a CEO using this line to urge his board to sell a star subsidiary? In our view, what makes sense in business also makes sense in stocks: An investor should ordinarily hold a small piece of an outstanding business with the same tenacity that an owner would exhibit if he owned all of that business.

Earlier I mentioned the financial results that could have been achieved by investing $40 in The Coca-Cola Co. in 1919.[22] In 1938, more than 50 years after the introduction of Coke, and long after the drink was firmly established as an American icon, *Fortune* did an excellent story on the company. In the second paragraph the writer reported: "Several times every year a weighty and serious

––––––––––––––

[22] [A separate paragraph from this 1993 letter contained the following:]

Let me add a lesson from history: Coke went public in 1919 at $40 per share. By the end of 1920 the market, coldly reevaluating Coke's future prospects, had battered the stock down by more than 50%, to $19.50. At yearend 1993, that single share, with dividends reinvested, was worth more than $2.1 million.

investor looks long and with profound respect at Coca-Cola's record, but comes regretfully to the conclusion that he is looking too
late. The specters of saturation and competition rise before him."

Yes, competition there was in 1938 and in 1993 as well. But
it's worth noting that in 1938 The Coca-Cola Co. sold 207 million
cases of soft drinks (if its gallonage then is converted into the 192-
ounce cases used for measurement today) and in 1993 it sold about
10.7 billion cases, a 50-fold increase in physical volume from a company that in 1938 was already dominant in its very major industry.
Nor was the party over in 1938 for an investor: Though the $40
invested in 1919 in one share had (with dividends reinvested)
turned into $3,277 by the end of 1938, a fresh $40 then invested in
Coca-Cola stock would have grown to $25,000 by yearend 1993.

I can't resist one more quote from that 1938 *Fortune* story: "It
would be hard to name any company comparable in size to Coca-
Cola and selling, as Coca-Cola does, an unchanged product that
can point to a ten-year record anything like Coca-Cola's." In the 55
years that have since passed, Coke's product line has broadened
somewhat, but it's remarkable how well that description still fits.

Charlie and I decided long ago that in an investment lifetime
it's too hard to make hundreds of smart decisions. That judgment
became ever more compelling as Berkshire's capital mushroomed
and the universe of investments that could significantly affect our
results shrank dramatically. Therefore, we adopted a strategy that
required our being smart—and not too smart at that—only a very
few times. Indeed, we'll now settle for one good idea a year.
(Charlie says it's my turn.)

The strategy we've adopted precludes our following standard
diversification dogma. Many pundits would therefore say the strategy must be riskier than that employed by more conventional investors. We disagree. We believe that a policy of portfolio
concentration may well *decrease* risk if it raises, as it should, both
the intensity with which an investor thinks about a business and the
comfort-level he must feel with its economic characteristics before
buying into it. In stating this opinion, we define risk, using diction-
ary terms, as "the possibility of loss or injury."

Academics, however, like to define investment "risk" differently, averring that it is the relative volatility of a stock or portfolio
of stocks—that is, their volatility as compared to that of a large
universe of stocks. Employing data bases and statistical skills,
these academics compute with precision the "beta" of a stock—its
relative volatility in the past—and then build arcane investment

and capital-allocation theories around this calculation. In their hunger for a single statistic to measure risk, however, they forget a fundamental principle: It is better to be approximately right than precisely wrong.

For owners of a business—and that's the way we think of shareholders—the academics' definition of risk is far off the mark, so much so that it produces absurdities. For example, under beta-based theory, a stock that has dropped very sharply compared to the market—as had Washington Post when we bought it in 1973—becomes "riskier" at the lower price than it was at the higher price. Would that description have then made any sense to someone who was offered the entire company at a vastly-reduced price?

In fact, the true investor *welcomes* volatility. Ben Graham explained why in Chapter 8 of *The Intelligent Investor*. There he introduced "Mr. Market," an obliging fellow [noted above] who shows up every day to either buy from you or sell to you, whichever you wish. The more manic-depressive this chap is, the greater the opportunities available to the investor. That's true because a wildly fluctuating market means that irrationally low prices will periodically be attached to solid businesses. It is impossible to see how the availability of such prices can be thought of as increasing the hazards for an investor who is totally free to either ignore the market or exploit its folly.

In assessing risk, a beta purist will disdain examining what a company produces, what its competitors are doing, or how much borrowed money the business employs. He may even prefer not to know the company's name. What he treasures is the price history of its stock. In contrast, we'll happily forgo knowing the price history and instead will seek whatever information will further our understanding of the company's business. After we buy a stock, consequently, we would not be disturbed if markets closed for a year or two. We don't need a daily quote on our 100% position in See's or H.H. Brown to validate our well-being. Why, then, should we need a quote on our 7% interest in Coke?

In our opinion, the real risk an investor must assess is whether his aggregate after-tax receipts from an investment (including those he receives on sale) will, over his prospective holding period, give him at least as much purchasing power as he had to begin with, plus a modest rate of interest on that initial stake. Though this risk cannot be calculated with engineering precision, it can in some cases be judged with a degree of accuracy that is useful. The primary factors bearing upon this evaluation are:

(1) The certainty with which the long-term economic characteristics of the business can be evaluated;

(2) The certainty with which management can be evaluated,
both as to its ability to realize the full potential of the business and to wisely employ its cash flows;

(3) The certainty with which management can be counted on
to channel the reward from the business to the shareholders rather than to itself;

(4) The purchase price of the business;

(5) The levels of taxation and inflation that will be experienced and that will determine the degree by which an investor's purchasing-power return is reduced from his gross
return.

These factors will probably strike many analysts as unbearably
fuzzy since they cannot be extracted from a data base of any kind.
But the difficulty of precisely quantifying these matters does not
negate their importance nor is it insuperable. Just as Justice Stewart found it impossible to formulate a test for obscenity but nevertheless asserted, "I know it when I see it," so also can investors—in
an inexact but useful way—"see" the risks inherent in certain investments without reference to complex equations or price
histories.

The theoretician bred on beta has no mechanism for differen-
tiating the risk inherent in, say, a single-product toy company selling pet rocks or hula hoops from that of another toy company
whose sole product is Monopoly or Barbie. But it's quite possible
for ordinary investors to make such distinctions if they have a reasonable understanding of consumer behavior and the factors that
create long-term competitive strength or weakness. Obviously,
every investor will make mistakes. But by confining himself to a
relatively few, easy-to-understand cases, a reasonably intelligent,
informed and diligent person can judge investment risks with a useful degree of accuracy.

In many industries, of course, Charlie and I can't determine
whether we are dealing with a "pet rock" or a "Barbie." We
couldn't solve this problem, moreover, even if we were to spend
years intensely studying those industries. Sometimes our own intellectual shortcomings would stand in the way of understanding,
and in other cases the nature of the industry would be the road-
block. For example, a business that must deal with fast-moving
technology is not going to lend itself to reliable evaluations of its
long-term economics. Did we foresee thirty years ago what would

transpire in the television-manufacturing or computer industries? Of course not. (Nor did most of the investors and corporate managers who enthusiastically entered those industries.) Why, then, should Charlie and I now think we can predict the future of other rapidly-evolving businesses? We'll stick instead with the easy cases. Why search for a needle buried in a haystack when one is sitting in plain sight?

Of course, some investment strategies—for instance, our efforts in arbitrage over the years—require wide diversification. If significant risk exists in a single transaction, overall risk should be reduced by making that purchase one of many mutually-independent commitments. Thus, you may consciously purchase a risky investment—one that indeed has a significant possibility of causing loss or injury—if you believe that your gain, weighted for probabilities, considerably exceeds your loss, comparably weighted, and if you can commit to a number of similar, but unrelated opportunities. Most venture capitalists employ this strategy. Should you choose to pursue this course, you should adopt the outlook of the casino that owns a roulette wheel, which will want to see lots of action because it is favored by probabilities, but will refuse to accept a single, huge bet.

Another situation requiring wide diversification occurs when an investor who does not understand the economics of specific businesses nevertheless believes it in his interest to be a long-term owner of American industry. That investor should both own a large number of equities and space out his purchases. By periodically investing in an index fund, for example, the know-nothing investor can actually out-perform most investment professionals. Paradoxically, when "dumb" money acknowledges its limitations, it ceases to be dumb.

On the other hand, if you are a know-something investor, able to understand business economics and to find five to ten sensibly-priced companies that possess important long-term competitive advantages, conventional diversification makes no sense for you. It is apt simply to hurt your results and increase your risk. I cannot understand why an investor of that sort elects to put money into a business that is his 20th favorite rather than simply adding that money to his top choices—the businesses he understands best and that present the least risk, along with the greatest profit potential. In the words of the prophet Mae West: "Too much of a good thing can be wonderful."

———————

We continually search for large businesses with understandable, enduring and mouth-watering economics that are run by able and shareholder-oriented managements. This focus doesn't guarantee results: We both have to buy at a sensible price and get business performance from our companies that validates our assessment. But this investment approach—searching for the superstars—offers us our only chance for real success. Charlie and I are simply not smart enough, considering the large sums we work with, to get great results by adroitly buying and selling portions of far-from-great businesses. Nor do we think many others can achieve long-term investment success by flitting from flower to flower. Indeed, we believe that according the name "investors" to institutions that trade actively is like calling someone who repeatedly engages in one-night stands a romantic.

If my universe of business possibilities was limited, say, to private companies in Omaha, I would, first, try to assess the long-term economic characteristics of each business; second, assess the quality of the people in charge of running it; and, third, try to buy into a few of the best operations at a sensible price. I certainly would not wish to own an equal part of every business in town. Why, then, should Berkshire take a different tack when dealing with the larger universe of public companies? And since finding great businesses and outstanding managers is so difficult, why should we discard proven products? Our motto is: "If at first you do succeed, quit trying."

John Maynard Keynes, whose brilliance as a practicing investor matched his brilliance in thought, wrote a letter to a business associate, F.C. Scott, on August 15, 1934 that says it all: "As time goes on, I get more and more convinced that the right method in investment is to put fairly large sums into enterprises which one thinks one knows something about and in the management of which one thoroughly believes. It is a mistake to think that one limits one's risk by spreading too much between enterprises about which one knows little and has no reason for special confidence. One's knowledge and experience are definitely limited and there are seldom more than two or three enterprises at any given time in which I personally feel myself entitled to put *full* confidence."

———

During 1987 the stock market was an area of much excitement but little net movement: The Dow advanced 2.3% for the year. You are aware, of course, of the roller coaster ride that produced this minor change. Mr. Market was on a manic rampage until October and then experienced a sudden, massive seizure.

We have "professional" investors, those who manage many billions, to thank for most of this turmoil. Instead of focusing on what businesses will do in the years ahead, many prestigious money managers now focus on what they expect other money managers to do in the days ahead. For them, stocks are merely tokens in a game, like the thimble and flatiron in Monopoly.

An extreme example of what their attitude leads to is "portfolio insurance," a money-management strategy that many leading investment advisors embraced in 1986-1987. This strategy—which is simply an exotically-labeled version of the small speculator's stop-loss order—dictates that ever-increasing portions of a stock portfolio, or their index-future equivalents, be sold as prices decline. The strategy says nothing else matters: A downtick of a given magnitude automatically produces a huge sell order. According to the Brady Report, $60 billion to $90 billion of equities were poised on this hair trigger in mid-October of 1987.

If you've thought that investment advisors were hired to invest, you may be bewildered by this technique. After buying a farm, would a rational owner next order his real estate agent to start selling off pieces of it whenever a neighboring property was sold at a lower price? Or would you sell your house to whatever bidder was available at 9:31 on some morning merely because at 9:30 a similar house sold for less than it would have brought on the previous day?

Moves like that, however, are what portfolio insurance tells a pension fund or university to make when it owns a portion of enterprises such as Ford or General Electric. The less these companies are being valued at, says this approach, the more vigorously they should be sold. As a "logical" corollary, the approach commands the institutions to repurchase these companies—*I'm not making this up*—once their prices have rebounded significantly. Considering that huge sums are controlled by managers following such Alice-in-Wonderland practices, is it any surprise that markets sometimes behave in aberrational fashion?

Many commentators, however, have drawn an incorrect conclusion upon observing recent events: They are fond of saying that the small investor has no chance in a market now dominated by the erratic behavior of the big boys. This conclusion is dead wrong: Such markets are ideal for any investor—small or large—so long as he sticks to his investment knitting. Volatility caused by money managers who speculate irrationally with huge sums will offer the true investor more chances to make intelligent investment moves. He can be hurt by such volatility only if he is forced, by either financial or psychological pressures, to sell at untoward times.

E. *"Value" Investing: A Redundancy*[23]

We really don't see many fundamental differences between the purchase of a controlled business and the purchase of marketable holdings. In each case we try to buy into businesses with favorable long-term economics. Our goal is to find an outstanding business at a sensible price, not a mediocre business at a bargain price. Charlie and I have found that making silk purses out of silk is the best that we can do; with sow's ears, we fail.

(It must be noted that your Chairman, always a quick study, required only 20 years to recognize how important it was to buy good businesses. In the interim, I searched for "bargains"—and had the misfortune to find some. My punishment was an education in the economics of short-line farm implement manufacturers, third-place department stores, and New England textile manufacturers.)

Of course, Charlie and I may misread the fundamental economics of a business. When that happens, we will encounter problems whether that business is a wholly-owned subsidiary or a marketable security, although it is usually far easier to exit from the latter. (Indeed, businesses can be misread: Witness the European reporter who, after being sent to this country to profile Andrew Carnegie, cabled his editor, "My God, you'll never believe the sort of money there is in running libraries.")

In making both control purchases and stock purchases, we try to buy not only good businesses, but ones run by high-grade, talented and likeable managers. If we make a mistake about the managers we link up with, the controlled company offers a certain advantage because we have the power to effect change. In practice, however, this advantage is somewhat illusory: Management changes, like marital changes, are painful, time-consuming and chancy.

I would say that the controlled company offers two main advantages. First, when we control a company we get to allocate capital, whereas we are likely to have little or nothing to say about this process with marketable holdings. This point can be important be-

---

[23] [Divided by hash lines: 1987; 1992; 1985.]

cause the heads of many companies are not skilled in capital alloca-tion. Their inadequacy is not surprising. Most bosses rise to the top because they have excelled in an area such as marketing, pro-duction, engineering, administration—or, sometimes, institutional politics.

Once they become CEOs, they face new responsibilities. They now must make capital allocation decisions, a critical job that they may have never tackled and that is not easily mastered. To stretch the point, it's as if the final step for a highly-talented musician was not to perform at Carnegie Hall but, instead, to be named Chair-man of the Federal Reserve.

The lack of skill that many CEOs have at capital allocation is no small matter: After ten years on the job, a CEO whose company annually retains earnings equal to 10% of net worth will have been responsible for the deployment of more than 60% of all the capital at work in the business.

CEOs who recognize their lack of capital-allocation skills (which not all do) will often try to compensate by turning to their staffs, management consultants, or investment bankers. Charlie and I have frequently observed the consequences of such "help." On balance, we feel it is more likely to accentuate the capital-allo-cation problem than to solve it.

In the end, plenty of unintelligent capital allocation takes place in corporate America. (That's why you hear so much about "restructuring.") Berkshire, however, has been fortunate. At the companies that are our major non-controlled holdings, capital has generally been well-deployed and, in some cases, brilliantly so.

The second advantage of a controlled company over a market-able security has to do with taxes. Berkshire, as a corporate holder, absorbs some significant tax costs through the ownership of partial positions that we do not when our ownership is 80% or greater. Such tax disadvantages have long been with us, but changes in the tax code caused them to increase significantly dur-ing [1986]. As a consequence, a given business result can now de-liver Berkshire financial results that are as much as 50% better if they come from an 80%-or-greater holding rather than from a lesser holding.

The disadvantages of owning marketable securities are some-times offset by a huge advantage: Occasionally the stock market offers us the chance to buy non-controlling pieces of extraordinary businesses at truly ridiculous prices—dramatically below those commanded in negotiated transactions that transfer control. For example, we purchased Washington Post stock in 1973 at $5.63 per share, and per-share operating earnings in 1987 after taxes were $10.30. Similarly, our GEICO stock was purchased in 1976, 1979 and 1980 at an average of $6.67 per share, and after-tax operating earnings per share last year were $9.01. In cases such as these, Mr. Market has proven to be a mighty good friend.

Our equity-investing strategy remains little changed from what it was when we said in the 1977 annual report: "We select our marketable equity securities in much the way we would evaluate a business for acquisition in its entirety. We want the business to be one (a) that we can understand; (b) with favorable long-term prospects; (c) operated by honest and competent people; and (d) available at a very attractive price." We have seen cause to make only one change in this creed: Because of both market conditions and our size, we now substitute "an attractive price" for "a very attractive price."

But how, you will ask, does one decide what's "attractive"? In answering this question, most analysts feel they must choose between two approaches customarily thought to be in opposition: "value" and "growth." Indeed, many investment professionals see any mixing of the two terms as a form of intellectual cross-dressing.

We view that as fuzzy thinking (in which, it must be confessed, I myself engaged some years ago). In our opinion, the two approaches are joined at the hip: Growth is *always* a component in the calculation of value, constituting a variable whose importance can range from negligible to enormous and whose impact can be negative as well as positive.

In addition, we think the very term "value investing" is redundant. What is "investing" if it is not the act of seeking value at least sufficient to justify the amount paid? Consciously paying more for a stock than its calculated value—in the hope that it can soon be sold for a still-higher price—should be labeled speculation (which is neither illegal, immoral nor—in our view—financially fattening).

Whether appropriate or not, the term "value investing" is widely used. Typically, it connotes the purchase of stocks having attributes such as a low ratio of price to book value, a low price-earnings ratio, or a high dividend yield. Unfortunately, such characteristics, even if they appear in combination, are far from determinative as to whether an investor is indeed buying something for what it is worth and is therefore truly operating on the principle of obtaining value in his investments. Correspondingly, opposite characteristics—a high ratio of price to book value, a high price-earnings ratio, and a low dividend yield—are in no way inconsistent with a "value" purchase.

Similarly, business growth, per se, tells us little about value. It's true that growth often has a positive impact on value, sometimes one of spectacular proportions. But such an effect is far from certain. For example, investors have regularly poured money into the domestic airline business to finance profitless (or worse) growth. For these investors, it would have been far better if Orville had failed to get off the ground at Kitty Hawk: The more the industry has grown, the worse the disaster for owners.

Growth benefits investors only when the business in point can invest at incremental returns that are enticing—in other words, only when each dollar used to finance the growth creates over a dollar of long-term market value. In the case of a low-return business requiring incremental funds, growth hurts the investor.

In *The Theory of Investment Value*, written over 50 years ago, John Burr Williams set forth the equation for value, which we condense here: *The value of any stock, bond or business today is determined by the cash inflows and outflows—discounted at an appropriate interest rate—that can be expected to occur during the remaining life of the asset.* Note that the formula is the same for stocks as for bonds. Even so, there is an important, and difficult to deal with, difference between the two: A bond has a coupon and maturity date that define future cash flows; but in the case of equities, the investment analyst must himself estimate the future "coupons." Furthermore, the quality of management affects the bond coupon only rarely—chiefly when management is so inept or dishonest that payment of interest is suspended. In contrast, the ability of management can dramatically affect the equity "coupons."

The investment shown by the discounted-flows-of-cash calculation to be the cheapest is the one that the investor should purchase—irrespective of whether the business grows or doesn't, displays volatility or smoothness in its earnings, or carries a high price or low [price] in relation to its current earnings and book value. Moreover, though the value equation has usually shown equities to be cheaper than bonds, that result is not inevitable: When bonds are calculated to be the more attractive investment, they should be bought.

Leaving the question of price aside, the best business to own is one that over an extended period can employ large amounts of incremental capital at very high rates of return. The worst business to own is one that must, or *will*, do the opposite—that is, consistently employ ever-greater amounts of capital at very low rates of return. Unfortunately, the first type of business is very hard to find: Most high-return businesses need relatively little capital. Shareholders of such a business usually will benefit if it pays out most of its earnings in dividends or makes significant stock repurchases.

Though the mathematical calculations required to evaluate equities are not difficult, an analyst—even one who is experienced and intelligent—can easily go wrong in estimating future "coupons." At Berkshire, we attempt to deal with this problem in two ways. First, we try to stick to businesses we believe we understand. That means they must be relatively simple and stable in character. If a business is complex or subject to constant change, we're not smart enough to predict future cash flows. Incidentally, that shortcoming doesn't bother us. What counts for most people in investing is not how much they know, but rather how realistically they define what they don't know. An investor needs to do very few things right as long as he or she avoids big mistakes.

Second, and equally important, we insist on a margin of safety in our purchase price. If we calculate the value of a common stock to be only slightly higher than its price, we're not interested in buying. We believe this margin-of-safety principle, so strongly emphasized by Ben Graham, to be the cornerstone of investment success.

[A]n intelligent investor in common stocks will do better in the secondary market than he will do buying new issues. The reason has to do with the way prices are set in each instance. The secondary market, which is periodically ruled by mass folly, is constantly setting a "clearing" price. No matter how foolish that price may be, it's what counts for the holder of a stock or bond who needs or wishes to sell, of whom there are always going to be a few at any moment. In many instances, shares worth x in business value have sold in the market for $\frac{1}{2}x$ or less.

The new-issue market, on the other hand, is ruled by controlling stockholders and corporations, who can usually select the timing of offerings or, if the market looks unfavorable, can avoid an offering altogether. Understandably, these sellers are not going to offer any bargains, either by way of a public offering or in a negotiated transaction: It's rare you'll find x for $\frac{1}{2}x$ here. Indeed, in the case of common-stock offerings, selling shareholders are often motivated to unload only when they feel the market is overpaying. (These sellers, of course, would state that proposition somewhat differently, averring instead that they simply resist selling when the market is underpaying for their goods.)

Right after yearend, Berkshire purchased 3 million shares of Capital Cities/ABC, Inc. ("Cap Cities") at $172.50 per share, the market price of such shares at the time the commitment was made early in March, 1985. I've been on record for many years about the management of Cap Cities: I think it is the best of any publicly-owned company in the country. And Tom Murphy and Dan Burke are not only great managers, they are precisely the sort of fellows that you would want your daughter to marry. It is a privilege to be associated with them—and also a lot of fun, as any of you who know them will understand.

Our purchase of stock helped Cap Cities finance the $3.5 billion acquisition of American Broadcasting Companies. For Cap Cities, ABC is a major undertaking whose economics are likely to be unexciting over the next few years. This bothers us not an iota; we can be very patient. (No matter how great the talent or effort, some things just take time: you can't produce a baby in one month by getting nine women pregnant.)

As evidence of our confidence, we have executed an unusual agreement: for an extended period Tom, as CEO (or Dan, should he be CEO) votes our stock. This arrangement was initiated by Charlie and me, not by Tom. We also have restricted ourselves in various ways regarding sale of our shares. The object of these restrictions is to make sure that our block does not get sold to anyone who is a large holder (or intends to become a large holder) without the approval of management, an arrangement similar to ones we initiated some years ago at GEICO and Washington Post.

Since large blocks frequently command premium prices, some might think we have injured Berkshire financially by creating such restrictions. Our view is just the opposite. We feel the long-term economic prospects for these businesses—and, thus, for ourselves as owners—are enhanced by the arrangements. With them in place, the first-class managers with whom we have aligned ourselves can focus their efforts entirely upon running the businesses and maximizing long-term values for owners. Certainly this is much better than having those managers distracted by "revolving-door capitalists" hoping to put the company "in play." (Of course, some managers place their own interests above those of the company and its owners and deserve to be shaken up—but, in making investments, we try to steer clear of this type.)

Today, corporate instability is an inevitable consequence of widely-diffused ownership of voting stock. At any time a major holder can surface, usually mouthing reassuring rhetoric but frequently harboring uncivil intentions. By circumscribing our blocks of stock as we often do, we intend to promote stability where it otherwise might be lacking. That kind of certainty, combined with a good manager and a good business, provides excellent soil for a rich financial harvest. That's the economic case for our arrangements.

The human side is just as important. We don't want managers we like and admire—and who have welcomed a major financial commitment by us—to ever lose any sleep wondering whether surprises might occur because of our large ownership. I have told them there will be no surprises, and these agreements put Berkshire's signature where my mouth is. That signature also means the managers have a corporate commitment and therefore need not worry if my personal participation in Berkshire's affairs ends prematurely (a term I define as any age short of three digits).

Our Cap Cities purchase was made at a full price, reflecting the very considerable enthusiasm for both media stocks and media properties that has developed in recent years (and that, in the case of some property purchases, has approached a mania). It's no field for bargains. However, our Cap Cities investment allies us with an exceptional combination of properties and people—and we like the opportunity to participate in size.

Of course, some of you probably wonder why we are now buying Cap Cities at $172.50 per share given that your Chairman, in a characteristic burst of brilliance, sold Berkshire's holdings in the same company at $43 per share in 1978-80. Anticipating your question, I spent much of 1985 working on a snappy answer that would reconcile these acts.

A little more time, please.

F. *Intelligent Investing*[24]

Inactivity strikes us as intelligent behavior. Neither we nor most business managers would dream of feverishly trading highly-profitable subsidiaries because a small move in the Federal Reserve's discount rate was predicted or because some Wall Street pundit had reversed his views on the market. Why, then, should we behave differently with our minority positions in wonderful

---

[24] [Divided by hash lines: 1996; 1999; 1997.]

businesses? The art of investing in public companies successfully is little different from the art of successfully acquiring subsidiaries. In each case you simply want to acquire, at a sensible price, a business with excellent economics and able, honest management. Thereafter, you need only monitor whether these qualities are being preserved.

When carried out capably, an investment strategy of that type will often result in its practitioner owning a few securities that will come to represent a very large portion of his portfolio. This investor would get a similar result if he followed a policy of purchasing an interest in, say, 20% of the future earnings of a number of outstanding college basketball stars. A handful of these would go on to achieve NBA stardom, and the investor's take from them would soon dominate his royalty stream. To suggest that this investor should sell off portions of his most successful investments simply because they have come to dominate his portfolio is akin to suggesting that the Bulls trade Michael Jordan because he has become so important to the team.

In studying the investments we have made in both subsidiary companies and common stocks, you will see that we favor businesses and industries unlikely to experience major change. The reason for that is simple: Making either type of purchase, we are searching for operations that we believe are virtually certain to possess enormous competitive strength ten or twenty years from now. A fast-changing industry environment may offer the chance for huge wins, but it precludes the certainty we seek.

I should emphasize that, as citizens, Charlie and I welcome change: Fresh ideas, new products, innovative processes and the like cause our country's standard of living to rise, and that's clearly good. As investors, however, our reaction to a fermenting industry is much like our attitude toward space exploration: We applaud the endeavor but prefer to skip the ride.

Obviously all businesses change to some extent. Today, See's is different in many ways from what it was in 1972 when we bought it: It offers a different assortment of candy, employs different machinery and sells through different distribution channels. But the reasons why people today buy boxed chocolates, and why they buy them from us rather than from someone else, are virtually unchanged from what they were in the 1920s when the See family was building the business. Moreover, these motivations are not likely to change over the next 20 years, or even 50.

We look for similar predictability in marketable securities. Take Coca-Cola: The zeal and imagination with which Coke products are sold burgeoned under Roberto Goizueta, who [did] an absolutely incredible job in creating value for his shareholders. Aided by Don Keough and Doug Ivester, Roberto rethought and improved every aspect of the company. But the fundamentals of the business—the qualities that underlie Coke's competitive dominance and stunning economics—have remained constant through the years.

I was recently studying the 1896 report of Coke (and you think that you are behind in your reading!). At that time Coke, though it was already the leading soft drink, had been around for only a decade. But its blueprint for the next 100 years was already drawn. Reporting sales of $148,000 that year, Asa Candler, the company's president, said: "We have not lagged in our efforts to go into all the world teaching that Coca-Cola is the article, par excellence, for the health and good feeling of all people." Though "health" may have been a reach, I love the fact that Coke still relies on Candler's basic theme today—a century later. Candler went on to say, just as Roberto could now, "No article of like character has ever so firmly entrenched itself in public favor." Sales of syrup that year, incidentally, were 116,492 gallons versus about 3.2 billion in 1996.

I can't resist one more Candler quote: "Beginning this year about March 1st . . . we employed ten traveling salesmen by means of which, with systematic correspondence from the office, we covered almost the territory of the Union." That's my kind of sales force.

Companies such as Coca-Cola might well be labeled "The Inevitables." Forecasters may differ a bit in their predictions of exactly how much soft drink or shaving-equipment business these companies will be doing in ten or twenty years. Nor is our talk of inevitability meant to play down the vital work that these companies must continue to carry out, in such areas as manufacturing, distribution, packaging and product innovation. In the end, however, no sensible observer—not even these companies' most vigorous competitors, assuming they are assessing the matter honestly— questions that Coke will dominate worldwide for an investment lifetime. Indeed, dominance will probably strengthen.

Obviously many companies in high-tech businesses or embryonic industries will grow much faster in percentage terms than will The Inevitables. But I would rather be certain of a good result than hopeful of a great one.

Of course, Charlie and I can identify only a few Inevitables, even after a lifetime of looking for them. Leadership alone provides no certainties: Witness the shocks some years back at General Motors, IBM and Sears, all of which had enjoyed long periods of seeming invincibility. Though some industries or lines of business exhibit characteristics that endow leaders with virtually insurmountable advantages, and that tend to establish Survival of the Fattest as almost a natural law, most do not. Thus, for every Inevitable, there are dozens of Impostors, companies now riding high but vulnerable to competitive attacks. Considering what it takes to be an Inevitable, Charlie and I recognize that we will never be able to come up with a Nifty Fifty or even a Twinkling Twenty. To the Inevitables in our portfolio, therefore, we add a few "Highly Probables."

You can, of course, pay too much for even the best of businesses. The overpayment risk surfaces periodically and, in our opinion, may now be quite high for the purchasers of virtually all stocks, The Inevitables included. Investors making purchases in an overheated market need to recognize that it may often take an extended period for the value of even an outstanding company to catch up with the price they paid.

A far more serious problem occurs when the management of a great company gets sidetracked and neglects its wonderful base business while purchasing other businesses that are so-so or worse. When that happens, the suffering of investors is often prolonged. Unfortunately, that is precisely what transpired years ago at Coke. (Would you believe that a few decades back they were growing shrimp at Coke?) Loss of focus is what most worries Charlie and me when we contemplate investing in businesses that in general look outstanding. All too often, we've seen value stagnate in the presence of hubris or of boredom that caused the attention of managers to wander. That's not going to happen again at Coke, however—not given current and prospective managements.

*   *   *   *   *

Let me add a few thoughts about your own investments. Most investors, both institutional and individual, will find that the best way to own common stocks is through an index fund that charges minimal fees. Those following this path are sure to beat the net results (after fees and expenses) delivered by the great majority of investment professionals.

Should you choose, however, to construct your own portfolio, there are a few thoughts worth remembering. Intelligent investing is not complex, though that is far from saying that it is easy. What an investor needs is the ability to correctly evaluate selected businesses. Note that word "selected": You don't have to be an expert on every company, or even many. You only have to be able to evaluate companies within your circle of competence. The size of that circle is not very important; knowing its boundaries, however, is vital.

To invest successfully, you need not understand beta, efficient markets, modern portfolio theory, option pricing, or emerging markets. You may, in fact, be better off knowing nothing of these. That, of course, is not the prevailing view at most business schools, whose finance curriculum tends to be dominated by such subjects. In our view, though, investment students need only two well-taught courses—How to Value a Business, and How to Think About Market Prices.

Your goal as an investor should simply be to purchase, at a rational price, a part interest in an easily-understandable business whose earnings are virtually certain to be materially higher five, ten and twenty years from now. Over time, you will find only a few companies that meet these standards—so when you see one that qualifies, you should buy a meaningful amount of stock. You must also resist the temptation to stray from your guidelines: If you aren't willing to own a stock for ten years, don't even think about owning it for ten minutes. Put together a portfolio of companies whose aggregate earnings march upward over the years, and so also will the portfolio's market value.

Though it's seldom recognized, this is the exact approach that has produced gains for Berkshire shareholders: Our look-through earnings have grown at a good clip over the years, and our stock price has risen correspondingly. Had those gains in earnings not materialized, there would have been little increase in Berkshire's value.

[S]everal of the companies in which we have large investments had disappointing business results last year. Nevertheless, we believe these companies have important competitive advantages that will endure over time. This attribute, which makes for good long-term investment results, is one Charlie and I occasionally believe we can identify. More often, however, we can't—not at least with a high degree of conviction. This explains, by the way, why we don't own stocks of tech companies, even though we share the general view that our society will be transformed by their products and services. Our problem—which we can't solve by studying up—is that we have no insights into which participants in the tech field possess a truly *durable* competitive advantage.

Our lack of tech insights, we should add, does not distress us. After all, there are a great many business areas in which Charlie and I have no special capital-allocation expertise. For instance, we bring nothing to the table when it comes to evaluating patents, manufacturing processes or geological prospects. So we simply don't get into judgments in those fields.

If we have a strength, it is in recognizing when we are operating well within our circle of competence and when we are approaching the perimeter. Predicting the long-term economics of companies that operate in fast-changing industries is simply far beyond our perimeter. If others claim predictive skill in those industries—and seem to have their claims validated by the behavior of the stock market—we neither envy nor emulate them. Instead, we just stick with what we understand. If we stray, we will have done so inadvertently, not because we got restless and substituted hope for rationality. Fortunately, it's almost certain there will be opportunities from time to time for Berkshire to do well within the circle we've staked out.

Right now, the prices of the fine businesses we already own are just not that attractive. In other words, we feel much better about the businesses than their stocks. That's why we haven't added to our present holdings. Nevertheless, we haven't yet scaled back our portfolio in a major way: If the choice is between a questionable business at a comfortable price or a comfortable business at a questionable price, we much prefer the latter. What really gets our attention, however, is a comfortable business at a comfortable price.

Our reservations about the prices of securities we own apply also to the general level of equity prices. We have never attempted to forecast what the stock market is going to do in the next month or the next year, and we are not trying to do that now. But [as of late 1999] equity investors currently seem wildly optimistic in their expectations about future returns.

We see the growth in corporate profits as being largely tied to the business done in the country (GDP), and we see GDP growing at a real rate of about 3%. In addition, we have hypothesized 2% inflation. Charlie and I have no particular conviction about the

accuracy of 2%. However, it's the market's view: Treasury Infla-
tion-Protected Securities (TIPS) yield about two percentage points
less than the standard treasury bond, and if you believe inflation
rates are going to be higher than that, you can profit by simply
buying TIPS and shorting Governments.

If profits do indeed grow along with GDP, at about a 5% rate,
the valuation placed on American business is unlikely to climb by
much more than that. Add in something for dividends, and you
emerge with returns from equities that are dramatically less than
most investors have either experienced in the past or expect in the
future. If investor expectations become more realistic—and they
almost certainly will—the market adjustment is apt to be severe,
particularly in sectors in which speculation has been concentrated.

Berkshire will someday have opportunities to deploy major
amounts of cash in equity markets—we are confident of that. But,
as the song goes, "Who knows where or when?" Meanwhile, if anyone starts explaining to you what is going on in the truly-manic
portions of this "enchanted" market, you might remember still another line of song: "Fools give you reasons, wise men never try."

[At times when prices are high for both businesses and stocks],
we try to exert a Ted Williams kind of discipline. In his book *The
Science of Hitting*, Ted explains that he carved the strike zone into
77 cells, each the size of a baseball. Swinging only at balls in his
"best" cell, he knew, would allow him to bat .400; reaching for balls
in his "worst" spot, the low outside corner of the strike zone, would
reduce him to .230. In other words, waiting for the fat pitch would
mean a trip to the Hall of Fame; swinging indiscriminately would
mean a ticket to the minors.

If they are in the strike zone at all, the business "pitches" we
now see are just catching the lower outside corner. If we swing, we
will be locked into low returns. But if we let all of today's balls go
by, there can be no assurance that the next ones we see will be
more to our liking. Perhaps the attractive prices of the past were
the aberrations, not the full prices of today. Unlike Ted, we can't
be called out if we resist three pitches that are barely in the strike
zone; nevertheless, just standing there, day after day, with my bat
on my shoulder is not my idea of fun.

G. *Cigar Butts and the Institutional Imperative*[25]

To quote Robert Benchley, "Having a dog teaches a boy fidelity, perseverance, and to turn around three times before lying down." Such are the shortcomings of experience. Nevertheless, it's a good idea to review past mistakes before committing new ones. So let's take a quick look at the last 25 years.

• My first mistake, of course, was in buying control of Berkshire. Though I knew its business—textile manufacturing—to be unpromising, I was enticed to buy because the price looked cheap. Stock purchases of that kind had proved reasonably rewarding in my early years, though by the time Berkshire came along in 1965 I was becoming aware that the strategy was not ideal.

If you buy a stock at a sufficiently low price, there will usually be some hiccup in the fortunes of the business that gives you a chance to unload at a decent profit, even though the long-term performance of the business may be terrible. I call this the "cigar butt" approach to investing. A cigar butt found on the street that has only one puff left in it may not offer much of a smoke, but the "bargain purchase" will make that puff all profit.

Unless you are a liquidator, that kind of approach to buying businesses is foolish. First, the original "bargain" price probably will not turn out to be such a steal after all. In a difficult business, no sooner is one problem solved than another surfaces—never is there just one cockroach in the kitchen. Second, any initial advantage you secure will be quickly eroded by the low return that the business earns. For example, if you buy a business for $8 million that can be sold or liquidated for $10 million and promptly take either course, you can realize a high return. But the investment will disappoint if the business is sold for $10 million in ten years and in the interim has annually earned and distributed only a few percent on cost. Time is the friend of the wonderful business, the enemy of the mediocre.

You might think this principle is obvious, but I had to learn it the hard way—in fact, I had to learn it several times over. Shortly after purchasing Berkshire, I acquired a Baltimore department store, Hochschild, Kohn, buying through a company called Diversified Retailing that later merged with Berkshire. I bought at a substantial discount from book value, the people were first-class, and the deal included some extras—unrecorded real estate values and a significant LIFO inventory cushion. How could I miss? So-o-o—

---

[25] [1989.]

three years later I was lucky to sell the business for about what I had paid.

• That leads right into a related lesson: Good jockeys will do well on good horses, but not on broken-down nags. Both Berkshire's textile business and Hochschild, Kohn had able and honest people running them. The same managers employed in a business with good economic characteristics would have achieved fine records. But they were never going to make any progress while running in quicksand.[26]

I've said many times that when a management with a reputation for brilliance tackles a business with a reputation for bad economics, it is the reputation of the business that remains intact. I just wish I hadn't been so energetic in creating examples. My behavior has matched that admitted by Mae West: "I was Snow White, but I drifted."

• A further related lesson: Easy does it. After 25 years of buying and supervising a great variety of businesses, Charlie and I have *not* learned how to solve difficult business problems. What we have learned is to avoid them. To the extent we have been successful, it is because we concentrated on identifying one-foot hurdles that we could step over rather than because we acquired any ability to clear seven-footers.

The finding may seem unfair, but in both business and investments it is usually far more profitable to simply stick with the easy and obvious than it is to resolve the difficult. On occasion, tough problems *must* be tackled. In other instances, a great investment opportunity occurs when a marvelous business encounters a one-time huge, but solvable, problem as was the case many years back at both American Express and GEICO. Overall, however, we've done better by avoiding dragons than by slaying them.

• My most surprising discovery: the overwhelming importance in business of an unseen force that we might call "the institutional imperative." In business school, I was given no hint of the imperative's existence and I did not intuitively understand it when I entered the business world. I thought then that decent, intelligent, and experienced managers would automatically make rational business decisions. But I learned over time that isn't so. Instead, rationality frequently wilts when the institutional imperative comes into play.

---

[26] [*See* the essay The Anxieties of Business Change in Part I.C.]

For example: (1) As if governed by Newton's First Law of Motion, an institution will resist any change in its current direction; (2) Just as work expands to fill available time, corporate projects or acquisitions will materialize to soak up available funds; (3) Any business craving of the leader, however foolish, will be quickly supported by detailed rate-of-return and strategic studies prepared by his troops; and (4) The behavior of peer companies, whether they are expanding, acquiring, setting executive compensation or whatever, will be mindlessly imitated.

Institutional dynamics, not venality or stupidity, set businesses on these courses, which are too often misguided. After making some expensive mistakes because I ignored the power of the imperative, I have tried to organize and manage Berkshire in ways that minimize its influence. Furthermore, Charlie and I have attempted to concentrate our investments in companies that appear alert to the problem.

• After some other mistakes, I learned to go into business only with people whom I like, trust, and admire. As I noted before, this policy of itself will not ensure success: A second-class textile or department-store company won't prosper simply because its managers are [people] that you would be pleased to see your [children] marry. However, an owner—or investor—can accomplish wonders if he manages to associate himself with such people in businesses that possess decent economic characteristics. Conversely, we do not wish to join with managers who lack admirable qualities, no matter how attractive the prospects of their business. We've never succeeded in making a good deal with a bad person.

• Some of my worst mistakes were not publicly visible. These were stock and business purchases whose virtues I understood and yet didn't make. It's no sin to miss a great opportunity outside one's area of competence. But I have passed on a couple of really big purchases that were served up to me on a platter and that I was fully capable of understanding. For Berkshire's shareholders, myself included, the cost of this thumb-sucking has been huge.

• Our consistently-conservative financial policies may appear to have been a mistake, but in my view were not. In retrospect, it is clear that significantly higher, though still conventional, leverage ratios at Berkshire would have produced considerably better returns on equity than the 23.8% we have actually averaged. Even in 1965, perhaps we could have judged there to be a 99% probability that higher leverage would lead to nothing but good. Correspondingly, we might have seen only a 1% chance that some shock factor, external or internal, would cause a conventional debt ratio to produce a result falling somewhere between temporary anguish and default.

We wouldn't have liked those 99:1 odds—and never will. A small chance of distress or disgrace cannot, in our view, be offset by a large chance of extra returns. If your actions are sensible, you are certain to get good results; in most such cases, leverage just moves things along faster. Charlie and I have never been in a big hurry: We enjoy the process far more than the proceeds—though we have learned to live with those also.

H.   *Life and Debt*[27]

Except for token amounts, we shun debt, turning to it for only three purposes: (1) We occasionally use repos as a part of certain short-term investing strategies that incorporate ownership of U.S. government (or agency) securities. Purchases of this kind are highly opportunistic and involve only the most liquid of securities. (2) We borrow money against portfolios of interest-bearing receivables whose risk characteristics we understand. (3) [Subsidiaries, such as Berkshire Hathaway Energy, may incur debt that appears on Berkshire's consolidated balance sheet, but Berkshire does not guarantee the obligation.]

From a risk standpoint, it is far safer to have earnings from ten diverse and uncorrelated utility operations that cover interest charges by, say, a 2:1 ratio than it is to have far greater coverage provided by a single utility. A catastrophic event can render a single utility insolvent—witness what Katrina did to the local electric utility in New Orleans—no matter how conservative its debt policy. A geographical disaster—say, an earthquake in a Western state—can't have the same effect on MidAmerican. And even a worrier like Charlie can't think of an event that would systemically decrease utility earnings in any major way. Because of MidAmerican's ever-widening diversity of regulated earnings, it will always utilize major amounts of debt.

And that's about it. We are not interested in incurring any significant debt at Berkshire for acquisitions or operating purposes. Conventional business wisdom, of course, would argue that we are being too conservative and that there are added profits that could be safely earned if we injected moderate leverage into our balance sheet. Maybe so. But many of Berkshire's hundreds of thousands

---

[27] [2005; 2010.]

of investors have a large portion of their net worth in our stock (among them, it should be emphasized, a large number of our board and key managers) and a disaster for the company would be a disaster for them.

Moreover, there are people who have been permanently injured to whom we owe insurance payments that stretch out for fifty years or more. To these and other constituencies we have promised total security, whatever comes: financial panics, stock-exchange closures (an extended one occurred in 1914) or even domestic nuclear, chemical or biological attacks. We are quite willing to accept huge risks. Indeed, more than any other insurer, we write high-limit policies that are tied to single catastrophic events.

We also own a large investment portfolio whose market value could fall dramatically and quickly under certain conditions (as happened on October 19, 1987). Whatever occurs, though, Berkshire will have the net worth, the earnings streams and the liquidity to handle the problem with ease. Any other approach is dangerous. Over the years, a number of very smart people have learned the hard way that a long string of impressive numbers multiplied by a single zero always equals zero. That is not an equation whose effects I would like to experience personally, and I would like even less to be responsible for imposing its penalties upon others.

Unquestionably, some people have become very rich through the use of borrowed money. However, that's also been a way to get very poor. When leverage works, it magnifies your gains. Your spouse thinks you're clever, and your neighbors get envious. But leverage is addictive. Once having profited from its wonders, very few people retreat to more conservative practices. And [to repeat] as we all learned in third grade—and some relearned in 2008—any series of positive numbers, however impressive the numbers may be, evaporates when multiplied by a single zero. History tells us that leverage all too often produces zeroes, even when it is employed by very smart people.

Leverage, of course, can be lethal to businesses as well. Companies with large debts often assume that these obligations can be refinanced as they mature. That assumption is usually valid. Occasionally, though, either because of company-specific problems or a worldwide shortage of credit, maturities must actually be met by payment. For that, only cash will do the job.

Borrowers then learn that credit is like oxygen. When either is abundant, its presence goes unnoticed. When either is missing, that's *all* that is noticed. Even a short absence of credit can bring a company to its knees. In September 2008, in fact, its overnight disappearance in many sectors of the economy came dangerously close to bringing our entire country to its knees.

At Berkshire, we will hold at least $10 billion of cash, excluding that held at our regulated utility and railroad businesses. Because of that commitment, we customarily keep at least $20 billion on hand so that we can both withstand unprecedented insurance losses (our largest to date having been about $3 billion from Katrina, the insurance industry's most expensive catastrophe) and quickly seize acquisition or investment opportunities, even during times of financial turmoil.

We keep our cash largely in U.S. Treasury bills and avoid other short-term securities yielding a few more basis points, a policy we adhered to long before the frailties of commercial paper and money market funds became apparent in September 2008. We agree with investment writer Ray DeVoe's observation, "More money has been lost reaching for yield than at the point of a gun." At Berkshire, we don't rely on bank lines, and we don't enter into contracts that could require postings of collateral except for amounts that are tiny in relation to our liquid assets.

By being so cautious in respect to leverage, we penalize our returns by a minor amount. Having loads of liquidity, though, lets us sleep well. Moreover, during the episodes of financial chaos that occasionally erupt in our economy, we will be equipped both financially and emotionally to play offense while others scramble for survival.

That's what allowed us to invest $15.6 billion in 25 days of panic following the Lehman bankruptcy in 2008.

III. Investment Alternatives

In addition to our permanent common stock holdings, we hold large quantities of marketable securities in our insurance companies. In selecting these, we can choose among five major categories: (1) long-term common stock investments, (2) medium-term fixed-income securities, (3) long-term fixed income securities, (4) short-term cash equivalents, and (5) short-term arbitrage commitments [as discussed in the essay Arbitrage in Part II.C].

We have no particular bias when it comes to choosing from these categories. We just continuously search among them for the highest after-tax returns as measured by "mathematical expectation," limiting ourselves always to investment alternatives we think we understand. Our criteria have nothing to do with maximizing immediately reportable earnings; our goal, rather, is to maximize eventual net worth.[28]

A. *Surveying the Field*[29]

Investment possibilities are both many and varied. There are three major categories, however, and it's important to understand the characteristics of each. So let's survey the field.

Investments that are denominated in a given currency include money-market funds, bonds, mortgages, bank deposits, and other instruments. Most of these currency-based investments are thought of as "safe." In truth they are among the most dangerous of assets. Their beta may be zero, but their risk is huge.

Over the past century these instruments have destroyed the purchasing power of investors in many countries, even as the holders continued to receive timely payments of interest and principal. This ugly result, moreover, will forever recur. Governments determine the ultimate value of money, and systemic forces will sometimes cause them to gravitate to policies that produce inflation. From time to time such policies spin out of control.

Even in the U.S., where the wish for a stable currency is strong, the dollar has fallen a staggering 86% in value since 1965, when I took over management of Berkshire. It takes no less than $7 today to buy what $1 did at that time. Consequently, a tax-free institution would have needed 4.3% interest annually from bond investments over that period to simply maintain its purchasing

---

[28] [Introductory essay, 1987; repeated without the first sentence in 1988 and 1989.]
[29] [2011.]

power. Its managers would have been kidding themselves if they thought of *any* portion of that interest as "income."

For tax-paying investors, the picture has been far worse. During the same 47-year period, continuous rolling of U.S. Treasury bills produced 5.7% annually. That sounds satisfactory. But if an individual investor paid personal income taxes at a rate averaging 25%, this 5.7% return would have yielded *nothing* in the way of real income. This investor's visible income tax would have stripped him of 1.4 points of the stated yield, and the invisible inflation tax would have devoured the remaining 4.3 points. It's noteworthy that the implicit inflation "tax" was more than triple the explicit income tax that our investor probably thought of as his main burden. "In God We Trust" may be imprinted on our currency, but the hand that activates our government's printing press has been all too human.

High interest rates, of course, can compensate purchasers for the inflation risk they face with currency-based investments—and indeed, rates in the early 1980s did that job nicely. Current rates, however, do not come close to offsetting the purchasing-power risk that investors assume. Right now bonds should come with a warning label.

Under today's conditions, therefore, I do not like currency-based investments. Even so, Berkshire holds significant amounts of them, primarily of the short-term variety. At Berkshire the need for ample liquidity occupies center stage and will *never* be slighted, however inadequate rates may be. Accommodating this need, we primarily hold U.S. Treasury bills, the only investment that can be counted on for liquidity under the most chaotic of economic conditions. Our working level for liquidity is $20 billion; $10 billion is our absolute minimum.

Beyond the requirements that liquidity and regulators impose on us, we will purchase currency-related securities only if they offer the possibility of unusual gain—either because a particular credit is mispriced, as can occur in periodic junk-bond debacles, or because rates rise to a level that offers the possibility of realizing substantial capital gains on high-grade bonds when rates fall. Though we've exploited both opportunities in the past—and may do so again—we are now 180 degrees removed from such prospects. Today, a wry comment that Wall Streeter Shelby Cullom Davis made long ago seems apt: "Bonds promoted as offering risk-free returns are now priced to deliver return-free risk."

The second major category of investments involves assets that will never produce anything, but that are purchased in the buyer's hope that someone else—who also knows that the assets will be forever unproductive—will pay more for them in the future. Tulips, of all things,. briefly became a favorite of such buyers in the 17th century.

This type of investment requires an expanding pool of buyers, who, in turn, are enticed because they believe the buying pool will expand still further. Owners are *not* inspired by what the asset itself can produce—it will remain lifeless forever—but rather by the belief that others will desire it even more avidly in the future.

The major asset in this category is gold, currently a huge favorite of investors who fear almost all other assets, especially paper money (of whose value, as noted, they are right to be fearful). Gold, however, has two significant shortcomings, being neither of much use nor procreative. True, gold has some industrial and decorative utility, but the demand for these purposes is both limited and incapable of soaking up new production. Meanwhile, if you own one ounce of gold for an eternity, you will still own one ounce at its end.

What motivates most gold purchasers is their belief that the ranks of the fearful will grow. During the past decade that belief has proved correct. Beyond that, the rising price has on its own generated additional buying enthusiasm, attracting purchasers who see the rise as validating an investment thesis. As "bandwagon" investors join any party, they create their own truth—*for a while*.

Over the past 15 years, both Internet stocks and houses have demonstrated the extraordinary excesses that can be created by combining an initially sensible thesis with well-publicized rising prices. In these bubbles, an army of originally skeptical investors succumbed to the "proof" delivered by the market, and the pool of buyers—for a time—expanded sufficiently to keep the bandwagon rolling. But bubbles blown large enough inevitably pop.

Today the world's gold stock is about 170,000 metric tons. If all of this gold were melded together, it would form a cube of about 68 feet per side. (Picture it fitting comfortably within a baseball infield.) At $1,750 per ounce—gold's price as I write this—its value would be $9.6 trillion. Call this cube pile A.

Let's now create a pile B costing an equal amount. For that, we could buy *all* U.S. cropland (400 million acres with output of about $200 billion annually), plus 16 Exxon Mobils (the world's most profitable company, one earning more than $40 billion annually). After these purchases, we would have about $1 trillion left over for walking-around money (no sense feeling strapped after this buying binge). Can you imagine an investor with $9.6 trillion selecting pile A over pile B?

Beyond the staggering valuation given the existing stock of gold, current prices make today's annual production of gold command about $160 billion. Buyers—whether jewelry and industrial users, frightened individuals, or speculators—must continually absorb this additional supply to merely maintain an equilibrium at present prices.

A century from now the 400 million acres of farmland will have produced staggering amounts of corn, wheat, cotton, and other crops—and will continue to produce that valuable bounty, whatever the currency may be. Exxon Mobil will probably have delivered trillions of dollars in dividends to its owners and will also hold assets worth many more trillions (and, remember, you get *16* Exxons). The 170,000 tons of gold will be unchanged in size and still incapable of producing anything. You can fondle the cube, but it will not respond.

Admittedly, when people a century from now are fearful, it's likely many will still rush to gold. I'm confident, however, that the $9.6 trillion current valuation of pile A will compound over the century at a rate far inferior to that achieved by pile B.

Our first two categories enjoy maximum popularity at peaks of fear: Terror over economic collapse drives individuals to currency-based assets, most particularly U.S. obligations, and fear of currency collapse fosters movement to sterile assets such as gold. We heard "cash is king" in late 2008, just when cash should have been deployed rather than held. Similarly, we heard "cash is trash" in the early 1980s just when fixed-dollar investments were at their most attractive level in memory. On those occasions, investors who required a supportive crowd paid dearly for that comfort.

My own preference—and you knew this was coming—is our third category: investment in productive assets, whether businesses, farms, or real estate. Ideally, these assets should have the ability in inflationary times to deliver output that will retain its purchasing-power value while requiring a minimum of new capital investment. Farms, real estate, and many businesses such as Coca-Cola, IBM and our own See's Candy meet that double-barreled test. Certain other companies—think of our regulated utilities, for example—fail it because inflation places heavy capital requirements on them. To earn more, their owners must invest more. Even so, these investments will remain superior to nonproductive or currency-based assets.

Whether the currency a century from now is based on gold, seashells, shark teeth, or a piece of paper (as today), people will be willing to exchange a couple of minutes of their daily labor for a Coca-Cola or some See's peanut brittle. In the future the U.S. population will move more goods, consume more food, and require more living space than it does now. People will forever exchange what they produce for what others produce.

Our country's businesses will continue to efficiently deliver goods and services wanted by our citizens. Metaphorically, these commercial "cows" will live for centuries and give ever greater quantities of "milk" to boot. Their value will be determined not by the medium of exchange but rather by their capacity to deliver milk. Proceeds from the sale of the milk will compound for the owners of the cows, just as they did during the 20th century when the Dow increased from 66 to 11,497 (and paid loads of dividends as well). Berkshire's goal will be to increase its ownership of first-class businesses. Our first choice will be to own them in their entirety—but we will also be owners by way of holding sizable amounts of marketable stocks. I believe that over any extended period of time this category of investing will prove to be the runaway winner among the three we've examined. More important, it will be *by far* the safest.

B.   *Junk Bonds and the Dagger Thesis*[30]

Investing in junk bonds and investing in stocks are alike in certain ways: Both activities require us to make a price-value calculation and also to scan hundreds of securities to find the very few that have attractive reward/risk ratios. But there are important differences between the two disciplines as well. In stocks, we expect every commitment to work out well because we concentrate on conservatively financed businesses with competitive strengths, run by able and honest people. If we buy into these companies at sensible prices, losses should be rare. Indeed, during the 38 years we have run the company's affairs, gains from the equities we manage at Berkshire (that is, excluding those managed at General Re and GEICO) have exceeded losses by a ratio of about 100 to one.

---

[30] [Divided by hash lines: 2002; 1990; 1990 Wesco Financial Corporation Letter to Shareholders, by Charles T. Munger. Reprinted with permission.]

Purchasing junk bonds, we are dealing with enterprises that are far more marginal. These businesses are usually overloaded with debt and often operate in industries characterized by low returns on capital. Additionally, the quality of management is sometimes questionable. Management may even have interests that are directly counter to those of debt-holders. Therefore, we expect that we will have occasional large losses in junk issues. So far, however, we have done reasonably well in this field.

Lethargy bordering on sloth remains the cornerstone of our investment style: This year we neither bought nor sold a share of five of our six major holdings. The exception was Wells Fargo, a superbly-managed, high-return banking operation in which we increased our ownership to just under 10%, the most we can own without the approval of the Federal Reserve Board. About one-sixth of our position was bought in 1989, the rest in 1990. [By 2015, Berkshire owned approximately 25% of Wells Fargo's outstanding common stock.]

The banking business is no favorite of ours. When assets are twenty times equity—a common ratio in this industry—mistakes that involve only a small portion of assets can destroy a major portion of equity. And mistakes have been the rule rather than the exception at many major banks. Most have resulted from a managerial failing that we [call] the "institutional imperative:"[31] the tendency of executives to mindlessly imitate the behavior of their peers, no matter how foolish it may be to do so. In their lending, many bankers played follow-the-leader with lemming-like zeal; now they are experiencing a lemming-like fate.

Because leverage of 20:1 magnifies the effects of managerial strengths and weaknesses, we have no interest in purchasing shares of a poorly-managed bank at a "cheap" price. Instead, our only interest is in buying into well-managed banks at fair prices.

With Wells Fargo, we think we have obtained the best managers in the business, Carl Reichardt and Paul Hazen. In many ways the combination of Carl and Paul reminds me of another—Tom Murphy and Dan Burke at Capital Cities/ABC. First, each pair is stronger than the sum of its parts because each partner understands, trusts and admires the other. Second, both managerial teams pay able people well, but abhor having a bigger head count than is needed. Third, both attack costs as vigorously when profits

---

[31] [*See* the essay Cigar Butts and the Institutional Imperative in Part II.G.]

are at record levels as when they are under pressure. Finally, both stick with what they understand and let their abilities, not their egos, determine what they attempt. (Thomas J. Watson Sr. of IBM followed the same rule: "I'm no genius," he said. "I'm smart in spots—but I stay around those spots.")

Our purchases of Wells Fargo in 1990 were helped by a chaotic market in bank stocks. The disarray was appropriate: Month by month the foolish loan decisions of once well-regarded banks were put on public display. As one huge loss after another was unveiled—often on the heels of managerial assurances that all was well—investors understandably concluded that no bank's numbers were to be trusted. Aided by their flight from bank stocks, we purchased our 10% interest in Wells Fargo for $290 million, less than five times after-tax earnings, and less than three times pre-tax earnings.

Wells Fargo is big—it has $56 billion in assets—and has been earning more than 20% on equity and 1.25% on assets. Our purchase of one-tenth of the bank may be thought of as roughly equivalent to our buying 100% of a $5 billion bank with identical financial characteristics. But were we to make such a purchase, we would have to pay about twice the $290 million we paid for Wells Fargo. Moreover, that $5 billion bank, commanding a premium price, would present us with another problem: We would not be able to find a Carl Reichardt to run it. In recent years, Wells Fargo executives have been more avidly recruited than any others in the banking business; no one however, has been able to hire the dean.

Of course, ownership of a bank—or about any other business—is far from riskless. California banks face the specific risk of a major earthquake, which might wreak enough havoc on borrowers to in turn destroy the banks lending to them. A second risk is systemic—the possibility of a business contraction or financial panic so severe that it would endanger almost every highly-leveraged institution, no matter how intelligently run. Finally, the market's major fear of the moment is that West Coast real estate values will tumble because of overbuilding and deliver huge losses to banks that have financed the expansion. Because it is a leading real estate lender, Wells Fargo is thought to be particularly vulnerable.

None of these eventualities can be ruled out. The probability of the first two occurring, however, is low and even a meaningful drop in real estate values is unlikely to cause major problems for well-managed institutions. Consider some mathematics: Wells

Fargo currently earns well over $1 billion pre-tax annually after expensing more than $300 million for loan losses. If 10% of all $48 billion of the bank's loans—not just its real estate loans—were hit by problems in 1991, and these produced losses (including foregone interest) averaging 30% of principal, the company would roughly break even.

A year like that—which we consider only a low-level possibility, not a likelihood—would not distress us. In fact, at Berkshire we would love to acquire businesses or invest in capital projects that produced no return for a year, but that could then be expected to earn 20% on growing equity. Nevertheless, fears of a California real estate disaster similar to that experienced in New England caused the price of Wells Fargo stock to fall almost 50% within a few months during 1990. Even though we had bought some shares at the prices prevailing before the fall, we welcomed the decline because it allowed us to pick up many more shares at the new, panic prices.

We will be buying businesses—or small parts of businesses, called stocks—year in, year out as long as I live (and longer, if Berkshire's directors attend the seances I have scheduled). Given these intentions, declining prices for businesses benefit us, and rising prices hurt us.

The most common cause of low prices is pessimism—sometimes pervasive, sometimes specific to a company or industry. We *want* to do business in such an environment, not because we like pessimism but because we like the prices it produces. It's optimism that is the enemy of the rational buyer.

None of this means, however, that a business or stock is an intelligent purchase simply because it is unpopular; a contrarian approach is just as foolish as a follow-the-crowd strategy. What's required is thinking rather than polling. Unfortunately, Bertrand Russell's observation about life in general applies with unusual force in the financial world: "Most men would rather die than think. Many do."

*   *   *   *   *

Our other major portfolio change last year was large additions to our holdings of RJR Nabisco bonds, securities that we first bought in late 1989. At yearend 1990 we had $440 million invested in these securities, an amount that approximated market value. (As I write this, however, their market value has risen by more than $150 million.)

Just as buying into the banking business is unusual for us, so is the purchase of below-investment-grade bonds. But opportunities that interest us and that are also large enough to have a worthwhile impact on Berkshire's results are rare. Therefore, we will look at any category of investment, so long as we understand the business we're buying into and believe that price and value may differ significantly. (Woody Allen, in another context, pointed out the advantage of open-mindedness: "I can't understand why more people aren't bi-sexual because it doubles your chances for a date on Saturday night.")

In the past we have bought a few below-investment-grade bonds with success, though these were all old-fashioned "fallen angels"—bonds that were initially of investment grade but that were downgraded when the issuers fell on bad times.

A kind of bastardized fallen angel burst onto the investment scene in the 1980s—"junk bonds" that were far below investment-grade when issued. As the decade progressed, new offerings of manufactured junk became ever junkier and ultimately the predictable outcome occurred: Junk bonds lived up to their name. In 1990—even before the recession dealt its blows—the financial sky became dark with the bodies of failing corporations.

The disciples of debt assured us that this collapse wouldn't happen: Huge debt, we were told, would cause operating managers to focus their efforts as never before, much as a dagger mounted on the steering wheel of a car could be expected to make its driver proceed with intensified care. We'll acknowledge that such an attention-getter would produce a very alert driver. But another certain consequence would be a deadly—and unnecessary—accident if the car hit even the tiniest pothole or sliver of ice. The roads of business are riddled with potholes; a plan that requires dodging them all is a plan for disaster.

In the final chapter of *The Intelligent Investor* Ben Graham forcefully rejected the dagger thesis: "Confronted with a challenge to distill the secret of sound investment into three words, we venture the motto, Margin of Safety." Forty-two years after reading that, I still think those are the right three words. The failure of investors to heed this simple message caused them staggering losses as the 1990s began.

At the height of the debt mania, capital structures were concocted that guaranteed failure: In some cases, so much debt was issued that even highly favorable business results could not produce the funds to service it. One particularly egregious "kill-'emat-birth" case a few years back involved the purchase of a mature television station in Tampa, bought with so much debt that the interest on it exceeded the station's *gross revenues*. Even if you assume that all labor, programs and services were donated rather than purchased, this capital structure required revenues to explode—or else the station was doomed to go broke. (Many of the bonds that financed the purchase were sold to now-failed savings and loan associations; as a taxpayer, you are picking up the tab for this folly.)

All of this seems impossible now. When these misdeeds were done, however, dagger-selling investment bankers pointed to the "scholarly" research of academics, which reported that over the years the higher interest rates received from low-grade bonds had more than compensated for their higher rate of default. Thus, said the friendly salesmen, a diversified portfolio of junk bonds would produce greater net returns than would a portfolio of high-grade bonds. (Beware of past-performance "proofs" in finance: If history books were the key to riches, the Forbes 400 would consist of librarians.)

There was a flaw in the salesmen's logic—one that a first-year student in statistics is taught to recognize. An assumption was being made that the universe of newly-minted junk bonds was identical to the universe of low-grade fallen angels and that, therefore, the default experience of the latter group was meaningful in predicting the default experience of the new issues. (That was an error similar to checking the historical death rate from Kool-Aid before drinking the version served at Jonestown.)

The universes were of course dissimilar in several vital respects. For openers, the manager of a fallen angel almost invariably yearned to regain investment-grade status and worked toward that goal. The junk-bond operator was usually an entirely different breed. Behaving much as a heroin user might, he devoted his energies not to finding a cure for his debt-ridden condition, but rather to finding another fix. Additionally, the fiduciary sensitivities of the executives managing the typical fallen angel were often, though not always, more finely developed than were those of the junk-bond-issuing financiopath.

Wall Street cared little for such distinctions. As usual, the Street's enthusiasm for an idea was proportional not to its merit, but rather to the revenue it would produce. Mountains of junk bonds were sold by those who didn't care to those who didn't think—and there was no shortage of either.

Junk bonds remain a mine field, even at prices that today are often a small fraction of issue price. As we said last year, we have never bought a new issue of a junk bond. (The only time to buy these is on a day with no "y" in it.) We are, however, willing to look at the field, now that it is in disarray.

In the case of RJR Nabisco, we feel the Company's credit is considerably better than was generally perceived for a while and that the yield we receive, as well as the potential for capital gain, more than compensates for the risk we incur (though that is far from nil). RJR has made asset sales at favorable prices, has added major amounts of equity, and in general is being run well.

However, as we survey the field, most low-grade bonds still look unattractive. The handiwork of the Wall Street of the 1980s is even worse than we had thought: Many important businesses have been mortally wounded. We will, though, keep looking for opportunities as the junk market continues to unravel.

It is interesting to compare Wesco's approach (deliberate non-diversification of investments in an attempt to be more skillful per transaction) with an approach promoted for years by Michael Milken to help sell junk bonds. The Milken approach, supported by theories of many finance professors, argued that (1) market prices were efficient in a world where investors get paid extra for enduring volatility (wide swings in outcomes); (2) therefore, the prices at which new issues of junk bonds came to market were fair in a probabilistic sense (meaning that the high promised interest rates covered increased statistical expectancy of loss) and also provided some premium return to cover volatility exposure; and (3) therefore, if a savings and loan association (or other institution) arranged diversification, say, by buying, without much examination, a large part of each new Milken issue of junk bonds, the association would work itself into the sure-to-get-better-than-average-results position of a gambling house proprietor with a "house" edge. This type of theorizing has now wreaked havoc at institutions, governed by true-believers, which backed their conclusions by buying Milken's "bonds." Contrary to the theorizing, widely diversified purchases of such "bonds" have in most cases produced dismal results. We can all understand why Milken behaved as he did and believed what he had to believe in order to maintain an endurable self-image. But how can we explain why anyone else believed that Milken was paid 5% commissions to put "bond" buyers in the position of the house in Las Vegas? We suggest this cause: many of the foolish buyers, and their advisers, were trained by finance professors who pushed beloved models (efficient market theory and modern portfolio theory) way too far, while they ignored other models that would have warned of danger. This is a common type of "expert" error.

C.   *Zero-Coupon Bonds and Ski Masks*[32]

Berkshire issued $902.6 million principal amount of Zero-Coupon Convertible Subordinated Debentures, which are now listed on the New York Stock Exchange. Salomon Brothers handled the underwriting in superb fashion, providing us helpful advice and a flawless execution.

Most bonds, of course, require regular payments of interest, usually semi-annually. A zero-coupon bond, conversely, requires no current interest payments; instead, the investor receives his yield by purchasing the security at a significant discount from maturity value. The effective interest rate is determined by the original issue price, the maturity value, and the amount of time between issuance and maturity.

In our case, the bonds were issued at 44.314% of maturity value and are due in 15 years. For investors purchasing the bonds, that is the mathematical equivalent of a 5.5% current payment compounded semi-annually. Because we received only 44.31 cents on the dollar, our proceeds from this offering were $400 million (less about $9.5 million of offering expenses).

The bonds were issued in denominations of $10,000 and each bond is convertible into .4515 shares of Berkshire Hathaway. Because a $10,000 bond cost $4,431, this means that the conversion price was $9,815 per Berkshire share, a 15% premium to the market price then existing. Berkshire can call the bonds at any time after September 28, 1992 at their accreted value (the original issue price plus 5.5% compounded semi-annually) and on two specified days, September 28 of 1994 and 1999, the bondholders can require Berkshire to buy the securities at their accreted value.

For tax purposes, Berkshire is entitled to deduct the 5.5% interest accrual each year, even though we make no payments to the bondholders. Thus the net effect to us, resulting from the reduced taxes, is positive cash flow. That is a very significant benefit. Some unknowable variables prevent us from calculating our exact effective rate of interest, but under all circumstances it will be well below 5.5%. There is meanwhile a symmetry to the tax law: Any taxable holder of the bonds must pay tax each year on the 5.5% interest, even though he receives no cash.

Neither our bonds nor those of certain other companies that issued similar bonds last year (notably Loews and Motorola) resemble the great bulk of zero-coupon bonds that have been issued in recent years. Of these, Charlie and I have been, and will continue to be, outspoken critics. As I will later explain, such bonds have often been used in the most deceptive of ways and with deadly consequences to investors. But before we tackle that subject, let's travel back to Eden, to a time when the apple had not yet been bitten.

If you're my age you bought your first zero-coupon bonds during World War II, by purchasing the famous Series E U.S. Savings Bond, the most widely-sold bond issue in history. (After the war, these bonds were held by one out of two U.S. households.) Nobody, of course, called the Series E a zero-coupon bond, a term in fact that I doubt had been invented. But that's precisely what the Series E was.

These bonds came in denominations as small as $18.75. That amount purchased a $25 obligation of the United States government due in 10 years, terms that gave the buyer a compounded annual return of 2.9%. At the time, this was an attractive offer: the 2.9% rate was higher than that generally available on Government bonds and the holder faced no market-fluctuation risk, since he could at any time cash in his bonds with only a minor reduction in interest.

A second form of zero-coupon U.S. Treasury issue, also benign and useful, surfaced in the last decade. One problem with a normal bond is that even though it pays a given interest rate—say 10%—the holder cannot be assured that a compounded 10% return will be realized. For that rate to materialize, each semi-annual coupon must be reinvested at 10% as it is received. If current interest rates are, say, only 6% or 7% when these coupons come due, the holder will be unable to compound his money over the life of the bond at the advertised rate. For pension funds or other investors with long-term liabilities, "reinvestment risk" of this type can be a serious problem. Savings Bonds might have solved it, except that they are issued only to individuals and are unavailable in large denominations. What big buyers needed was huge quantities of "Savings Bond Equivalents."

Enter some ingenious and, in this case, highly useful investment bankers (led, I'm happy to say, by Salomon Brothers). They created the instrument desired by "stripping" the semi-annual coupons from standard Government issues. Each coupon, once detached, takes on the essential character of a Savings Bond since it represents a single sum due sometime in the future. For example, if you strip the 40 semi-annual coupons from a U.S. Government Bond due in the year 2010, you will have 40 zero-coupon bonds, with maturities from six months to 20 years, each of which can then be bundled with other coupons of like maturity and marketed. If current interest rates are, say, 10% for all maturities, the six-month issue will sell for 95.24% of maturity value and the 20-year issue will sell for 14.20%. The purchaser of any given maturity is thus guaranteed a compounded rate of 10% for his entire holding period. Stripping of government bonds has occurred on a large scale in recent years, as long-term investors, ranging from pension funds to individual IRA accounts, recognized these high-grade, zero-coupon issues to be well suited to their needs.

But as happens in Wall Street all too often, what the wise do in the beginning, fools do in the end. In the last few years zero-coupon bonds (and their functional equivalent, pay-in-kind bonds, which distribute additional PIK bonds semi-annually as interest instead of paying cash) have been issued in enormous quantities by ever-junkier credits. To these issuers, zero (or PIK) bonds offer one overwhelming advantage: It is impossible to default on a promise to pay nothing. Indeed, if LDC governments had issued no debt in the 1970s other than long-term zero-coupon obligations, they would now have a spotless record as debtors.

This principle at work—that you need not default for a long time if you solemnly promise to pay nothing for a long time—has not been lost on promoters and investment bankers seeking to finance ever-shakier deals. But its acceptance by lenders took a while: When the leveraged buy-out craze began some years back, purchasers could borrow only on a reasonably sound basis, in which conservatively-estimated free cash flow—that is, operating earnings plus depreciation and amortization less normalized capital expenditures—was adequate to cover both interest and modest reductions in debt.

Later, as the adrenalin of deal-makers surged, businesses began to be purchased at prices so high that all free cash flow necessarily had to be allocated to the payment of interest. That left nothing for the paydown of debt. In effect, a Scarlett O'Hara "I'll think about it tomorrow" position in respect to principal payments was taken by borrowers and accepted by a new breed of lender, the buyer of original-issue junk bonds. Debt now became something to be refinanced rather than repaid. The change brings to mind a *New Yorker* cartoon in which the grateful borrower rises to shake the hand of the bank's lending officer and gushes: "I don't know how I'll ever repay you."

Soon borrowers found even the new, lax standards intolerably binding. To induce lenders to finance even sillier transactions, they introduced an abomination, EBDIT—Earnings Before Depreciation, Interest and Taxes—as the test of a company's ability to pay interest. Using this sawed-off yardstick, the borrower ignored depreciation as an expense on the theory that it did not require a current cash outlay.

Such an attitude is clearly delusional. At 95% of American businesses, capital expenditures that over time roughly approximate depreciation are a necessity and are every bit as real an expense as labor or utility costs. Even a high school dropout knows that to finance a car he must have income that covers not only interest and operating expenses, but also realistically-calculated depreciation. He would be laughed out of the bank if he started talking about EBDIT.

Capital outlays at a business can be skipped, of course, in any given month, just as a human can skip a day or even a week of eating. But if the skipping becomes routine and is not made up, the body weakens and eventually dies. Furthermore, a start and-stop feeding policy will over time produce a less healthy organism, human or corporate, than that produced by a steady diet. As businessmen, Charlie and I relish having competitors who are unable to fund capital expenditures.

You might think that waving away a major expense such as depreciation in an attempt to make a terrible deal look like a good one hits the limits of Wall Street's ingenuity. If so, you haven't been paying attention during the past few years. Promoters needed to find a way to justify even pricier acquisitions. Otherwise, they risked—heaven forbid—losing deals to other promoters with more "imagination."

So, stepping through the Looking Glass, promoters and their investment bankers proclaimed that EBDIT should now be measured against cash interest only, which meant that interest accruing on zero-coupon or PIK bonds could be ignored when the financial feasibility of a transaction was being assessed. This approach not only relegated depreciation expense to the let's-ignore-it corner, but gave similar treatment to what was usually a significant portion of interest expense. To their shame, many professional investment managers went along with this nonsense, though they usually were careful to do so only with clients' money, not their own. (Calling these managers "professionals" is actually too kind; they should be designated "promotees.")

Under this new standard, a business earning, say, $100 million pre-tax and having debt on which $90 million of interest must be paid currently, might use a zero-coupon of PIK issue to incur another $60 million of annual interest that would accrue and compound but not come due for some years. The rate on these issues would typically be very high, which means that the situation in year 2 might be $90 million cash interest plus $69 million accrued interest, and so on as the compounding proceeds. Such high-rate reborrowing schemes, which a few years ago were appropriately confined to the waterfront, soon became models of finance at virtually all major investment banking houses.

When they make these offerings, investment bankers display their humorous side: They dispense income and balance sheet projections extending five or more years into the future for companies they barely had heard of a few months earlier. If you are shown such schedules, I suggest that you join the fun: Ask the investment banker for the one-year budgets that his own firm prepared as the last few years began and then compare these with what actually happened.

Some time ago Ken Galbraith, in his witty and insightful *The Great Crash*, coined a new economic term: "the bezzle," defined as the current amount of undiscovered embezzlement. This financial creature has a magical quality: The embezzlers are richer by the amount of the bezzle, while the embezzlees do not yet feel poorer.

Professor Galbraith astutely pointed out that this sum should be added to the National Wealth so that we might know the Psychic National Wealth. Logically, a society that wanted to feel enormously prosperous would both encourage its citizens to embezzle and try not to detect the crime. By this means, "wealth" would balloon though not an erg of productive work had been done.

The satirical nonsense of the bezzle is dwarfed by the real-world nonsense of the zero-coupon bond. With zeros, one party to a contract can experience "income" without his opposite experiencing the pain of expenditure. In our illustration, a company capable of earning only $100 million dollars annually—and therefore capable of paying only that much in interest—magically creates "earnings" for bondholders of $150 million. As long as major investors willingly don their Peter Pan wings and repeatedly say "I believe," there is no limit to how much "income" can be created by the zero-coupon bond.

Wall Street welcomed this invention with the enthusiasm less-enlightened folk might reserve for the wheel or the plow. Here, finally, was an instrument that would let the Street make deals at prices no longer limited by actual earning power. The result, obviously, would be more transactions: Silly prices will always attract sellers. And, as Jesse Unruh might have put it, transactions are the mother's milk of finance.

The zero-coupon or PIK bond possesses an additional attraction for the promoter and investment banker, which is that the time elapsing between folly and failure can be stretched out. This is no small benefit. If the period before all costs must be faced is long, promoters can create a string of foolish deals—and take in lots of fees—before any chickens come home to roost from their earlier ventures.

But in the end, alchemy, whether it is metallurgical or financial, fails. A base business can not be transformed into a golden business by tricks of accounting or capital structure. The man claiming to be a financial alchemist may become rich. But gullible investors rather than business achievements will usually be the source of his wealth.

Whatever their weaknesses, we should add, many zero-coupon and PIK bonds will not default. We have in fact owned some and may buy more if their market becomes sufficiently distressed. (We've not, however, even considered buying a new issue from a weak credit.) No financial instrument is evil per se; it's just that some variations have far more potential for mischief than others.

The blue ribbon for mischief-making should go to the zero-coupon issuer unable to make its interest payments on a current basis. Our advice: Whenever an investment banker starts talking about EBDIT—or whenever someone creates a capital structure that does not allow all interest, both payable and accrued, to be comfortably met out of current cash flow net of ample capital expenditures—zip up your wallet. Turn the tables by suggesting that the promoter and his high-priced entourage accept zero-coupon fees, deferring their take until the zero-coupon bonds have been paid in full. See then how much enthusiasm for the deal endures.

Our comments about investment bankers may seem harsh. But Charlie and I—in our hopelessly old-fashioned way—believe that they should perform a gatekeeping role, guarding investors against the promoter's propensity to indulge in excess. Promoters, after all, have throughout time exercised the same judgment and restraint in accepting money that alcoholics have exercised in accepting liquor. At a minimum, therefore, the banker's conduct should rise to that of a responsible bartender who, when necessary, refuses the profit from the next drink to avoid sending a drunk out on the highway. In recent years, unfortunately, many leading investment firms have found bartender morality to be an intolerably restrictive standard. Lately, those who have traveled the high road in Wall Street have not encountered heavy traffic.

One distressing footnote: The cost of the zero-coupon folly will not be borne solely by the direct participants. Certain savings and loan associations were heavy buyers of such bonds, using cash that came from FSLIC-insured deposits. Straining to show splendid earnings, these buyers recorded—but did not receive— ultra-high interest income on these issues. Many of these associations are now in major trouble. Had their loans to shaky credits worked, the owners of the associations would have pocketed the profits. In the many cases in which the loans will fail, the taxpayer will pick up the bill. To paraphrase Jackie Mason, at these associations it was the managers who should have been wearing the ski masks.

D. *Preferred Stock*[33]

We only want to link up with people whom we like, admire, and trust. John Gutfreund at Salomon, Colman Mockler, Jr. at Gillette, Ed Colodny at USAir, and Andy Sigler at Champion meet this test in spades.

They in turn have demonstrated some confidence in us, insisting in each case that our preferreds have unrestricted voting rights on a fully-converted basis, an arrangement that is far from standard in corporate finance. In effect they are trusting us to be intelligent owners, thinking about tomorrow *instead* of today, just as we are trusting them to be intelligent managers, thinking about tomorrow *as well* as today.

The preferred-stock structures we have negotiated will provide a mediocre return for us if industry economics hinder the perform-

---

[33] [Divided by hash lines: 1989; 1994; 1996; 1990; 1995; 1997.]

ance of our investees, but will produce reasonably attractive results for us if they can earn a return comparable to that of American industry in general. We believe that Gillette, under Colman's management, will far exceed that return and believe that John, Ed, and Andy will reach it unless industry conditions are harsh.

Under almost any conditions, we expect these preferreds to return us our money plus dividends. If that is all we get, though, the result will be disappointing, because we will have given up flexibility and consequently will have missed some significant opportunities that are bound to present themselves during the decade. Under that scenario, we will have obtained only a preferred-stock yield during a period when the typical preferred stock will have held no appeal for us whatsoever. The only way Berkshire can achieve satisfactory results from its four preferred issues is to have the common stocks of the investee companies do well.

Good management and at least tolerable industry conditions will be needed if that is to happen. But we believe Berkshire's investment will also help and that the other shareholders of each investee will profit over the years ahead from our preferred-stock purchase. The help will come from the fact that each company now has a major, stable, and interested shareholder whose Chairman and Vice Chairman have, through Berkshire's investments, indirectly committed a very large amount of their own money to these undertakings. In dealing with our investees, Charlie and I will be supportive, analytical, and objective. We recognize that we are working with experienced CEOs who are very much in command of their own business but who nevertheless, at certain moments, appreciate the chance to test their thinking on someone without ties to their industry or to decisions of the past.

As a group, these convertible preferreds will not produce the returns we can achieve when we find a business with wonderful economic prospects that is unappreciated by the market. Nor will the returns be as attractive as those produced when we make our favorite form of capital deployment, the acquisition of 80% or more of a fine business with a fine management. But both opportunities are rare, particularly in a size befitting our present and anticipated resources.

In summation, Charlie and I feel that our preferred stock investments should produce returns moderately above those achieved by most fixed-income portfolios and that we can play a minor but enjoyable and constructive role in the investee companies.

Mistakes occur at the time of decision. We can only make our mistake-*du-jour* award, however, when the foolishness of a decision becomes obvious. By this measure, 1994 was a vintage year with keen competition for the gold medal. Here, I would like to tell you that the mistakes I will describe originated with Charlie. But whenever I try to explain things that way, my nose begins to grow.

And the nominees are . . .

Late in 1993 I sold 10 million shares of Cap Cities at $63; at year-end 1994, the price was $85¼. (The difference is $222.5 million for those of you who wish to avoid the pain of calculating the damage yourself.) When we purchased the stock at $17.25 in 1986, I told you that I had previously sold our Cap Cities holdings at $4.30 per share during 1978-80, and added that I was at a loss to explain my earlier behavior.[34] Now I've become a repeat offender. Maybe it's time to get a guardian appointed.

Egregious as it is, the Cap Cities decision earns only a silver medal. Top honors go to a mistake I made five years ago that fully ripened in 1994: Our $358 million purchase of USAir preferred stock, on which the dividend was suspended in September. [T]his deal [w]as an "unforced error," meaning that I was neither pushed into the investment nor misled by anyone when making it. Rather, this was a case of sloppy analysis, a lapse that may have been caused by the fact that we were buying a senior security or by hubris. Whatever the reason, the mistake was large.

Before this purchase, I simply failed to focus on the problems that would inevitably beset a carrier whose costs were both high and extremely difficult to lower. In earlier years, these life-threatening costs posed few problems. Airlines were then protected from competition by regulation, and carriers could absorb high costs because they could pass them along by way of fares that were also high.

When deregulation came along, it did not immediately change the picture: The capacity of low-cost carriers was so small that the high-cost lines could, in large part, maintain their existing fare structures. During this period, with the longer-term problems largely invisible but slowly metastasizing, the costs that were non-sustainable became further embedded.

---

[34] [*See* the essay "Value" Investing: A Redundancy in Part II.E. The per share figures in the two essays differ because of stock splits.]

As the seat capacity of the low-cost operators expanded, their fares began to force the old-line, high-cost airlines to cut their own. The day of reckoning for these airlines could be delayed by infusions of capital (such as ours into USAir), but eventually a fundamental rule of economics prevailed: In an unregulated commodity business, a company must lower its costs to competitive levels or face extinction. This principle should have been obvious to your Chairman, but I missed it.

Seth Schofield, [then] CEO of USAir, has worked diligently to correct the company's historical cost problems but, to date, has not managed to do so. In part, this is because he has had to deal with a moving target, the result of certain major carriers having obtained labor concessions and other carriers having benefitted from "fresh-start" costs that came out of bankruptcy proceedings. (As Herb Kelleher, CEO of Southwest Airlines, has said: "Bankruptcy court for airlines has become a health spa.") Additionally, it should be no surprise to anyone that those airline employees who contractually receive above-market salaries will resist any reduction in these as long as their checks continue to clear.

Despite this difficult situation, USAir may yet achieve the cost reductions it needs to maintain its viability long-term. But it is far from sure that will happen.

Accordingly, we wrote our USAir investment down to $89.5 million, or 25¢ on the dollar, at yearend 1994. This valuation reflects both a possibility that our preferred will have its value fully or largely restored and an opposite possibility that the stock will eventually become worthless. Whatever the outcome, we will heed a prime rule of investing: You don't have to make it back the way that you lost it.

The accounting effects of our USAir writedown are complicated. On our balance sheet, we carry all stocks at estimated market value. Therefore, at the end of last year's third quarter, we were carrying our USAir preferred at $89.5 million, or 25% of cost. In other words, our net worth was at that time reflecting a value for USAir that was far below our $358 million cost.

But in the fourth quarter, we concluded that the decline in value was, in accounting terms, "other than temporary," and that judgment required us to send the writedown of $268.5 million through our income statement. The amount had no other fourth-quarter effect. That is, it did not reduce our net worth, because the diminution of value had already been reflected there.

Charlie and I will not stand for reelection to USAir's board at the upcoming annual meeting. Should Seth wish to consult with us, however, we will be pleased to be of any help that we can.

———————

When Richard Branson, the wealthy owner of Virgin Atlantic Airways, was asked how to become a millionaire, he had a quick answer: "There's really nothing to it. Start as a billionaire and then buy an airline." Unwilling to accept Branson's proposition on faith, your Chairman decided in 1989 to test it by investing $358 million in a 9¼% preferred stock of USAir.

I liked and admired Ed Colodny, the company's then-CEO, and I still do. But my analysis of USAir's business was both superficial and wrong. I was so beguiled by the company's long history of profitable operations, and by the protection that ownership of a senior security seemingly offered me, that I overlooked the crucial point: USAir's revenues would increasingly feel the effects of an unregulated, fiercely competitive market whereas its cost structure was a holdover from the days when regulation protected profits. These costs, if left unchecked, portended disaster, however reassuring the airline's past record might be.

To rationalize its costs, however, USAir needed major improvements in its labor contracts—and that's something most airlines have found it extraordinarily difficult to get, short of credibly threatening, or actually entering, bankruptcy. USAir was to be no exception. Immediately after we purchased our preferred stock, the imbalance between the company's costs and revenues began to grow explosively. In the 1990-1994 period, USAir lost an aggregate of $2.4 billion, a performance that totally wiped out the book equity of its common stock.

For much of this period, the company paid us our preferred dividends, but in 1994 payment was suspended. A bit later, with the situation looking particularly gloomy, we wrote down our investment by 75%, to $89.5 million. Thereafter, during much of 1995, I offered to sell our shares at 50% of face value. Fortunately, I was unsuccessful.

Mixed in with my many mistakes at USAir was one thing I got right: Making our investment, we wrote into the preferred contract a somewhat unusual provision stipulating that "penalty dividends"—to run five percentage points over the prime rate—would be accrued on any arrearages. This meant that when our 9¼% dividend was omitted for two years, the unpaid amounts compounded at rates ranging between 13¼% and 14%.

Facing this penalty provision, USAir had every incentive to pay arrearages just as promptly as it could. And in the second half of 1996, when USAir turned profitable, it indeed began to pay, giving us $47.9 million. We owe Stephen Wolf, the company's CEO, a huge thank-you for extracting a performance from the airline that permitted this payment. Even so, USAir's performance has recently been helped significantly by an industry tailwind that may be cyclical in nature. The company still has basic cost problems that must be solved.

In any event, the prices of USAir's publicly-traded securities tell us that our preferred stock is now probably worth its par value of $358 million, give or take a little. In addition, we have over the years collected an aggregate of $240.5 million in dividends (including $30 million received in 1997).

Early in 1996, before any accrued dividends had been paid, I tried once more to unload our holdings—this time for about $335 million. You're lucky: I again failed in my attempt to snatch defeat from the jaws of victory.

In another context, a friend once asked me: "If you're so rich, why aren't you smart?" After reviewing my sorry performance with USAir, you may conclude he had a point.

In making the USAir purchase, your Chairman displayed exquisite timing: I plunged into the business at almost the exact moment that it ran into severe problems. (No one pushed me; in tennis parlance, I committed an "unforced error.") The company's troubles were brought on both by industry conditions and by the post-merger difficulties it encountered in integrating Piedmont, an affliction I should have expected since almost all airline mergers have been followed by operational turmoil.

In short order, Ed Colodny and Seth Schofield resolved the second problem: The airline now gets excellent marks for service. Industry-wide problems have proved to be far more serious. Since our purchase, the economics of the airline industry have deteriorated at an alarming pace, accelerated by the kamikaze pricing tactics of certain carriers. The trouble this pricing has produced for all carriers illustrates an important truth: In a business selling a commodity-type product, it's impossible to be a lot smarter than your dumbest competitor.

However, unless the industry is decimated during the next few years, our USAir investment should work out all right. Ed and Seth decisively addressed the current turbulence by making major changes in operations. Even so, our investment is now less secure than at the time I made it.

Our convertible preferred stocks are relatively simple securities, yet I should warn you that, if the past is any guide, you may from time to time read inaccurate or misleading statements about them. Last year, for example, several members of the press calculated the value of all our preferreds as equal to that of the common stock into which they are convertible. By their logic, that is, our Salomon preferred, convertible into common at $38, would be worth 60% of face value if Salomon common were selling at $22.80. But there is a small problem with this line of reasoning: Using it, one must conclude that all of the value of a convertible preferred resides in the conversion privilege and that value of a non-convertible preferred of Salomon would be zero, no matter what its coupon or terms for redemption.

The point you should keep in mind is that most of the value of our convertible preferreds is derived from their fixed-income characteristics. That means the securities cannot be worth less than the value they would possess as non-convertible preferreds and may be worth more because of their conversion options.

Berkshire made five private purchases of convertible preferred stocks during the 1987-91 period and the time seems right to discuss their status.

In each case we had the option of sticking with these preferreds as fixed-income securities or converting them into common stock. Initially, their value to us came primarily from their fixed-income characteristics. The option we had to convert was a kicker.

Our $300 million private purchase of American Express "Percs" was a modified form of common stock whose fixed-income characteristics contributed only a minor portion of its initial value. Three years after we bought them, the Percs automatically were converted to common stock. In contrast, [our other convertible preferred stocks] were set to become common stocks only if we wished them to—a crucial difference.

When we purchased our convertible securities, I told you that we expected to earn after-tax returns from them that "moderately" exceeded what we could earn from the medium-term fixed-income securities they replaced. We beat this expectation—but only because of the performance of a single issue. I also told you that these securities, as a group, would "not produce the returns we can achieve when we find a business with wonderful economic prospects." Unfortunately, that prediction was fulfilled. Finally, I said that "under almost any conditions, we expect these preferreds to return us our money plus dividends." That's one I would like to have back. Winston Churchill once said that "eating my words has never given me indigestion." My assertion, however, that it was almost impossible for us to lose money on our preferreds has caused me some well-deserved heartburn.

Our best holding has been Gillette, which we told you from the start was a superior business. Ironically, though, this is also the purchase in which I made my biggest mistake—of a kind, however, never recognized on financial statements.

We paid $600 million in 1989 for Gillette preferred shares that were convertible into 48 million (split-adjusted) common shares. Taking an alternative route with the $600 million, I probably could have purchased 60 million shares of common from the company. The market on the common was then about $10.50, and given that this would have been a huge private placement carrying important restrictions, I probably could have bought the stock at a discount of at least 5%. I can't be sure about this, but it's likely that Gillette's management would have been just as happy to have Berkshire opt for common.

But I was far too clever to do that. Instead, for less than two years, we received some extra dividend income (the difference between the preferred's yield and that of the common), at which point the company—quite properly—called the issue, moving to do that as quickly as was possible. If I had negotiated for common rather than preferred, we would have been better off at yearend 1995 by $625 million, minus the "excess" dividends of about $70 million.

In the case of Champion, the ability of the company to call our preferred at 115% of cost forced a move out of us last August that we would rather have delayed. In this instance, we converted our shares just prior to the pending call and offered them to the company at a modest discount.

Charlie and I have never had a conviction about the paper industry—actually, I can't remember ever owning the common stock of a paper producer in my 54 years of investing—so our choice in August was whether to sell in the market or to the company. Our Champion capital gain was moderate—about 19% after tax from a six-year investment—but the preferred delivered us a good after-tax dividend yield throughout our holding period. (That said, many press accounts have overstated the after-tax yields earned by property-casualty insurance companies on dividends paid to them. What the press has failed to take into account is a change in the tax law that took effect in 1987 and that significantly reduced the dividends received credit applicable to insurers.)

Our First Empire preferred [was to] be called on March 31, 1996, the earliest date allowable. We are comfortable owning stock in well-run banks, and we will convert and keep our First Empire common shares. Bob Wilmers, CEO of the company, is an outstanding banker, and we love being associated with him.

Our other two preferreds have been disappointing, though the Salomon preferred has modestly outperformed the fixed-income securities for which it was a substitute. However, the amount of management time Charlie and I have devoted to this holding has been vastly greater than its economic significance to Berkshire. Certainly I never dreamed I would take a new job at age 60—Salomon interim chairman, that is—because of an earlier purchase of a fixed-income security.

Soon after our purchase of the Salomon preferred in 1987, I wrote that I had "no special insights regarding the direction or future profitability of investment banking." Even the most charitable commentator would conclude that I have since proved my point.

To date, our option to convert into Salomon common has not proven of value. Furthermore, the Dow Industrials have doubled since I committed to buy the preferred, and the brokerage group has performed equally as well. That means my decision to go with Salomon because I saw value in the conversion option must be graded as very poor. Even so, the preferred has continued under some trying conditions to deliver as a fixed-income security, and the 9% dividend is currently quite attractive.

Unless the preferred is converted, its terms require redemption of 20% of the issue on October 31 of each year, 1995-99, and $140 million of our original $700 million was taken on schedule last year. (Some press reports labeled this a sale, but a senior security that matures is not "sold.") Though we did not elect to convert the preferred that matured last year, we have four more bites at the conversion apple, and I believe it quite likely that we will yet find value in our right to convert.

———————————

The common stocks of both Gillette and First Empire [into which Berkshire's preferreds had been converted] have risen substantially, in line with the companies' excellent performance. At year end, the $600 million we put into Gillette in 1989 had appreciated to $4.8 billion, and the $40 million we committed to First Empire in 1991 had risen to $236 million.

Our two laggards [USAir and Salomon], meanwhile, have come to life in a very major way. In a transaction that finally rewarded its long-suffering shareholders, Salomon recently merged into Travelers Group. All of Berkshire's shareholders—including me, very personally—owe a huge debt to Deryck Maughan and Bob Denham for, first, playing key roles in saving Salomon from extinction following its 1991 scandal and, second, restoring the vitality of the company to a level that made it an attractive acquisition for Travelers. I have often said that I wish to work with executives that I like, trust and admire. No two fit that description better than Deryck and Bob.

Berkshire's final results from its Salomon investment won't be tallied for some time, but it is safe to say that they will be far better than I anticipated two years ago. Looking back, I think of my Salomon experience as having been both fascinating and instructional, though for a time in 1991-92 [when serving as its chairman] I felt like the drama critic who wrote: "I would have enjoyed the play except that I had an unfortunate seat. It faced the stage."

The resuscitation of US Airways borders on the miraculous. Those who have watched my moves in this investment know that I have compiled a record that is unblemished by success. I was wrong in originally purchasing the stock, and I was wrong later, in repeatedly trying to unload our holdings at 50 cents on the dollar.

Two changes at the company coincided with its remarkable rebound: (1) Charlie and I left the board of directors and (2) Stephen Wolf became CEO. Fortunately for our egos, the second event was the key: Stephen Wolf's accomplishments at the airline have been phenomenal.

There still is much to do at US Airways, but survival is no longer an issue. Consequently, the company made up the dividend arrearages on our preferred during 1997, adding extra payments to compensate us for the delay we suffered. The company's common stock, furthermore, has risen from a low of $4 to a recent high of $73.

Our preferred has been called for redemption on March 15. But the rise in the company's stock has given our conversion rights, which we thought worthless not long ago, great value. It is now almost certain that our US Airways shares will produce a decent profit—that is, if my cost for Maalox is excluded—and the gain could even prove indecent.

Next time I make a big, dumb decision, Berkshire shareholders will know what to do: *Phone Mr. Wolf.*

*   *   *   *   *

In addition to the convertible preferreds, we purchased one other private placement in 1991, $300 million of American Express Percs. This security was essentially a common stock that featured a tradeoff in its first three years: We received extra dividend payments during that period, but we were also capped in the price appreciation we could realize. Despite the cap, this holding has proved extraordinarily profitable thanks to a move by your Chairman that combined luck and skill—110% luck, the balance skill.

Our Percs were due to convert into common stock in August 1994, and in the month before I was mulling whether to sell upon conversion. One reason to hold was Amex's outstanding CEO, Harvey Golub, who seemed likely to maximize whatever potential the company had (a supposition that has since been proved—in spades). But the size of that potential was in question: Amex faced relentless competition from a multitude of card-issuers, led by Visa. Weighing the arguments, I leaned toward sale.

Here's where I got lucky. During that month of decision, I played golf at Prouts Neck, Maine with Frank Olson, CEO of Hertz. Frank is a brilliant manager, with intimate knowledge of the card business. So from the first tee on I was quizzing him about the industry. By the time we reached the second green, Frank had convinced me that Amex's corporate card was a terrific franchise, and I had decided not to sell. On the back nine I turned buyer, and in a few months Berkshire owned 10% of the company.

We now have a $3 billion gain in our Amex shares, and I naturally feel very grateful to Frank. But George Gillespie, our mutual friend, says that I am confused about where my gratitude should go. After all, he points out, it was he who arranged the game and assigned me to Frank's foursome.

E.   *Derivatives*[35]

Charlie and I are of one mind in how we feel about derivatives and the trading activities that go with them: We view them as time

---

[35] [2002; 2005; 2006; 2008.]

bombs, both for the parties that deal in them and the economic system.

Having delivered that thought, which I'll get back to, let me retreat to explaining derivatives, though the explanation must be general because the word covers an extraordinarily wide range of financial contracts. Essentially, these instruments call for money to change hands at some future date, with the amount to be determined by one or more reference items, such as interest rates, stock prices or currency values. If, for example, you are either long or short an S&P 500 futures contract, you are a party to a very simple derivatives transaction—with your gain or loss *derived* from movements in the index. Derivatives contracts are of varying duration (running sometimes to 20 or more years) and their value is often tied to several variables.

Unless derivatives contracts are collateralized or guaranteed, their ultimate value also depends on the creditworthiness of the counterparties to them. In the meantime, though, before a contract is settled, the counterparties record profits and losses—often huge in amount—in their current earnings statements without so much as a penny changing hands.

The range of derivatives contracts is limited only by the imagination of man (or sometimes, so it seems, madmen). At Enron, for example, newsprint and broadband derivatives, due to be settled many years in the future, were put on the books. Or say you want to write a contract speculating on the number of twins to be born in Nebraska in 2020. No problem—at a price, you will easily find an obliging counterparty.

When we purchased Gen Re, it came with General Re Securities, a derivatives dealer that Charlie and I didn't want, judging it to be dangerous. We failed in our attempts to sell the operation, however, and are now terminating it.

But closing down a derivatives business is easier said than done. In fact, the reinsurance and derivatives businesses are similar: Like Hell, both are easy to enter and almost impossible to exit. In either industry, once you write a contract—which may require a large payment decades later—you are usually stuck with it. True, there are methods by which the risk can be laid off with others. But most strategies of that kind leave you with residual liability.

Another commonality of reinsurance and derivatives is that both generate reported earnings that are often wildly overstated. That's true because today's earnings are in a significant way based on estimates whose inaccuracy may not be exposed for many years.

Errors will usually be honest, reflecting only the human tendency to take an optimistic view of one's commitments. But the parties to derivatives also have enormous incentives to cheat in accounting for them. Those who trade derivatives are usually paid (in whole or part) on "earnings" calculated by mark-to-market accounting. But often there is no real market (think about our contract involving twins) and "mark-to-model" is utilized.

This substitution can bring on large-scale mischief. As a general rule, contracts involving multiple reference items and distant settlement dates increase the opportunities for counterparties to use fanciful assumptions. In the twins scenario, for example, the two parties to the contract might well use differing models allowing *both* to show substantial profits for many years. In extreme cases, mark-to-model degenerates into what I would call mark-to-myth.

Of course, both internal and outside auditors review the numbers, but that's no easy job. For example, General Re Securities at year-end (after ten months of winding down its operation) had 14,384 contracts outstanding, involving 672 counterparties around the world. Each contract had a plus or minus value derived from one or more reference items, including some of mind-boggling complexity. Valuing a portfolio like that, expert auditors could easily and honestly have widely varying opinions.

The valuation problem is far from academic: In recent years, some huge-scale frauds and near-frauds have been facilitated by derivatives trades. In the energy and electric utility sectors, for example, companies used derivatives and trading activities to report great "earnings"—until the roof fell in when they actually tried to convert the derivatives-related receivables on their balance sheets into cash. "Mark-to-market" then turned out to be truly "mark-to-myth."

I can assure you that the marking errors in the derivatives business have not been symmetrical. Almost invariably, they have favored either the trader who was eyeing a multi-million dollar bonus or the CEO who wanted to report impressive "earnings" (or both). The bonuses were paid, and the CEO profited from his options. Only much later did shareholders learn that the reported earnings were a sham.

Another problem about derivatives is that they can exacerbate trouble that a corporation has run into for completely unrelated reasons. This pile-on effect occurs because many derivatives contracts require that a company suffering a credit downgrade immediately supply collateral to counterparties. Imagine, then, that a company is downgraded because of general adversity and that its derivatives instantly kick in with *their* requirement, imposing an unexpected and enormous demand for cash collateral on the company. The need to meet this demand can then throw the company into a liquidity crisis that may, in some cases, trigger still more downgrades. It all becomes a spiral that can lead to a corporate meltdown.

Derivatives also create a daisy-chain risk that is akin to the risk run by insurers or reinsurers that lay off much of their business with others. In both cases, huge receivables from many counterparties tend to build up over time. A participant may see himself as prudent, believing his large credit exposures to be diversified and therefore not dangerous. Under certain circumstances, though, an exogenous event that causes the receivable from Company A to go bad will also affect those from Companies B through Z. History teaches us that a crisis often causes problems to correlate in a manner undreamed of in more tranquil times.

In banking, the recognition of a "linkage" problem was one of the reasons for the formation of the Federal Reserve System. Before the Fed was established, the failure of weak banks would sometimes put sudden and unanticipated liquidity demands on previously-strong banks, causing them to fail in turn. The Fed now insulates the strong from the troubles of the weak. But there is no central bank assigned to the job of preventing the dominoes toppling in insurance or derivatives. In these industries, firms that are fundamentally solid can become troubled simply because of the travails of other firms further down the chain. When a "chain reaction" threat exists within an industry, it pays to minimize links of any kind. That's how we conduct our reinsurance business, and it's one reason we are exiting derivatives.

Many people argue that derivatives reduce systemic problems, in that participants who can't bear certain risks are able to transfer them to stronger hands. These people believe that derivatives act to stabilize the economy, facilitate trade, and eliminate bumps for individual participants. And, on a micro level, what they say is often true. Indeed, at Berkshire, I sometimes engage in large-scale derivatives transactions in order to facilitate certain investment strategies.

Charlie and I believe, however, that the macro picture is dangerous and getting more so. Large amounts of risk, particularly credit risk, have become concentrated in the hands of relatively few derivatives dealers, who in addition trade extensively with one other. The troubles of one could quickly infect the others. On top of that, these dealers are owed huge amounts by non-dealer counterparties. Some of these counterparties, as I've mentioned, are linked in ways that could cause them to contemporaneously run into a problem because of a single event (such as the implosion of the telecom industry or the precipitous decline in the value of merchant power projects). Linkage, when it suddenly surfaces, can trigger serious systemic problems.

Indeed, in 1998, the leveraged and derivatives-heavy activities of a single hedge fund, Long-Term Capital Management, caused the Federal Reserve anxieties so severe that it hastily orchestrated a rescue effort. In later Congressional testimony, Fed officials acknowledged that, had they not intervened, the outstanding trades of LTCM—a firm unknown to the general public and employing only a few hundred people—could well have posed a serious threat to the stability of American markets. In other words, the Fed acted because its leaders were fearful of what might have happened to other financial institutions had the LTCM domino toppled. And this affair, though it paralyzed many parts of the fixed-income market for weeks, was far from a worst-case scenario.

One of the derivatives instruments that LTCM used was total-return swaps, contracts that facilitate 100% leverage in various markets, including stocks. For example, Party A to a contract, usually a bank, puts up all of the money for the purchase of a stock while Party B, without putting up any capital, agrees that at a future date it will receive any gain or pay any loss that the bank realizes.

Total-return swaps of this type make a joke of margin requirements. Beyond that, other types of derivatives severely curtail the ability of regulators to curb leverage and generally get their arms around the risk profiles of banks, insurers and other financial institutions. Similarly, even experienced investors and analysts encounter major problems in analyzing the financial condition of firms that are heavily involved with derivatives contracts. When Charlie and I finish reading the long footnotes detailing the derivatives activities of major banks, the only thing we understand is that we *don't* understand how much risk the institution is running.

The derivatives genie is now well out of the bottle, and these instruments will almost certainly multiply in variety and number until some event makes their toxicity clear. Knowledge of how dangerous they are has already permeated the electricity and gas businesses, in which the eruption of major troubles caused the use of derivatives to diminish dramatically. Elsewhere, however, the derivatives business continues to expand unchecked. Central banks and governments have so far found no effective way to control, or even monitor, the risks posed by these contracts.

Charlie and I believe Berkshire should be a fortress of financial strength—for the sake of our owners, creditors, policyholders and employees. We try to be alert to any sort of mega-catastrophe risk, and that posture may make us unduly apprehensive about the burgeoning quantities of long-term derivatives contracts and the massive amount of uncollateralized receivables that are growing alongside. In our view, however, derivatives are financial weapons of mass destruction, carrying dangers that, while now latent, are potentially lethal.

Long ago, Mark Twain said: "A man who tries to carry a cat home by its tail will learn a lesson that can be learned in no other way." If Twain were around now, he might try winding up a derivatives business. After a few days, he would opt for cats.

We lost $104 million pre-tax last year in our continuing attempt to exit Gen Re's derivative operation. Our aggregate losses since we began this endeavor total $404 million. Originally we had 23,218 contracts outstanding. By the start of 2005 we were down to 2,890. You might expect that our losses would have been stemmed by this point, but the blood has kept flowing. Reducing our inventory to 741 contracts last year cost us the $104 million mentioned above. [T]he rationale for establishing this unit in 1990 was Gen Re's wish to meet the needs of insurance clients.

Yet one of the contracts we liquidated in 2005 had a term of 100 years! It's difficult to imagine what "need" such a contract could fulfill except, perhaps, the need of a compensation-conscious trader to have a long-dated contract on his books. Long contracts, or alternatively those with multiple variables, are the most difficult to mark to market (the standard procedure used in accounting for derivatives) and provide the most opportunity for "imagination" when traders are estimating their value.

Small wonder that traders promote them. A business in which huge amounts of compensation flow from assumed numbers is obviously fraught with danger. When two traders execute a transaction that has several, sometimes esoteric, variables and a far-off settlement date, their respective firms must subsequently value these contracts whenever they calculate their earnings. A given contract may be valued at one price by Firm A and at another by

Firm B. You can bet that the valuation differences—and I'm personally familiar with several that were huge—tend to be tilted in a direction favoring higher earnings at each firm. It's a strange world in which two parties can carry out a paper transaction that each can promptly report as profitable.

I dwell on our experience in derivatives for two reasons. One is personal and unpleasant. The hard fact is that I have cost you a lot of money by not moving immediately to close down Gen Re's trading operation. Both Charlie and I knew at the time of the Gen Re purchase that it was a problem and told its management that we wanted to exit the business. It was my responsibility to make sure that happened. Rather than address the situation head on, however, I wasted several years while we attempted to sell the operation. That was a doomed endeavor because no realistic solution could have extricated us from the maze of liabilities that was going to exist for decades.

Our obligations were particularly worrisome because their potential to explode could not be measured. Moreover, if severe trouble occurred, we knew it was likely to correlate with problems elsewhere in financial markets. So I failed in my attempt to exit painlessly, and in the meantime more trades were put on the books. Fault me for dithering. (Charlie calls it thumb-sucking.) When a problem exists, whether in personnel or in business operations, the time to act is *now*.

The second reason I regularly describe our problems in this area lies in the hope that our experiences may prove instructive for managers, auditors and regulators. In a sense, we are a canary in this business coal mine and should sing a song of warning as we expire. The number and value of derivative contracts outstanding in the world continues to mushroom and is now a multiple of what existed in 1998, the last time that financial chaos erupted. Our experience should be particularly sobering because we were a better-than-average candidate to exit gracefully.

Additionally, we know of no bad behavior by anyone involved. It could be a different story for others in the future. Imagine, if you will, one or more firms (troubles often spread) with positions that are many multiples of ours attempting to liquidate in chaotic markets and under extreme, and well-publicized, pressures. This is a scenario to which much attention should be given now rather than after the fact. The time to have considered—and improved—the reliability of New Orleans' levees was before Katrina. When we finally wind up Gen Re Securities, my feelings about its departure will be akin to those expressed in a country song, "My wife ran away with my best friend, and I sure miss him a lot." [The 2006 letter indicates that Gen Re's derivative operation was finally closed.]

———————

[W]e have entered into [various] types of derivatives contracts. That may seem odd [given] the systemic problems that could result from the enormous growth in the use of derivatives. Why, you may wonder, are we fooling around with such potentially toxic material?

The answer is that derivatives, just like stocks and bonds, are sometimes wildly mis-priced. For many years, accordingly, we have selectively written derivative contracts—few in number but sometimes for large dollar amounts. We currently have 62 contracts outstanding. I manage them personally, and they are free of counterparty credit risk. So far, these derivative contracts have worked out well for us, producing pre-tax profits in the hundreds of millions of dollars. Though we will experience losses from time to time, we are likely to continue to earn—overall—significant profits from mis-priced derivatives.

———————

Derivatives are dangerous. They have dramatically increased the leverage and risks in our financial system. They have made it almost impossible for investors to understand and analyze our largest commercial banks and investment banks. They allowed Fannie Mae and Freddie Mac to engage in massive misstatements of earnings for years. So indecipherable were Freddie and Fannie that their federal regulator, OFHEO, whose more than 100 employees had no job except the oversight of these two institutions, totally missed their cooking of the books.

Indeed, recent events demonstrate that certain big-name CEOs (or former CEOs) at major financial institutions were simply incapable of managing a business with a huge, complex book of derivatives. Include Charlie and me in this hapless group: When Berkshire purchased General Re in 1998, we knew we could not get our minds around its book of 23,218 derivatives contracts, made with 884 counterparties (many of which we had never heard of). So we decided to close up shop. Though we were under no pressure and were operating in benign markets as we exited, it took us five years and more than $400 million in losses to largely complete the task. Upon leaving, our feelings about the business mirrored a line in a country song: "I liked you better before I got to know you so well."

Improved "transparency"—a favorite remedy of politicians, commentators and financial regulators for averting future train wrecks—won't cure the problems that derivatives pose. I know of no reporting mechanism that would come close to describing and measuring the risks in a huge and complex portfolio of derivatives. Auditors can't audit these contracts, and regulators can't regulate them.

For a case study on regulatory effectiveness, let's look harder at the Freddie and Fannie example. These giant institutions were created by Congress, which retained control over them, dictating what they could and could not do. To aid its oversight, Congress created OFHEO in 1992, admonishing it to make sure the two behemoths were behaving themselves. With that move, Fannie and Freddie became the most intensely-regulated companies of which I am aware, as measured by manpower assigned to the task.

On June 15, 2003, OFHEO (whose annual reports are available on the Internet) sent its 2002 report to Congress—specifically to its four bosses in the Senate and House, among them none other than Messrs. Sarbanes and Oxley. The report's 127 pages included a self-congratulatory cover-line: "Celebrating 10 Years of Excellence." The transmittal letter and report were delivered nine days *after* the CEO and CFO of Freddie had resigned in disgrace and the COO had been fired. No mention of their departures was made in the letter, even while the report concluded, as it always did, that "Both Enterprises were financially sound and well managed."

In truth, both enterprises had engaged in massive accounting shenanigans for some time. Finally, in 2006, OFHEO issued a 340-page scathing chronicle of the sins of Fannie that, more or less, blamed the fiasco on every party but—you guessed it—Congress and OFHEO.

The Bear Stearns collapse highlights the counterparty problem embedded in derivatives transactions, a time bomb I first discussed in Berkshire's 2002 report [excerpted above]. On April 3, 2008, Tim Geithner, then the able president of the New York Fed, explained the need for a rescue: "The sudden discovery by Bear's derivative counterparties that important financial positions they had put in place to protect themselves from financial risk were no longer operative would have triggered substantial further dislocation in markets. This would have precipitated a rush by Bear's counterparties to liquidate the collateral they held against those positions and to attempt to replicate those positions in already very fragile markets." This is Fedspeak for "We stepped in to avoid a financial chain reaction of unpredictable magnitude." In my opinion, the Fed was right to do so.

A normal stock or bond trade is completed in a few days with one party getting its cash, the other its securities. Counterparty risk therefore quickly disappears, which means credit problems can't accumulate. This rapid settlement process is key to maintaining the integrity of markets. That, in fact, is a reason for NYSE and NAS-DAQ *shortening* the settlement period from five days to three days in 1995.

Derivatives contracts, in contrast, often go unsettled for years, or even decades, with counterparties building up huge claims against each other. "Paper" assets and liabilities—often hard to quantify—become important parts of financial statements though these items will not be validated for many years. Additionally, a frightening web of mutual dependence develops among huge financial institutions. Receivables and payables by the billions become concentrated in the hands of a few large dealers who are apt to be highly-leveraged in other ways as well. Participants seeking to dodge troubles face the same problem as someone seeking to avoid venereal disease: It's not just whom *you* sleep with, but also whom *they* are sleeping with.

Sleeping around, to continue our metaphor, can actually be useful for large derivatives dealers because it assures them government aid if trouble hits. In other words, only companies having problems that can infect the entire neighborhood—I won't mention names—are certain to become a concern of the state (an outcome, I'm sad to say, that is proper). From this irritating reality comes *The First Law of Corporate Survival* for ambitious CEOs who pile on leverage and run large and unfathomable derivatives books: Modest incompetence simply won't do; it's mindboggling screw-ups that are required.

F. *Foreign Currencies and Equities*[36]

During 2002 we entered the foreign currency market for the first time in my life, and in 2003 we enlarged our position, as I became increasingly bearish on the dollar. I should note that the cemetery for seers has a huge section set aside for macro forecast-

---

[36] [Divided by hash lines: 2003; 2004; 2005.]

ers. We have in fact made few macro forecasts at Berkshire, and we have seldom seen others make them with sustained success.

We have—and will continue to have—the bulk of Berkshire's net worth in U.S. assets. But in recent years our country's trade deficit has been force-feeding huge amounts of claims on, and ownership in, America to the rest of the world. For a time, foreign appetite for these assets readily absorbed the supply. Late in 2002, however, the world started choking on this diet, and the dollar's value began to slide against major currencies. Even so, prevailing exchange rates will not lead to a material letup in our trade deficit. So whether foreign investors like it or not, they will continue to be flooded with dollars. The consequences of this are anybody's guess. They could, however, be troublesome—and reach, in fact, well beyond currency markets.

As an American, I hope there is a benign ending to this problem. [P]erhaps the alarms I have raised will prove needless: Our country's dynamism and resiliency have repeatedly made fools of nay-sayers. But Berkshire holds many billions of cash-equivalents denominated in dollars. So I feel more comfortable owning foreign-exchange contracts that are at least a partial offset to that position.

Berkshire owned about $21.4 billion of foreign exchange contracts at year-end, spread among 12 currencies. [As mentioned in the preceding essay], holdings of this kind are a decided change for us. Before March 2002, neither Berkshire nor I had *ever* traded in currencies. But the evidence grows that our trade policies will put unremitting pressure on the dollar for many years to come—so since 2002 we've heeded that warning in setting our investment course. (As W.C. Fields once said when asked for a handout: "Sorry, son, all my money's tied up in currency.")

Be clear on one point: In no way does our thinking about currencies rest on doubts about America. We live in an extraordinarily rich country, the product of a system that values market economics, the rule of law and equality of opportunity. Our economy is far and away the strongest in the world and will continue to be. We are lucky to live here.

But our country's trade practices are weighing down the dollar. The decline in its value has already been substantial, but is nevertheless likely to continue. Without policy changes, currency markets could even become disorderly and generate spillover effects, both political and financial. No one knows whether these problems will materialize. But such a scenario is a far-from-remote possibility that policymakers should be considering *now*. Their bent, however, is to lean toward not-so-benign neglect: A 318-page Congressional study of the consequences of unremitting trade deficits was published in November 2000 and has been gathering dust ever since. The study was ordered after the deficit hit a then-alarming $263 billion in 1999; by last year it had risen to $618 billion.

Charlie and I, it should be emphasized, believe that true trade—that is, the exchange of goods and services with other countries—is enormously beneficial for both us and them. Last year we had $1.15 trillion of such honest-to-God trade and the more of this, the better. But, as noted, our country also purchased an additional $618 billion in goods and services from the rest of the world that was unreciprocated. That is a staggering figure and one that has important consequences.

The balancing item to this one-way pseudo-trade—in economics there is always an offset—is a transfer of wealth from the U.S. to the rest of the world. The transfer may materialize in the form of IOUs our private or governmental institutions give to foreigners, or by way of their assuming ownership of our assets, such as stocks and real estate. In either case, Americans end up owning a reduced portion of our country while non-Americans own a greater part. This force-feeding of American wealth to the rest of the world is now proceeding at the rate of $1.8 billion daily, an increase of 20% since I wrote you last year. Consequently, other countries and their citizens now own a net of about $3 trillion of the U.S. A decade ago their net ownership was negligible.

The mention of trillions numbs most brains. A further source of confusion is that the current account deficit (the sum of three items, the most important by far being the trade deficit) and our national budget deficit are often lumped as "twins." They are anything but. They have different causes and different consequences.

A budget deficit in no way reduces the portion of the national pie that goes to Americans. As long as other countries and their citizens have no net ownership of the U.S., 100% of our country's output belongs to our citizens under *any* budget scenario, even one involving a huge deficit.

As a rich "family" awash in goods, Americans will argue through their legislators as to how government should redistribute the national output—that is who pays taxes and who receives governmental benefits. If "entitlement" promises from an earlier day have to be reexamined, "family members" will angrily debate among themselves as to who feels the pain. Maybe taxes will go up; maybe promises will be modified; maybe more internal debt will be issued. But when the fight is finished, *all* of the family's huge pie remains available for its members, however it is divided. No slice must be sent abroad.

Large and persisting current account deficits produce an entirely different result. As time passes, and as claims against us grow, we own less and less of what we produce. In effect, the rest of the world enjoys an ever-growing royalty on American output. Here, we are like a family that consistently overspends its income. As time passes, the family finds that it is working more and more for the "finance company" and less for itself.

Should we continue to run current account deficits comparable to those now prevailing, the net ownership of the U.S. by other countries and their citizens a decade from now will amount to roughly $11 trillion. And, if foreign investors were to earn only 5% on that net holding, we would need to send a net of $.55 trillion of goods and services abroad *every year* merely to service the U.S. investments then held by foreigners. At that date, a decade out, our GDP would probably total about $18 trillion (assuming low inflation, which is far from a sure thing). Therefore, our U.S. "family" would then be delivering 3% of its annual output to the rest of the world simply as tribute for the overindulgences of the past. In this case, unlike that involving budget deficits, the sons would truly pay for the sins of their fathers.

This annual royalty paid the world—which would not disappear unless the U.S. massively under-consumed and began to run consistent and large trade surpluses—would undoubtedly produce significant political unrest in the U.S. Americans would still be living very well, indeed better than now because of the growth in our economy. But they would chafe at the idea of perpetually paying tribute to their creditors and owners abroad. A country that is now aspiring to an "Ownership Society" will not find happiness in—and I'll use hyperbole here for emphasis—a "Sharecropper's Society." But that's precisely where our trade policies, supported by Republicans and Democrats alike, are taking us.

Many prominent U.S. financial figures, both in and out of government, have stated that our current-account deficits cannot persist. For instance, the minutes of the Federal Reserve Open Market Committee of June 29-30, 2004 say: "The staff noted that outsized external deficits could not be sustained indefinitely." But, despite the constant hand-wringing by luminaries, they offer no substantive suggestions to tame the burgeoning imbalance.

[Sixteen months earlier, Buffett had] warned that "a gently declining dollar would not provide the answer." And so far it hasn't. Yet policymakers continue to hope for a "soft landing," meanwhile counseling other countries to stimulate (read "inflate") their economies and Americans to save more. In my view these admonitions miss the mark: There are deep-rooted structural problems that will cause America to continue to run a huge current-account deficit unless trade policies either change materially or the dollar declines by a degree that could prove unsettling to financial markets.

Proponents of the trade status quo are fond of quoting Adam Smith: "What is prudence in the conduct of every family can scarce be folly in that of a great kingdom. If a foreign country can supply us with a commodity cheaper than we ourselves can make it, better buy it of them with some part of the produce of our own industry, employed in a way in which we have some advantage."

I agree. Note, however, that Mr. Smith's statement refers to trade of *product* for product, not of *wealth* for product as our country is doing to the tune of $.6 trillion annually. Moreover, I am sure that he would never have suggested that "prudence" consisted of his "family" selling off part of its farm every day in order to finance its over-consumption. Yet that is just what the "great kingdom" called the United States is doing.

If the U.S. was running a $.6 trillion current-account *surplus*, commentators worldwide would violently condemn our policy, viewing it as an extreme form of "mercantilism"—a long-discredited economic strategy under which countries fostered exports, discouraged imports, and piled up treasure. I would condemn such a policy as well. But, in effect if not in intent, the rest of the world is practicing mercantilism in respect to the U.S., an act made possible by our vast store of assets and our pristine credit history. Indeed, the world would never let any other country use a credit card denominated in its own currency to the insatiable extent we are employing ours. Presently, most foreign investors are sanguine: they may view us as spending junkies, but they know we are *rich* junkies as well.

Our spendthrift behavior won't, however, be tolerated indefinitely. And though it's impossible to forecast just when and how the trade problem will be resolved, it's improbable that the resolution will foster an *increase* in the value of our currency relative to that of our trading partners.

We hope the U.S. adopts policies that will quickly and substantially reduce the current-account deficit. True, a prompt solution would likely cause Berkshire to record losses on its foreign-exchange contracts. But Berkshire's resources remain heavily concentrated in dollar-based assets, and both a strong dollar and a low-inflation environment are very much in our interest.

John Maynard Keynes said in his masterful *The General Theory*: "Worldly wisdom teaches that it is better for reputation to fail conventionally than to succeed unconventionally." (Or, to put it in less elegant terms, lemmings as a class may be derided but never does an *individual* lemming get criticized.) From a reputational standpoint, Charlie and I run a clear risk with our foreign-exchange commitment. But we believe in managing Berkshire as if we owned 100% of it ourselves. And, were that the case, we would not be following a dollar-only policy.

When we have a long-term position in stocks or bonds, year-to-year changes in value are reflected in our balance sheet but, as long as the asset is not sold, are rarely reflected in earnings. For example, our Coca-Cola holdings went from $1 billion in value early on to $13.4 billion at year end 1998 and have since declined to $8.1 billion—with none of these moves affecting our earnings statement. Long-term currency positions, however, are daily marked to market and therefore have an effect on earnings in every reporting period.

From the date we first entered into currency contracts, we are $2.0 billion in the black. We reduced our direct position in currencies somewhat during 2005. We partially offset this change, however, by purchasing equities whose prices are denominated in a variety of foreign currencies and that earn a large part of their profits internationally. Charlie and I prefer this method of acquiring non-dollar exposure. That's largely because of changes in interest rates: As U.S. rates have risen relative to those of the rest of the world, holding most foreign currencies now involves a significant negative "carry."

In contrast, the ownership of foreign equities is likely, over time, to create a positive carry—perhaps a substantial one. The underlying factors affecting the U.S. current account deficit continue to worsen, and no letup is in sight. Not only did our trade deficit—the largest and most familiar item in the current account—hit an all-time high in 2005, but we also can expect a second item—the balance of investment income—to soon turn negative. As foreigners increase their ownership of U.S. assets (or of claims against us) relative to U.S. investments abroad, these investors will begin earning more on their holdings than we do on ours.

Finally, the third component of the current account, unilateral transfers, is always negative. The U.S., it should be emphasized, is extraordinarily rich and will get richer. As a result, the huge imbalances in its current account may continue for a long time without their having noticeable deleterious effects on the U.S. economy or on markets. I doubt, however, that the situation will forever remain benign. Either Americans address the problem soon in a way we select, or at some point the problem will likely address us in an unpleasant way of its own.

G.   *Home Ownership: Practice and Policy*[37]

As is well-known, the U.S. went off the rails in its home-ownership and mortgage-lending policies, and for these mistakes our economy is now paying a huge price. All of us participated in the destructive behavior—government, lenders, borrowers, the media, rating agencies, you name it. At the core of the folly was the almost universal belief that the value of houses was certain to increase over time and that any dips would be inconsequential. The acceptance of this premise justified almost any price and practice in housing transactions. Homeowners everywhere felt richer and rushed to "monetize" the increased value of their homes by refinancings. These massive cash infusions fueled a consumption binge throughout our economy. It all seemed great fun while it lasted. (A largely unnoted fact: Large numbers of people who have "lost" their house through foreclosure have actually realized a profit because they carried out refinancings earlier that gave them cash in excess of their cost. In these cases, the evicted homeowner was the winner, and the victim was the lender.)

I will write here at some length about the mortgage operation of Clayton Homes because Clayton's recent experience may be useful in the public-policy debate about housing and mortgages.

Clayton is the largest company in the manufactured home industry, delivering 27,499 units last year. This came to about 34% of the industry's 81,889 total. Our share will likely grow in 2009, partly because much of the rest of the industry is in acute distress.

---

[37] [2011; 2008.]

Industry wide, units sold have steadily declined since they hit a peak of 372,843 in 1998.

At that time, much of the industry employed sales practices that were atrocious. Writing about the period somewhat later, I described it as involving "borrowers who shouldn't have borrowed being financed by lenders who shouldn't have lent."

To begin with, the need for meaningful down payments was frequently ignored. Sometimes fakery was involved. ("That certainly looks like a $2,000 cat to me" says the salesman who will receive a $3,000 commission if the loan goes through.) Moreover, impossible-to-meet monthly payments were being agreed to by borrowers who signed up because they had nothing to lose. The resulting mortgages were usually packaged ("securitized") and sold by Wall Street firms to unsuspecting investors. This chain of folly had to end badly, and it did.

Clayton, it should be emphasized, followed far more sensible practices in its own lending throughout that time. Indeed, no purchaser of the mortgages it originated and then securitized has ever lost a dime of principal or interest. But Clayton was the exception; industry losses were staggering. And the hangover continues to this day.

This 1997-2000 fiasco should have served as a canary-in-the-coal-mine warning for the far-larger conventional housing market. But investors, government and rating agencies learned exactly nothing from the manufactured-home debacle. Instead, in an eerie rerun of that disaster, the same mistakes were repeated with conventional homes in the 2004-07 period: Lenders happily made loans that borrowers couldn't repay out of their incomes, and borrowers just as happily signed up to meet those payments. Both parties counted on "house-price appreciation" to make this otherwise impossible arrangement work. It was Scarlett O'Hara all over again: "I'll think about it tomorrow." The consequences of this behavior are now reverberating through every corner of our economy.

Clayton's 198,888 borrowers, however, have continued to pay normally throughout the housing crash, handing us no unexpected losses. This is *not* because these borrowers are unusually creditworthy, a point proved by FICO scores (a standard measure of credit risk). Their median FICO score is 644, compared to a national median of 723, and about 35% are below 620, the segment usually designated "sub-prime." Many disastrous pools of mortgages on conventional homes are populated by borrowers with far better credit, as measured by FICO scores.

Yet at yearend, our delinquency rate on loans we have originated was 3.6%, up only modestly from 2.9% in 2006 and 2.9% in 2004. (In addition to our originated loans, we've also bought bulk portfolios of various types from other financial institutions.) Clayton's foreclosures during 2008 were 3.0% of originated loans compared to 3.8% in 2006 and 5.3% in 2004.

Why are our borrowers—characteristically people with modest incomes and far-from-great credit scores—performing so well? The answer is elementary, going right back to Lending 101. Our borrowers simply looked at how full-bore mortgage payments would compare with their actual—not hoped-for—income and then decided whether they could live with that commitment. Simply put, they took out a mortgage with the intention of paying it off, whatever the course of home prices.

Just as important is what our borrowers did *not* do. They did not count on making their loan payments by means of refinancing. They did not sign up for "teaser" rates that upon reset were outsized relative to their income. And they did not assume that they could always sell their home at a profit if their mortgage payments became onerous. Jimmy Stewart would have loved these folks.

Of course, a number of our borrowers will run into trouble. They generally have no more than minor savings to tide them over if adversity hits. The major cause of delinquency or foreclosure is the loss of a job, but death, divorce and medical expenses all cause problems. If unemployment rates rise—as they surely will in 2009—more of Clayton's borrowers will have troubles, and we will have larger, though still manageable, losses. But our problems will not be driven to any extent by the trend of home prices.

Commentary about the current housing crisis often ignores the crucial fact that most foreclosures do *not* occur because a house is worth less than its mortgage (so-called "upside-down" loans). Rather, foreclosures take place because borrowers can't pay the monthly payment that they agreed to pay. Homeowners who have made a meaningful down-payment—derived from savings and not from other borrowing—seldom walk away from a primary residence simply because its value today is less than the mortgage. Instead, they walk when they can't make the monthly payments.

Home ownership is a wonderful thing. My family and I have enjoyed my present home for 50 years, with more to come. But enjoyment and utility should be the primary motives for purchase, not profit or refi possibilities. And the home purchased ought to fit the income of the purchaser.

The present housing debacle should teach home buyers, lenders, brokers and government some simple lessons that will ensure stability in the future. Home purchases should involve an honest-to-God down payment of at least 10% and monthly payments that can be comfortably handled by the borrower's income. That income should be carefully verified.

Putting people into homes, though a desirable goal, shouldn't be our country's primary objective. Keeping them in their homes should be the ambition.

IV. COMMON STOCK

Occasional outbreaks of those two super-contagious diseases, fear and greed, will forever occur in the investment community. The timing of these epidemics will be unpredictable. And the market aberrations produced by them will be equally unpredictable, both as to duration and degree. Therefore, we never try to anticipate the arrival or departure of either disease. Our goal is more modest: we simply attempt to be fearful when others are greedy and to be greedy only when others are fearful.

As this is written, little fear is visible in Wall Street. Instead, euphoria prevails—and why not? What could be more exhilarating than to participate in a bull market in which the rewards to owners of businesses become gloriously uncoupled from the plodding performances of the businesses themselves. Unfortunately, however, stocks can't outperform businesses indefinitely.

Indeed, because of the heavy transaction and investment management costs they bear, stockholders as a whole and over the long term must inevitably underperform the companies they own. If American business, in aggregate, earns about 12% on equity annually, investors must end up earning significantly less. Bull markets can obscure mathematical laws, but they cannot repeal them.[38]

A.   *The Bane of Trading: Transaction Costs*[39]

It's been an easy matter for Berkshire and other owners of American equities to prosper over the years. Between December 31, 1899 and December 31, 1999, to give a really long-term example, the Dow rose from 66 to 11,497. (Guess what annual growth rate is required to produce this result; the surprising answer is at the end of this [essay].) This huge rise came about for a simple reason: Over the century American businesses did extraordinarily well and investors rode the wave of their prosperity. Businesses continue to do well. But now shareholders, through a series of self-inflicted wounds, are in a major way cutting the returns they will realize from their investments.

The explanation of how this is happening begins with a fundamental truth: With unimportant exceptions, such as bankruptcies in which some of a company's losses are borne by creditors, *the most that owners in aggregate can earn between now and Judgment Day*

---

[38] [Introductory essay, 1986.]

[39] [2005; Letter dated August 5, 1988 sent to Berkshire shareholders and reprinted 1988.]

is what their businesses in aggregate earn. True, by buying and selling that is clever or lucky, investor A may take more than his share of the pie at the expense of investor B. And, yes, all investors *feel* richer when stocks soar. But an owner can exit only by having someone take his place. If one investor sells high, another must buy high. For owners as a whole, there is simply no magic—no shower of money from outer space—that will enable them to extract wealth from their companies beyond that created by the companies themselves.

Indeed, owners must earn less than their businesses earn because of "frictional" costs. And that's my point: These costs are now being incurred in amounts that will cause shareholders to earn *far* less than they historically have.

To understand how this toll has ballooned, imagine for a moment that all American corporations are, and always will be, owned by a single family. We'll call them the Gotrocks. After paying taxes on dividends, this family—generation after generation— becomes richer by the aggregate amount earned by its companies. Today that amount is about $700 billion annually. Naturally, the family spends some of these dollars. But the portion it saves steadily compounds for its benefit. In the Gotrocks household everyone grows wealthier at the same pace, and all is harmonious.

But let's now assume that a few fast-talking Helpers approach the family and persuade each of its members to try to outsmart his relatives by buying certain of their holdings and selling them certain others. The Helpers—for a fee, of course—obligingly agree to handle these transactions. The Gotrocks still own all of corporate America; the trades just rearrange who owns what. So the family's annual gain in wealth diminishes, equaling the earnings of American business *minus* commissions paid. The more that family members trade, the smaller their share of the pie and the larger the slice received by the Helpers. This fact is not lost upon these broker-Helpers: Activity is their friend and, in a wide variety of ways, they urge it on.

After a while, most of the family members realize that they are not doing so well at this new "beat-my-brother" game. Enter another set of Helpers. These newcomers explain to each member of the Gotrocks clan that by himself he'll never outsmart the rest of the family. The suggested cure: "Hire a manager—yes, us—and get the job done professionally." These manager-Helpers continue to use the broker-Helpers to execute trades; the managers may even increase their activity so as to permit the brokers to prosper still more. Overall, a bigger slice of the pie now goes to the two classes of Helpers.

The family's disappointment grows. Each of its members is now employing professionals. Yet overall, the group's finances have taken a turn for the worse. The solution? More help, of course.

It arrives in the form of financial planners and institutional consultants, who weigh in to advise the Gotrocks on selecting manager-Helpers. The befuddled family welcomes this assistance. By now its members know they can pick neither the right stocks nor the right stock-pickers. Why, one might ask, should they expect success in picking the right consultant? But this question does not occur to the Gotrocks, and the consultant-Helpers certainly don't suggest it to them.

The Gotrocks, now supporting three classes of expensive Helpers, find that their results get worse, and they sink into despair. But just as hope seems lost, a fourth group—we'll call them the hyper-Helpers—appears. These friendly folk explain to the Gotrocks that their unsatisfactory results are occurring because the existing Helpers—brokers, managers, consultants—are not sufficiently motivated and are simply going through the motions. "What," the new Helpers ask, "can you expect from such a bunch of zombies?"

The new arrivals offer a breathtakingly simple solution: *Pay more money*. Brimming with self-confidence, the hyper-Helpers assert that huge contingent payments—in addition to stiff fixed fees—are what each family member must fork over in order to *really* outmaneuver his relatives.

The more observant members of the family see that some of the hyper-Helpers are really just manager-Helpers wearing new uniforms, bearing sewn-on sexy names like HEDGE FUND or PRIVATE EQUITY. The new Helpers, however, assure the Gotrocks that this change of clothing is all-important, bestowing on its wearers magical powers similar to those acquired by mild-mannered Clark Kent when he changed into his Superman costume. Calmed by this explanation, the family decides to pay up.

And that's where we are today: A record portion of the earnings that would go in their entirety to owners—if they all just stayed in their rocking chairs—is now going to a swelling army of Helpers. Particularly expensive is the recent pandemic of profit arrangements under which Helpers receive large portions of the winnings when they are smart or lucky, and leave family members with all of the losses—and large fixed fees to boot—when the Helpers are dumb or unlucky (or occasionally crooked).

A sufficient number of arrangements like this—heads, the Helper takes much of the winnings; tails, the Gotrocks lose and pay dearly for the privilege of doing so—may make it more accurate to call the family the Hadrocks. Today, in fact, the family's frictional costs of all sorts may well amount to 20% of the earnings of American business. In other words, the burden of paying Helpers may cause American equity investors, overall, to earn only 80% or so of what they would earn if they just sat still and listened to no one.

Long ago, Sir Isaac Newton gave us three laws of motion, which were the work of genius. But Sir Isaac's talents didn't extend to investing: He lost a bundle in the South Sea Bubble, explaining later, "I can calculate the movement of the stars, but not the madness of men." If he had not been traumatized by this loss, Sir Isaac might well have gone on to discover the Fourth Law of Motion: *For investors as a whole, returns decrease as motion increases.*

Here's the answer to the question posed at the beginning of this [essay]: To get very specific, the Dow increased from 65.73 to 11,497.12 in the 20th century, and that amounts to a gain of 5.3% compounded annually. (Investors would also have received dividends, of course.) To achieve an equal rate of gain in the 21st century, the Dow will have to rise by December 31, 2099 to—brace yourself—precisely 2,011,011.23. But I'm willing to settle for 2,000,000; six years into this century, the Dow has gained not at all.

———————

It is likely that in a few months Berkshire shares will be traded on the New York Stock Exchange. Our move there would be made possible by a new listing rule that the Exchange's Board of Governors has passed and asked the SEC to approve. If that approval is forthcoming, we expect to apply for a listing, which we believe will be granted.

Up to now, the Exchange has required newly-listed companies to have a minimum of 2,000 shareholders who each own 100 shares or more. The purpose of this rule is to insure that NYSE-listed companies enjoy the broad investor interest that facilitates an orderly market. The 100-share standard corresponds to the trading unit ("round lot") for all common stocks now listed on the Exchange.

Because [in 1988] Berkshire ha[d] relatively few shares outstanding (1,146,642), it [did] not have the number of 100-shares-or-more holders that the Exchange has required. A ten-share holding of Berkshire, however, represents a significant investment commitment. In fact, ten Berkshire shares have a value greater than that of 100 shares of any NYSE-listed stock. The Exchange, therefore, is willing to have Berkshire shares trade in *ten*-share "round lots."

The Exchange's proposed rule simply changes the 2,000 shareholder minimum from one measured by holders of 100 shares or more to one measured by holders of a round lot or more. Berkshire can easily meet this amended test.

Charlie and I are delighted at the prospect of listing, since we believe this move will benefit our shareholders. We have two criteria by which we judge what marketplace would be best for Berkshire stock. First, we hope for the stock to consistently trade at a price rationally related to its intrinsic business value. If it does, the investment result achieved by each shareholder will approximate Berkshire's business result during his period of ownership.

Such an outcome is far from automatic. Many stocks swing between levels of severe undervaluation and overvaluation. When this happens, owners are rewarded or penalized in a manner wildly at variance with how the business has performed during their period of ownership. We want to avoid such capricious results. Our goal is to have our shareholder-partners profit from the achievements of the business rather than from the foolish behavior of their co-owners.

Consistently rational prices are produced by rational owners, both current and prospective. All of our policies and communications are designed to attract the business-oriented long-term owner and to filter out possible buyers whose focus is short-term and market-oriented. To date we have been successful in this attempt, and Berkshire shares have consistently sold in an unusually narrow range around intrinsic business value. We do not believe that a NYSE listing will improve or diminish Berkshire's prospects for consistently selling at an appropriate price; the quality of our shareholders will produce a good result whatever the marketplace.

But we do believe that the listing will reduce transaction costs for Berkshire's shareholders—and that is important. Though we want to attract shareholders who will stay around for a long time, we also want to minimize the costs incurred by shareholders when they enter or exit. In the long run, the aggregate pre-tax rewards to our owners will equal the business gains achieved by the company less the transaction costs imposed by the marketplace—that is, commissions charged by brokers plus the net realized spreads of market-makers. Overall, we believe these transaction costs will be reduced materially by a NYSE listing.

[T]ransaction costs are very heavy for active stocks, often amounting to 10% or more of the earnings of a public company. In effect, these costs act as a hefty tax on owners, albeit one based on individual decisions to "change chairs" and one that is paid to the financial community rather than to Washington. Our policies and your investment attitude have reduced this "tax" on Berkshire owners to what we believe is the lowest level among large public companies. A NYSE listing should further reduce this cost for Berkshire's owners by narrowing the market-maker's spread.

One final comment: *You should clearly understand that we are not seeking a NYSE listing for the purpose of achieving a higher valuation on Berkshire shares. Berkshire should sell, and we hope will sell, on the NYSE at prices similar to those it would have commanded in the over-the-counter market, given similar economic circumstances.* The NYSE listing should not induce you to buy or sell; it simply should cut your costs somewhat should you decide to do either.

B.　*Attracting the Right Sort of Investor*[40]

Berkshire's shares were listed on the [NYSE] on November 29, 1988. Let me clarify one point not dealt with in the letter [set forth above]: Though our round lot for trading on the NYSE is ten shares, any number of shares from one on up can be bought or sold.

As the [foregoing] letter explains, our primary goal in listing was to reduce transaction costs, and we believe this goal is being achieved. Generally, the spread between the bid and asked price on the NYSE has been well below the spread that prevailed in the over-the-counter market.

Henderson Brothers, Inc., the specialist in our shares, is the oldest continuing specialist firm on the Exchange; its progenitor, William Thomas Henderson, bought his seat for $500 on September 8, 1861. (Recently, seats were selling for about $625,000.) Among the 54 firms acting as specialists, HBI ranks second in number of stocks assigned, with 83. We were pleased when Berkshire was allocated to HBI, and have been delighted with the firm's performance. Jim Maguire, Chairman of HBI, personally manages the trading in Berkshire, and we could not be in better hands.

---

[40] [1988.]

In two respects our goals probably differ somewhat from those of most listed companies. First, we do not want to maximize the price at which Berkshire shares trade. We wish instead for them to trade in a narrow range centered at intrinsic business value (which we hope increases at a reasonable—or, better yet, unreasonable—rate).

Second, we wish for very little trading activity. If we ran a private business with a few passive partners, we would be disappointed if those partners, and their replacements, frequently wanted to leave the partnership. Running a public company, we feel the same way.

Our goal is to attract long-term owners who, at the time of purchase, have no timetable or price target for sale but plan instead to stay with us indefinitely. We don't understand the CEO who wants lots of stock activity, for that can be achieved only if many of his owners are constantly exiting. At what other organization—school, club, church, etc.—do leaders cheer when members leave? (However if there were a broker whose livelihood depended upon the membership turnover in such organizations, you could be sure that there would be at least one proponent of activity, as in: "There hasn't been much going on in Christianity for a while; maybe we should switch to Buddhism next week.")

Of course, some Berkshire owners will need or want to sell from time to time, and we wish for good replacements who will pay them a fair price. Therefore we try, through our policies, performance, and communications, to attract new shareholders who understand our operations, share our time horizons, and measure us as we measure ourselves. If we can continue to attract this sort of shareholder—and, just as important, can continue to be uninteresting to those with short-term or unrealistic expectations—Berkshire shares should consistently sell at prices reasonably related to business value.[41]

---

41 [The following is from 1989:]

With more than a year behind him of trading Berkshire's stock on the New York Stock Exchange, our specialist, Jim Maguire of [HBI] continues his outstanding performance. Before we listed, dealer spreads often were 3% or more of market price. Jim has maintained the spread at 50 points or less, which at current prices is well under 1%. Shareholders who buy or sell benefit significantly from this reduction in transaction costs.

Because we are delighted by our experience with Jim, HBI and the NYSE, I said as much in ads that have been run in a series placed by the NYSE. Normally I shun testimonials, but I was pleased in this instance to publicly compliment the Exchange.

C. *Dividend Policy and Share Repurchases*[42]

Dividend policy is often reported to shareholders, but seldom explained. A company will say something like, "Our goal is to pay out 40% to 50% of earnings and to increase dividends at a rate at least equal to the rise in the CPI". And that's it—no analysis will be supplied as to why that particular policy is best for the owners of the business. Yet, allocation of capital is crucial to business and investment management. Because it is, we believe managers and owners should think hard about the circumstances under which earnings should be retained and under which they should be distributed.

The first point to understand is that all earnings are not created equal. In many businesses—particularly those that have high asset/profit ratios—inflation causes some or all of the reported earnings to become ersatz. The ersatz portion—let's call these earnings "restricted"—cannot, if the business is to retain its economic position, be distributed as dividends. Were these earnings to be paid out, the business would lose ground in one or more of the following areas: its ability to maintain its unit volume of sales, its long-term competitive position, its financial strength. No matter how conservative its payout ratio, a company that consistently distributes restricted earnings is destined for oblivion unless equity capital is otherwise infused.

Restricted earnings are seldom valueless to owners, but they often must be discounted heavily. In effect, they are conscripted by the business, no matter how poor its economic potential. (This retention-no-matter-how-unattractive-the-return situation was communicated unwittingly in a marvelously ironic way by Consolidated Edison a decade ago. At the time, a punitive regulatory policy was a major factor causing the company's stock to sell as low as one-fourth of book value: i.e., every time a dollar of earnings was retained for reinvestment in the business, that dollar was transformed into only 25¢ of market value. But, despite this gold-into-lead process, most earnings were reinvested in the business rather than paid to owners. Meanwhile, at construction and maintenance sites throughout New York, signs proudly proclaimed the corporate slogan, "Dig We Must".)

Restricted earnings need not concern us further in this dividend discussion. Let's turn to the much-more-valued unrestricted variety. These earnings may, with equal feasibility, be retained or

---

[42] [Divided by hash lines: 1984; 1984; 1999; 2011.]

distributed. In our opinion, management should choose whichever course makes greater sense for the owners of the business.

This principle is not universally accepted. For a number of reasons managers like to withhold unrestricted, readily distributable earnings from shareholders—to expand the corporate empire over which the managers rule, to operate from a position of exceptional financial comfort, etc. But we believe there is only one valid reason for retention. Unrestricted earnings should be retained only when there is a reasonable prospect—backed preferably by historical evidence or, when appropriate, by a thoughtful analysis of the future—that *for every dollar retained by the corporation, at least one dollar of market value will be created for owners.* This will happen only if the capital retained produces incremental earnings equal to, or above, those generally available to investors.

To illustrate, let's assume that an investor owns a risk-free 10% perpetual bond with one very unusual feature. Each year the investor can elect either to take his 10% coupon in cash, or to reinvest the coupon in more 10% bonds with identical terms: i.e., a perpetual life and coupons offering the same cash-or-reinvest options. If, in any given year, the prevailing interest rate on long-term, risk-free bonds is 5%, it would be foolish for the investor to take his coupon in cash since the 10% bonds he could instead choose would be worth considerably more than 100¢ on the dollar. Under these circumstances, the investor wanting to get his hands on cash should take his coupon in additional bonds and then immediately sell them. By doing that, he would realize more cash than if he had taken his coupon directly in cash. Assuming all bonds were held by rational investors, no one would opt for cash in an era of 5% interest, not even those bondholders needing cash for living purposes.

If, however, interest rates were 15%, no rational investor would want his money invested for him at 10%. Instead, the investor would choose to take his coupon in cash, even if his personal cash needs were nil. The opposite course—reinvestment of the coupon—would give an investor additional bonds with market value far less than the cash he could have elected. If he should want 10% bonds, he can simply take the cash received and buy them in the market, where they will be available at a large discount.

An analysis similar to that made by our hypothetical bondholder is appropriate for owners in thinking about whether a company's unrestricted earnings should be retained or paid out. Of course, the analysis is much more difficult and subject to error because the rate earned on reinvested earnings is not a contractual figure, as in our bond case, but rather a fluctuating figure. Owners must guess as to what the rate will average over the intermediate future. However, once an informed guess is made, the rest of the analysis is simple: you should wish your earnings to be reinvested if they can be expected to earn high returns, and you should wish them paid to you if low returns are the likely outcome of reinvestment.

Many corporate managers reason very much along these lines in determining whether subsidiaries should distribute earnings to their parent company. At that level, the managers have no trouble thinking like intelligent owners. But payout decisions at the parent company level often are a different story. Here managers frequently have trouble putting themselves in the shoes of their shareholder-owners.

With this schizoid approach, the CEO of a multi-divisional company will instruct Subsidiary A, whose earnings on incremental capital may be expected to average 5%, to distribute all available earnings in order that they may be invested in Subsidiary B, whose earnings on incremental capital are expected to be 15%. The CEO's business school oath will allow no lesser behavior. But if his own long-term record with incremental capital is 5%—and market rates are 10%—he is likely to impose a dividend policy on shareholders of the parent company that merely follows some historical or industry-wide payout pattern. Furthermore, he will expect managers of subsidiaries to give him a full account as to why it makes sense for earnings to be retained in their operations rather than distributed to the parent-owner. But seldom will he supply *his* owners with a similar analysis pertaining to the whole company.

In judging whether managers should retain earnings, shareholders should not simply compare total incremental earnings in recent years to total incremental capital because that relationship may be distorted by what is going on in a core business. During an inflationary period, companies with a core business characterized by extraordinary economics can use small amounts of incremental capital in that business at very high rates of return (as was discussed in last year's section on Goodwill).[43] But, unless they are experiencing tremendous unit growth, outstanding businesses by definition generate large amounts of excess cash. If a company

---

[43] [*See* the essay Economic versus Accounting Goodwill in Part VI.D.]

sinks most of this money in other businesses that earn low returns, the company's overall return on retained capital may nevertheless appear excellent because of the extraordinary returns being earned by the portion of earnings incrementally invested in the core business. The situation is analogous to a Pro-Am golf event: even if all of the amateurs are hopeless duffers, the team's best-ball score will be respectable because of the dominating skills of the professional.

Many corporations that consistently show good returns both on equity and on overall incremental capital have, indeed, employed a large portion of their retained earnings on an economically unattractive, even disastrous, basis. Their marvelous core businesses, however, whose earnings grow year after year, camouflage repeated failures in capital allocation elsewhere (usually involving high-priced acquisition of businesses that have inherently mediocre economics). The managers at fault periodically report on the lesson they have learned from the latest disappointment. They then usually seek out future lessons. (Failure seems to go to their heads.)

In such cases, shareholders would be far better off if earnings were retained only to expand the high-return business, with the balance paid in dividends or used to repurchase stock (an action that increases the owners' interest in the exceptional business while sparing them participation in subpar businesses). Managers of high-return businesses who consistently employ much of the cash thrown off by those businesses in other ventures with low returns should be held to account for those allocation decisions, regardless of how profitable the overall enterprise is.

Nothing in this discussion is intended to argue for dividends that bounce around from quarter to quarter with each wiggle in earnings or in investment opportunities. Shareholders of public corporations understandably prefer that dividends be consistent and predictable. Payments, therefore, should reflect long-term expectations for both earnings and returns on incremental capital. Since the long-term corporate outlook changes only infrequently, dividend patterns should change no more often. But over time distributable earnings that have been withheld by managers should earn their keep. If earnings have been unwisely retained, it is likely that managers, too, have been unwisely retained.

The companies in which we have our largest investments have all engaged in significant stock repurchases at times when wide discrepancies existed between price and value. As shareholders, we find this encouraging and rewarding for two important reasons—one that is obvious, and one that is subtle and not always understood. The obvious point involves basic arithmetic: major repurchases at prices well below per-share intrinsic business value immediately increase, in a highly significant way, that value. When companies purchase their own stock, they often find it easy to get $2 of present value for $1. Corporate acquisition programs almost never do as well and, in a discouragingly large number of cases, fail to get anything close to $1 of value for each $1 expended.

The other benefit of repurchases is less subject to precise measurement but can be fully as important over time. By making repurchases when a company's market value is well below its business value, management clearly demonstrates that it is given to actions that enhance the wealth of shareholders, rather than to actions that expand management's domain but that do nothing for (or even harm) shareholders. Seeing this, shareholders and potential shareholders increase their estimates of future returns from the business. This upward revision, in turn, produces market prices more in line with intrinsic business value. These prices are entirely rational. Investors should pay more for a business that is lodged in the hands of a manager with demonstrated pro-shareholder leanings than for one in the hands of a self-interested manager marching to a different drummer. (To make the point extreme, how much would you pay to be a minority shareholder of a company controlled by Robert Vesco?)

The key word is "demonstrated". A manager who consistently turns his back on repurchases, when these clearly are in the interests of owners, reveals more than he knows of his motivations. No matter how often or how eloquently he mouths some public relations-inspired phrase such as "maximizing shareholder wealth" (this season's favorite), the market correctly discounts assets lodged with him. His heart is not listening to his mouth—and, after a while, neither will the market.

———————

[A] number of shareholders have suggested to us that Berkshire repurchase its shares. Usually the requests were rationally based, but a few leaned on spurious logic.

There is only one combination of facts that makes it advisable for a company to repurchase its shares: First, the company has available funds—cash plus sensible borrowing capacity—beyond the near-term needs of the business and, second, finds its stock selling in the market below its intrinsic value, conservatively-calculated. To this we add a caveat: Shareholders should have been supplied all the information they need for estimating that value. Otherwise, insiders could take advantage of their uninformed partners and buy out their interests at a fraction of true worth. We have, on rare occasions, seen that happen. Usually, of course, chicanery is employed to drive stock prices up, not down.

The business "needs" that I speak of are of two kinds: First, expenditures that a company must make to maintain its competitive position (*e.g.*, the remodeling of stores at Helzberg's) and, second, optional outlays, aimed at business growth, that management expects will produce more than a dollar of value for each dollar spent (R. C. Willey's expansion into Idaho).

When available funds exceed needs of those kinds, a company with a growth-oriented shareholder population can buy new businesses or repurchase shares. If a company's stock is selling well below intrinsic value, repurchases usually make the most sense. In the mid-1970s, the wisdom of making these was virtually screaming at managements, but few responded. In most cases, those that did made their owners much wealthier than if alternative courses of action had been pursued. Indeed, during the 1970s (and, spasmodically, for some years thereafter) we searched for companies that were large repurchasers of their shares. This often was a tipoff that the company was both undervalued and run by a shareholder-oriented management.

That day is past. Now, repurchases are all the rage, but are all too often made for an unstated and, in our view, ignoble reason: to pump or support the stock price. The shareholder who chooses to sell today, of course, is benefitted by any buyer, whatever his origin or motives. But the *continuing* shareholder is penalized by repurchases above intrinsic value. Buying dollar bills for $1.10 is not good business for those who stick around.

Charlie and I admit that we feel confident in estimating intrinsic value for only a portion of traded equities and then only when we employ a range of values, rather than some pseudo-precise figure. Nevertheless, it appears to us that many companies now making repurchases are overpaying departing shareholders at the expense of those who stay. In defense of those companies, I would say that it is natural for CEOs to be optimistic about their own businesses. They also know a whole lot more about them than I do. However, I can't help but feel that too often today's repurchases are dictated by management's desire to "show confidence" or be in fashion rather than by a desire to enhance per-share value.

Sometimes, too, companies say they are repurchasing shares to offset the shares issued when stock options granted at much lower prices are exercised. This "buy high, sell low" strategy is one many unfortunate investors have employed—but never intentionally! Managements, however, seem to follow this perverse activity very cheerfully.

Of course, both option grants and repurchases may make sense—but if that's the case, it's not because the two activities are logically related. Rationally, a company's decision to repurchase shares or to issue them should stand on its own feet. Just because stock has been issued to satisfy options—or for any other reason— does not mean that stock should be repurchased at a price above intrinsic value. Correspondingly, a stock that sells well below intrinsic value should be repurchased whether or not stock has previously been issued (or may be because of outstanding options).

You should be aware that, at certain times in the past, I have erred in *not* making repurchases. My appraisal of Berkshire's value was then too conservative or I was too enthused about some alternative use of funds. We have therefore missed some opportunities—though Berkshire's trading volume at these points was too light for us to have done much buying, which means that the gain in our per-share value would have been minimal. (A repurchase of, say, 2% of a company's shares at a 25% discount from per-share intrinsic value produces only a $\frac{1}{2}$% gain in that value at most—and even less if the funds could alternatively have been deployed in value-building moves.)

Some of the letters we've received clearly imply that the writer is unconcerned about intrinsic value considerations but instead wants us to trumpet an intention to repurchase so that the stock will rise (or quit going down). If the writer wants to sell tomorrow, his thinking makes sense—for him!—but if he intends to hold, he should instead hope the stock falls and trades in enough volume for us to buy a lot of it. That's the only way a repurchase program can have any real benefit for a continuing shareholder.

We will not repurchase shares unless we believe Berkshire stock is selling well below intrinsic value, conservatively calculated. Nor will we attempt to talk the stock up or down. (Neither publicly or privately have I ever told anyone to buy or sell Berkshire shares.) Instead we will give all shareholders—and potential shareholders—the same valuation-related information we would wish to have if our positions were reversed.

Recently, when the A shares fell below $45,000, we considered making repurchases. We decided, however, to delay buying, if indeed we elect to do *any*, until shareholders have had the chance to review this report. If we do find that repurchases make sense, we will only rarely place bids on the New York Stock Exchange ("NYSE"). Instead, we will respond to offers made directly to us at or below the NYSE bid. If you wish to offer stock, have your broker call Mark Millard at 402-346-1400. When a trade occurs, the broker can either record it in the "third market" or on the NYSE. We will favor purchase of the B shares if they are selling at more than a 2% discount to the A. We will not engage in transactions involving fewer than 10 shares of A or 50 shares of B.

Please be clear about one point: We will *never* make purchases with the intention of stemming a decline in Berkshire's price. Rather we will make them if and when we believe that they represent an attractive use of the Company's money. At best, repurchases are likely to have only a very minor effect on the future rate of gain in our stock's intrinsic value.

Charlie and I favor repurchases when two conditions are met: first, a company has ample funds to take care of the operational and liquidity needs of its business; second, its stock is selling at a material discount to the company's intrinsic business value, conservatively calculated.

We have witnessed many bouts of repurchasing that failed our second test. Sometimes, of course, infractions—even serious ones—are innocent; many CEOs never stop believing their stock is cheap. In other instances, a less benign conclusion seems warranted. It doesn't suffice to say that repurchases are being made to offset the dilution from stock issuances or simply because a company has excess cash. Continuing shareholders are *hurt* unless shares are purchased below intrinsic value. The first law of capital allocation—whether the money is slated for acquisitions or share repurchases—is that what is smart at one price is dumb at another. (One CEO who always stresses the price/value factor in repurchase decisions is Jamie Dimon at J.P. Morgan; I recommend that you read his annual letter.)

Charlie and I have mixed emotions when Berkshire shares sell well below intrinsic value. We like making money for continuing shareholders, and there is no surer way to do that than by buying an asset—our own stock—that we know to be worth *at least* x for less than that—for .9x, .8x or even lower. (As one of our directors says, it's like shooting fish in a barrel, *after* the barrel has been drained and the fish have quit flopping.) Nevertheless, we don't enjoy cashing out partners at a discount, even though our doing so may give the selling shareholders a slightly higher price than they would receive if our bid was absent. When we are buying, therefore, we want those exiting partners to be fully informed about the value of the assets they are selling.

This discussion of repurchases offers me the chance to address the irrational reaction of many investors to changes in stock prices. When Berkshire buys stock in a company that is repurchasing shares, we hope for two events: First, we have the normal hope that earnings of the business will increase at a good clip for a long time to come; and second, we also hope that the stock *underperforms* in the market for a long time as well. A corollary to this second point: "Talking our book" about a stock we own—were that to be effective—would actually be harmful to Berkshire, not helpful as commentators customarily assume.

Let's use IBM as an example. As all business observers know, CEOs Lou Gerstner and Sam Palmisano did a superb job in moving IBM from near-bankruptcy twenty years ago to its prominence today. Their operational accomplishments were truly extraordinary.

But their financial management was equally brilliant, particularly in recent years as the company's financial flexibility improved. Indeed, I can think of no major company that has had better financial management, a skill that has materially increased the gains enjoyed by IBM shareholders. The company has used debt wisely, made value-adding acquisitions almost exclusively for cash and aggressively repurchased its own stock.

Today, IBM has 1.16 billion shares outstanding, of which we own about 63.9 million or 5.5%. Naturally, what happens to the company's earnings over the next five years is of enormous importance to us. Beyond that, the company will likely spend $50 billion or so in those years to repurchase shares. Our quiz for the day: What should a long-term shareholder, such as Berkshire, cheer for during that period?

I won't keep you in suspense. We should wish for IBM's stock price to *languish* throughout the five years.

Let's do the math. If IBM's stock price averages, say, $200 during the period, the company will acquire 250 million shares for its $50 billion. There would consequently be 910 million shares outstanding, and we would own about 7% of the company. If the stock conversely sells for an average of $300 during the five-year period, IBM will acquire only 167 million shares. That would leave about 990 million shares outstanding after five years, of which we would own 6.5%.

If IBM were to earn, say, $20 billion in the fifth year, our share of those earnings would be a full $100 million greater under the "disappointing" scenario of a lower stock price than they would have been at the higher price. At some later point our shares would be worth perhaps $11/2 billion more than if the "high-price" repurchase scenario had taken place.

The logic is simple: If you are going to be a net buyer of stocks in the future, either directly with your own money or indirectly (through your ownership of a company that is repurchasing shares), you are *hurt* when stocks rise. You benefit when stocks swoon. *Emotions*, however, too often complicate the matter: Most people, including those who will be net buyers in the future, take comfort in seeing stock prices advance. These shareholders resemble a commuter who rejoices after the price of gas increases, simply because his tank contains a day's supply.

Charlie and I don't expect to win many of you over to our way of thinking—we've observed enough human behavior to know the futility of that—but we do want you to be aware of our personal calculus. And here a confession is in order: In my early days I, too, rejoiced when the market rose. Then I read Chapter Eight of Ben Graham's *The Intelligent Investor*, the chapter dealing with how investors should view fluctuations in stock prices. Immediately the scales fell from my eyes, and low prices became my friend. Picking up that book was one of the luckiest moments in my life.

In the end, the success of our IBM investment will be determined primarily by its future earnings. But an important secondary factor will be how many shares the company purchases with the substantial sums it is likely to devote to this activity. And if repurchases ever reduce the IBM shares outstanding to 63.9 million, I will abandon my famed frugality and give Berkshire employees a paid holiday.

D. *Stock Splits and the Invisible Foot*[44]

We often are asked why Berkshire does not split its stock. The assumption behind this question usually appears to be that a split

---

44 [1983.]

would be a pro-shareholder action. We disagree. Let me tell you why.

One of our goals is to have Berkshire Hathaway stock sell at a price rationally related to its intrinsic business value. (But note "rationally related," not "identical": if well-regarded companies are generally selling in the market at large discounts from value, Berkshire might well be priced similarly.) The key to a rational stock price is rational shareholders, both current and prospective.

If the holders of a company's stock and/or the prospective buyers attracted to it are prone to make irrational or emotion-based decisions, some pretty silly stock prices are going to appear periodically. Manic-depressive personalities produce manic-depressive valuations. Such aberrations may help us in buying and selling the stocks of other companies. But we think it is in both your interest and ours to minimize their occurrence in the market for Berkshire.

To obtain only high quality shareholders is no cinch. Mrs. Astor could select her 400, but anyone can buy any stock. Entering members of a shareholder "club" cannot be screened for intellectual capacity, emotional stability, moral sensitivity or acceptable dress. Shareholder eugenics, therefore, might appear to be a hopeless undertaking.

In large part, however, we feel that high quality ownership can be attracted and maintained if we consistently communicate our business and ownership philosophy—*along with no other conflicting messages*—and then let self selection follow its course. For example, self selection will draw a far different crowd to a musical event advertised as an opera than one advertised as a rock concert—even though anyone can buy a ticket to either.

Through our policies and communications—our "advertisements"—we try to attract investors who will understand our operations, attitudes and expectations. (And, fully as important, we try to dissuade those who won't.) We want those who think of themselves as business owners and invest in companies with the intention of staying a long time. And, we want those who keep their eyes focused on business results, not market prices.

Investors possessing those characteristics are in a small minority, but we have an exceptional collection of them. I believe well over 90%—probably over 95%—of our shares are held by those who were shareholders of Berkshire five years ago. And I would guess that over 95% of our shares are held by investors for whom the holding is at least double the size of their next largest. Among companies with at least several thousand public shareholders and more than $1 billion of market value, we are almost certainly the leader in the degree to which our shareholders think and act like owners. Upgrading a shareholder group that possesses these characteristics is not easy.

Were we to split the stock or take other actions focusing on stock price rather than business value, we would attract an entering class of buyers inferior to the exiting class of sellers. Would a potential one-share purchaser be better off if we split 100 for 1 so he could buy 100 shares? Those who think so and who would buy the stock because of the split or in anticipation of one would definitely downgrade the quality of our present shareholder group. (Could we really improve our shareholder group by trading some of our present clear-thinking members for impressionable new ones who, preferring paper to value, feel wealthier with nine $10 bills than with one $100 bill?) People who buy for non-value reasons are likely to sell for non-value reasons. Their presence in the picture will accentuate erratic price swings unrelated to underlying business developments.

We will try to avoid policies that attract buyers with a short-term focus on our stock price and try to allow policies that attract informed long-term investors focusing on business values. Just as you purchased your Berkshire shares in a market populated by rational informed investors, you deserve a chance to sell—should you ever want to—in the same kind of market. We will work to keep it in existence.

One of the ironies of the stock market is the emphasis on activity. Brokers, using terms such as "marketability" and "liquidity", sing the praises of companies with high share turnover (those who cannot fill your pocket will confidently fill your ear). But investors should understand that what is good for the croupier is not good for the customer. A hyperactive stock market is the pickpocket of enterprise.

For example, consider a typical company earning, say, 12% on equity. Assume a very high turnover rate in its shares of 100% per year. If a purchase and sale of the stock trades at book value, the owners of our hypothetical company will pay, in aggregate, 2% of the company's net worth annually for the privilege of transferring ownership. This activity does nothing for the earnings of the business, and means that 1/6 of them are lost to the owners through the "frictional" cost of transfer. (And this calculation does not count option trading, which would increase frictional costs still further.)

All that makes for a rather expensive game of musical chairs. Can you imagine the agonized cry that would arise if a governmental unit were to impose a new 16⅔% tax on earnings of corporations or investors? By market activity, investors can impose upon themselves the equivalent of such a tax.

(We are aware of the pie-expanding argument that says that such activities improve the rationality of the capital allocation process. We think that this argument is specious and that, on balance, hyperactive equity markets subvert rational capital allocation and act as pie shrinkers. Adam Smith felt that all noncollusive acts in a free market were guided by an invisible hand that led an economy to maximum progress; our view is that casino-type markets and hair-trigger investment management act as an invisible foot that trips up and slows down a forward-moving economy.)

E. *Shareholder Strategies*[45]

Late last year Berkshire's stock price crossed $10,000. Several shareholders have mentioned to me that the high price causes them problems: They like to give shares away each year and find themselves impeded by the tax rule that draws a distinction between annual gifts of $10,000 or under to a single individual and those above $10,000. That is, those gifts no greater than $10,000 are completely tax-free; those above $10,000 require the donor to use up a portion of his or her lifetime exemption from gift and estate taxes, or, if that exemption has been exhausted, to pay gift taxes.

I can suggest three ways to address this problem. The first would be useful to a married shareholder, who can give up to $20,000 annually to a single recipient, as long as the donor files a gift tax return containing his or her spouse's written consent to gifts made during the year.

Secondly, a shareholder, married or not, can make a bargain sale. Imagine, for example, that Berkshire is selling for $12,000 and that one wishes to make only a $10,000 gift. In that case, sell the stock to the giftee for $2,000. (Caution: You will be taxed on the amount, if any, by which the sales price to your giftee exceeds your tax basis.)

Finally, you can establish a partnership with people to whom you are making gifts, fund it with Berkshire shares, and simply give percentage interests in the partnership away each year. These in-

---

45 [1992.]

terests can be for any value that you select. If the value is $10,000 or less, the gift will be tax-free.

We issue the customary warning: Consult with your own tax advisor before taking action on any of the more esoteric methods of gift-making.

We hold to the view about stock splits that we set forth in the [preceding essay]. Overall, we believe our owner-related policies—including the no-split policy—have helped us assemble a body of shareholders that is the best associated with any widely-held American corporation. Our shareholders think and behave like rational long-term owners and view the business much as Charlie and I do. Consequently, our stock consistently trades in a price range that is sensibly related to intrinsic value.

Additionally, we believe that our shares turn over far less actively than do the shares of any other widely-held company. The frictional costs of trading—which act as a major "tax" on the owners of many companies—are virtually non-existent at Berkshire. (The market-making skills of Jim Maguire, our New York Stock Exchange specialist, definitely help to keep these costs low.) Obviously a split would not change this situation dramatically. Nonetheless, there is no way that our shareholder group would be upgraded by the new shareholders enticed by a split. Instead we believe that modest degradation would occur.

F. *Berkshire's Recapitalization*[46]

At the Annual Meeting you will be asked to approve a recapitalization of Berkshire, creating two classes of stock. If the plan is adopted, our existing common stock will be designated as Class A Common Stock and a new Class B Common Stock will be authorized.

Each share of the "B" will have the rights of 1/30th of an "A" share with these exceptions: First, a B share will have 1/200th of the vote of an A share (rather than 1/30th of the vote). Second, the B will not be eligible to participate in Berkshire's shareholder-designated charitable contributions program.

When the recapitalization is complete, each share of A will become convertible, at the holder's option and at any time, into 30 shares of B. This conversion privilege will not extend in the oppo-

---

[46] [Divided by hash lines: 1995; 1996. The Class B was later split in connection with Berkshire's acquisition of BNSF so that it has 1/1,500th of the economic rights of a Class A share and 1/10,000th of the voting rights.]

site direction. That is, holders of B shares will not be able to convert them into A shares.

We expect to list the B shares on the New York Stock Exchange, where they will trade alongside the A stock. To create the shareholder base necessary for a listing—and to ensure a liquid market in the B stock—Berkshire expects to make a public offering for cash of at least $100 million of new B shares. The offering will be made only by means of a prospectus.

The market will ultimately determine the price of the B shares. Their price, though, should be in the neighborhood of 1/30th of the price of the A shares.

Class A shareholders who wish to give gifts may find it convenient to convert a share or two of their stock into Class B shares. Additionally, arbitrage-related conversions will occur if demand for the B is strong enough to push its price to slightly above 1/30th of the price of A.

However, because the Class A stock will entitle its holders to full voting rights, these shares will be superior to the Class B shares and we would expect most shareholders to remain holders of the Class A—which is precisely what the Buffett and Munger families plan to do, except in those instances when we ourselves might convert a few shares to facilitate gifts. The prospect that most shareholders will stick to the A stock suggests that it will enjoy a somewhat more liquid market than the B.

There are tradeoffs for Berkshire in this recapitalization. But they do not arise from the proceeds of the offering—we will find constructive uses for the money—nor in any degree from the price at which we will sell the B shares. As I write this—with Berkshire stock at $36,000—Charlie and I do not believe it undervalued. Therefore, the offering we propose will not diminish the per-share intrinsic value of our existing stock. Let me also put our thoughts about valuation more baldly: Berkshire is selling at a price at which Charlie and I would not consider buying it.

What Berkshire will incur by way of the B stock are certain added costs, including those involving the mechanics of handling a larger number of shareholders. On the other hand, the stock should be a convenience for people wishing to make gifts. And those of you who have hoped for a split have gained a do-it-yourself method of bringing one about.

We are making this move, though, for other reasons—having to do with the appearance of expense-laden unit trusts purporting to be low-priced "clones" of Berkshire and sure to be aggressively marketed. The idea behind these vehicles is not new: In recent years, a number of people have told me about their wish to create an "all-Berkshire" investment fund to be sold at a low dollar price. But until recently, the promoters of these investments heard out my objections and backed off.

I did not discourage these people because I prefer large investors over small. Were it possible, Charlie and I would love to turn $1,000 into $3,000 for multitudes of people who would find that gain an important answer to their immediate problems.

In order to quickly triple small stakes, however, we would have to just as quickly turn our present market capitalization of $43 billion into $129 billion (roughly the market cap of General Electric, America's most highly valued company). *We can't come close to doing that*. The very best we hope for is—on average—to double Berkshire's per-share intrinsic value every five years, and we may well fall far short of that goal.

In the end, Charlie and I do not care whether our shareholders own Berkshire in large or small amounts. What we wish for are shareholders of any size who are knowledgeable about our operations, share our objectives and long-term perspective, and are aware of our limitations, most particularly those imposed by our large capital base.

The unit trusts that have recently surfaced fly in the face of these goals. They would be sold by brokers working for big commissions, would impose other burdensome costs on their shareholders, and would be marketed *en masse* to unsophisticated buyers, apt to be seduced by our past record and beguiled by the publicity Berkshire and I have received in recent years. The sure outcome: a multitude of investors destined to be disappointed.

Through our creation of the B stock—a low-denomination product far superior to Berkshire-only trusts—we hope to make the clones unmerchandisable.

But both present and prospective Berkshire shareholders should pay special attention to one point: Though the per-share intrinsic value of our stock has grown at an excellent rate during the past five years, its market price has grown still faster. The stock, in other words, has outperformed the business.

That kind of market overperformance cannot persist indefinitely, neither for Berkshire nor any other stock. *Inevitably, there will be periods of underperformance as well*. The price volatility that results, though endemic to public markets, is not to our liking. What we would prefer instead is to have the market price of Berkshire precisely track its intrinsic value. Were the stock to do that, every shareholder would benefit during his period of ownership in exact proportion to the progress Berkshire itself made in the period.

Obviously, the market behavior of Berkshire's stock will never conform to this ideal. But we will come closer to this goal than we would otherwise if our present and prospective shareholders are informed, business-oriented and not exposed to high-commission salesmanship when making their investment decisions. To that end, we are better off if we can blunt the merchandising efforts of the unit trust—and that is the reason we are creating the B stock.

———————————

[W]e made two good-sized offerings through Salomon [during 1996], both with interesting aspects. The first was our sale in May of 517,500 shares of Class B Common, which generated net proceeds of $565 million. As I have told you before, we made this sale in response to the threatened creation of unit trusts that would have marketed themselves as Berkshire look-alikes. In the process, they would have used our past, and definitely nonrepeatable, record to entice naive small investors and would have charged these innocents high fees and commissions.

I think it would have been quite easy for such trusts to have sold many billions of dollars worth of units, and I also believe that early marketing successes by these trusts would have led to the formation of others. (In the securities business, whatever can be sold will be sold.) The trusts would have meanwhile indiscriminately poured the proceeds of their offerings into a supply of Berkshire shares that is fixed and limited. The likely result: a speculative bubble in our stock. For at least a time, the price jump would have been self-validating, in that it would have pulled new waves of naive and impressionable investors into the trusts and set off still more buying of Berkshire shares.

Some Berkshire shareholders choosing to exit might have found that outcome ideal, since they could have profited at the expense of the buyers entering with false hopes. Continuing shareholders, however, would have suffered once reality set in, for at that point Berkshire would have been burdened with both hundreds of thousands of unhappy, indirect owners (trustholders, that is) and a stained reputation.

Our issuance of the B shares not only arrested the sale of the trusts, but provided a low-cost way for people to invest in Berkshire if they still wished to after hearing the warnings we issued. To blunt the enthusiasm that brokers normally have for pushing new issues—because that's where the money is—we arranged for our offering to carry a commission of only 1½%, the lowest payoff that we have ever seen in common stock underwriting. Additionally, we made the amount of the offering open-ended, thereby repelling the typical IPO buyer who looks for a short-term price spurt arising from a combination of hype and scarcity.

Overall, we tried to make sure that the B stock would be purchased only by investors with a long-term perspective. Those efforts were generally successful: Trading volume in the B shares immediately following the offering—a rough index of "flipping"—was far below the norm for a new issue. In the end we added about 40,000 shareholders, most of whom we believe both understand what they own and share our time horizons.

Salomon could not have performed better in the handling of this unusual transaction. Its investment bankers understood perfectly what we were trying to achieve and tailored every aspect of the offering to meet these objectives. The firm would have made far more money—perhaps ten times as much—if our offering had been standard in its make-up. But the investment bankers involved made no attempt to tweak the specifics in that direction. Instead they came up with ideas that were counter to Salomon's financial interest but that made it much more certain Berkshire's goals would be reached. Terry Fitzgerald captained this effort, and we thank him for the job that he did.

Given that background, it won't surprise you to learn that we again went to Terry when we decided late in the year to sell an issue of Berkshire notes that can be exchanged for a portion of the Salomon shares that we hold. In this instance, once again, Salomon did an absolutely first-class job, selling $500 million principal amount of five-year notes for $447.1 million. Each $1,000 note is exchangeable into 17.65 shares and is callable in three years at accreted value. Counting the original issue discount and a 1% coupon, the securities will provide a yield of 3% to maturity for holders who do not exchange them for Salomon stock. But it seems quite likely that the notes will be exchanged before their maturity. If that happens, our interest cost will be about 1.1% for the period prior to exchange.

In recent years, it has been written that Charlie and I are unhappy about all investment-banking fees. That's dead wrong. We have paid a great many fees over the last 30 years—beginning with the check we wrote to Charlie Heider upon our purchase of National Indemnity in 1967—and we are delighted to make payments that are commensurate with performance. In the case of the 1996 transactions at Salomon Brothers we more than got our money's worth.

G. *Berkshire's Dividend Policy*[47]

A number of Berkshire shareholders—including some of my good friends—would like Berkshire to pay a cash dividend. It puzzles them that we relish the dividends we receive from most of the stocks that Berkshire owns, but pay out nothing ourselves. So let's examine when dividends do and don't make sense for shareholders.

A profitable company can allocate its earnings in various ways (which are not mutually exclusive). A company's management should first examine reinvestment possibilities offered by its current business—projects to become more efficient, expand territorially, extend and improve product lines or to otherwise widen the economic moat separating the company from its competitors.

I ask the managers of our subsidiaries to unendingly focus on moat-widening opportunities, and they find many that make economic sense. But sometimes our managers misfire. The usual cause of failure is that they start with the answer they want and then work backwards to find a supporting rationale. Of course, the process is subconscious; that's what makes it so dangerous.

Your chairman has not been free of this sin. In Berkshire's 1986 annual report, I described how twenty years of management effort and capital improvements in our original textile business were an exercise in futility. I *wanted* the business to succeed and *wished* my way into a series of bad decisions. (I even bought *another* New England textile company.) But wishing makes dreams come true only in Disney movies; it's poison in business.

Despite such past miscues, our first priority with available funds will always be to examine whether they can be *intelligently* deployed in our various businesses. Our record $12.1 billion of fixed-asset investments and bolt-on acquisitions in 2012 demonstrate that this is a fertile field for capital allocation at Berkshire. And here we have an advantage: Because we operate in so many areas of the economy, we enjoy a range of choices far wider than that open to most corporations. In deciding what to do, we can water the flowers and skip over the weeds.

---

[47] [Divided by hash lines 2012; 2014, 50th Anniversary section.]

Even after we deploy hefty amounts of capital in our current operations, Berkshire will regularly generate a lot of additional cash. Our next step, therefore, is to search for acquisitions unrelated to our current businesses. Here our test is simple: Do Charlie and I think we can effect a transaction that is likely to leave our shareholders wealthier on a per-share basis than they were prior to the acquisition?

I have made plenty of mistakes in acquisitions and will make more. Overall, however, our record is satisfactory, which means that our shareholders are *far* wealthier today than they would be if the funds we used for acquisitions had instead been devoted to share repurchases or dividends.

But, to use the standard disclaimer, past performance is no guarantee of future results. That's particularly true at Berkshire: Because of our present size, making acquisitions that are both meaningful and sensible is now more difficult than it has been during most of our years.

Nevertheless, a large deal still offers us possibilities to add materially to per-share intrinsic value. BNSF is a case in point: It is now worth considerably more than our carrying value. Had we instead allocated the funds required for this purchase to dividends or repurchases, you and I would have been worse off. Though large transactions of the BNSF kind will be rare, there are still some whales in the ocean.

The third use of funds—repurchases—is sensible for a company when its shares sell at a meaningful discount to conservatively calculated intrinsic value. Indeed, disciplined repurchases are the *surest* way to use funds intelligently: It's hard to go wrong when you're buying dollar bills for 80¢ or less. We explained our criteria for repurchases [earlier in Section C of this Part] and, if the opportunity presents itself, we will buy large quantities of our stock. We originally said we would not pay more than 110% of book value, but that proved unrealistic. Therefore, we increased the limit to 120% in December when a large block became available at about 116% of book value.

But never forget: In repurchase decisions, price is all-important. Value is *destroyed* when purchases are made above intrinsic value. The directors and I believe that continuing shareholders are benefitted in a meaningful way by purchases up to our 120% limit.

And that brings us to dividends. Here we have to make a few assumptions and use some math. The numbers will require careful reading, but they are essential to understanding the case for and against dividends. So bear with me.

We'll start by assuming that you and I are the equal owners of a business with $2 million of net worth. The business earns 12% on tangible net worth—$240,000—and can reasonably expect to earn the same 12% on reinvested earnings. Furthermore, there are outsiders who always wish to buy into our business at 125% of net worth. Therefore, the value of what we each own is now $1.25 million.

You would like to have the two of us shareholders receive one-third of our company's annual earnings and have two-thirds be reinvested. That plan, you feel, will nicely balance your needs for both current income and capital growth. So you suggest that we pay out $80,000 of current earnings and retain $160,000 to increase the future earnings of the business. In the first year, your dividend would be $40,000, and as earnings grew and the one- third payout was maintained, so too would your dividend. In total, dividends and stock value would increase 8% each year (12% earned on net worth less 4% of net worth paid out).

After ten years our company would have a net worth of $4,317,850 (the original $2 million compounded at 8%) and your dividend in the upcoming year would be $86,357. Each of us would have shares worth $2,698,656 (125% of our half of the company's net worth). And we would live happily ever after—with dividends and the value of our stock continuing to grow at 8% annually.

There is an alternative approach, however, that would leave us even happier. Under this scenario, we would leave *all* earnings in the company and each sell 3.2% of our shares annually. Since the shares would be sold at 125% of book value, this approach would produce the same $40,000 of cash initially, a sum that would grow annually. Call this option the "sell-off" approach.

Under this "sell-off" scenario, the net worth of our company increases to $6,211,696 after ten years ($2 million compounded at 12%). Because we would be selling shares each year, our *percentage* ownership would have declined, and, after ten years, we would each own 36.12% of the business. Even so, your share of the net worth of the company at that time would be $2,243,540. And, remember, every dollar of net worth attributable to each of us can be sold for $1.25. Therefore, the market value of your remaining shares would be $2,804,425, about 4% greater than the value of your shares if we had followed the dividend approach.

Moreover, your annual cash receipts from the sell-off policy would now be running 4% more than you would have received under the dividend scenario. Voila!—you would have both more cash to spend annually *and* more capital value.

This calculation, of course, assumes that our hypothetical company can earn an average of 12% annually on net worth and that its shareholders can sell their shares for an average of 125% of book value. To that point, the S&P 500 earns considerably more than 12% on net worth and sells at a price far above 125% of that net worth. Both assumptions also seem reasonable for Berkshire, though certainly not assured.

There also is a possibility that the assumptions will be exceeded. If they are, the argument for the sell-off policy becomes even stronger. Over Berkshire's history—admittedly one that won't come close to being repeated—the sell-off policy would have produced results for shareholders *dramatically* superior to the dividend policy.

Aside from the favorable math, there are two further—*and important*—arguments for a sell-off policy. First, dividends impose a specific cash-out policy upon all shareholders. If, say, 40% of earnings is the policy, those who wish 30% or 50% will be thwarted. Our shareholders cover the waterfront in their desires for cash. It is safe to say, however, that a great many of them—perhaps even most of them—are in a net-savings mode and logically should prefer no payment at all.

The sell-off alternative, on the other hand, lets each shareholder make his own choice between cash receipts and capital build-up. One shareholder can elect to cash out, say, 60% of annual earnings while other shareholders elect 20% or nothing at all. Of course, a shareholder in our dividend-paying scenario could turn around and use his dividends to purchase more shares. But he would take a beating in doing so: He would both incur taxes and also pay a 25% premium to get his dividend reinvested. (Keep remembering, open-market purchases of the stock take place at 125% of book value.)

The second disadvantage of the dividend approach is of equal importance: The tax consequences for *all* taxpaying shareholders are inferior—usually *far* inferior—to those under the sell-off program. Under the dividend program, all of the cash received by shareholders each year is taxed whereas the sell-off program results in tax on only the gain portion of the cash receipts.

Let me end this math exercise—and I can hear you cheering as I put away the dentist drill—by using my own case to illustrate how a shareholder's regular disposals of shares can be accompanied by an *increased* investment in his or her business. For the last seven years, I have annually given away about $4\frac{1}{4}\%$ of my Berkshire shares. Through this process, my original position of 712,497,000 B-equivalent shares (split-adjusted) has decreased to 528,525,623 shares. Clearly my ownership *percentage* of the company has significantly decreased.

Yet my investment in the business has actually increased: The book value of my current interest in Berkshire considerably exceeds the book value attributable to my holdings of seven years ago. (The actual figures are $28.2 billion for 2005 and $40.2 billion for 2012.) In other words, I now have *far* more money working for me at Berkshire even though my ownership of the company has materially decreased.

———————

Berkshire truly has an owner base unlike that of any other giant corporation. That fact was demonstrated in spades at last year's annual meeting, where the shareholders were offered a proxy resolution: "RESOLVED: Whereas the corporation has more money than it needs and since the owners unlike Warren are not multi billionaires, the board shall consider paying a meaningful annual dividend on the shares."

The sponsoring shareholder of that resolution never showed up at the meeting, so his motion was not officially proposed. Nevertheless, the proxy votes had been tallied, and they were enlightening. Not surprisingly, the A shares—owned by relatively few shareholders, each with a large economic interest— voted "no" on the dividend question by a margin of 89 to 1. The remarkable vote was that of our B shareholders. They number in the hundreds of thousands—perhaps even totaling one million—and they voted 660,759,855 "no" and 13,927,026 "yes," a ratio of about 47 to 1.

Our directors recommended a "no" vote but the company did not otherwise attempt to influence shareholders. Nevertheless, 98% of the shares voting said, in effect, "Don't send us a dividend but instead reinvest all of the earnings." To have our fellow owners—large and small—be so in sync with our managerial philosophy is both remarkable and rewarding.

V. MERGERS AND ACQUISITIONS

Of all our activities at Berkshire, the most exhilarating for Charlie and me is the acquisition of a business with excellent economic characteristics and a management that we like, trust and admire. Such acquisitions are not easy to make but we look for them constantly. In the search, we adopt the same attitude one might find appropriate in looking for a spouse: It pays to be active, interested, and open-minded, but it does not pay to be in a hurry.

In the past, I've observed that many acquisition-hungry managers were apparently mesmerized by their childhood reading of the story about the frog-kissing princess. Remembering her success, they pay dearly for the right to kiss corporate toads, expecting wondrous transfigurations. Initially, disappointing results only deepen their desire to round up new toads. ("Fanaticism," said [Santayana], "consists of redoubling your effort when you've forgotten your aim.") Ultimately, even the most optimistic manager must face reality. Standing knee-deep in unresponsive toads, he then announces an enormous "restructuring" charge. In this corporate equivalent of a Head Start program, the CEO receives the education but the stockholders pay the tuition.

In my early days as a manager I, too, dated a few toads. They were cheap dates—I've never been much of a sport—but my results matched those of acquirers who courted higher-priced toads. I kissed and they croaked.

After several failures of this type, I finally remembered some useful advice I once got from a golf pro (who, like all pros who have had anything to do with my game, wishes to remain anonymous). Said the pro: "Practice doesn't make perfect; practice makes permanent." And thereafter I revised my strategy and tried to buy good businesses at fair prices rather than fair businesses at good prices.[48]

A. *Bad Motives and High Prices*[49]

As our history indicates, we are comfortable both with total ownership of businesses and with marketable securities representing small portions of businesses. We continually look for ways to employ large sums in each area. (But we try to avoid small commitments—"If something's not worth doing at all, it's not worth

---

[48] [Introductory essay, 1992.]
[49] [Divided by hash lines: 1981; 1982; 1997; 1994.]

doing well".) Indeed, the liquidity requirements of our insurance businesses mandate major investments in marketable securities.

Our acquisition decisions will be aimed at maximizing real economic benefits, not at maximizing either managerial domain or reported numbers for accounting purposes. (In the long run, managements stressing accounting appearance over economic substance usually achieve little of either.)

Regardless of the impact upon immediately reportable earnings, we would rather buy 10% of Wonderful Business T at X per share than 100% of T at 2X per share. Most corporate managers prefer just the reverse, and have no shortage of stated rationales for their behavior.

However, we suspect three motivations—usually unspoken—to be, singly or in combination, the important ones in most high-premium takeovers:

(1) Leaders, business or otherwise, seldom are deficient in animal spirits and often relish increased activity and challenge. At Berkshire, the corporate pulse never beats faster than when an acquisition is in prospect.

(2) Most organizations, business or otherwise, measure themselves, are measured by others, and compensate their managers far more by the yardstick of size than by any other yardstick. (Ask a Fortune 500 manager where his corporation stands on that famous list and, invariably, the number responded will be from the list ranked by size of sales; he may well not even know where his corporation places on the list *Fortune* just as faithfully compiles ranking the same 500 corporations by profitability.)

(3) Many managements apparently were overexposed in impressionable childhood years to the story in which the imprisoned handsome prince is released from a toad's body by a kiss from a beautiful princess. Consequently, they are certain their managerial kiss will do wonders for the profitability of Company T(arget).

Such optimism is essential. Absent that rosy view, why else should the shareholders of Company A(cquisitor) want to own an interest in T at the 2X takeover cost rather than at the X market price they would pay if they made direct purchases on their own?

In other words, investors can always buy toads at the going price for toads. If investors instead bankroll princesses who wish to pay double for the right to kiss the toad, those kisses had better pack some real dynamite. We've observed many kisses but very few miracles. Nevertheless, many managerial princesses remain serenely confident about the future potency of their kisses—even after their corporate backyards are knee-deep in unresponsive toads. In fairness, we should acknowledge that some acquisition records have been dazzling. Two major categories stand out.

The first involves companies that, through design or accident, have purchased only businesses that are particularly well adapted to an inflationary environment. Such favored business must have two characteristics: (1) an ability to increase prices rather easily (even when product demand is flat and capacity is not fully utilized) without fear of significant loss of either market share or unit volume, and (2) an ability to accommodate large dollar volume increases in business (often produced more by inflation than by real growth) with only minor additional investment of capital. Managers of ordinary ability, focusing solely on acquisition possibilities meeting these tests, have achieved excellent results in recent decades. However, very few enterprises possess both characteristics, and competition to buy those that do has now become fierce to the point of being self-defeating.

The second category involves the managerial superstars—[those] who can recognize that rare prince who is disguised as a toad, and who have managerial abilities that enable them to peel away the disguise. We salute such managers as Ben Heineman at Northwest Industries, Henry Singleton at Teledyne, Erwin Zaban at National Service Industries, and especially Tom Murphy at Capital Cities Communications (a real managerial "twofer", whose acquisition efforts have been properly focused in Category 1 and whose operating talents also make him a leader of Category 2). From both direct and vicarious experience, we recognize the difficulty and rarity of these executives' achievements. (So do they; these champs have made very few deals in recent years, and often have found repurchase of their own shares to be the most sensible employment of corporate capital.)

Your Chairman, unfortunately, does not qualify for Category 2. And, despite a reasonably good understanding of the economic factors compelling concentration in Category 1, our actual acquisition activity in that category has been sporadic and inadequate. Our preaching was better than our performance. (We neglected the Noah principle: predicting rain doesn't count, building arks does.)

We have tried occasionally to buy toads at bargain prices with results that have been chronicled in past reports. Clearly our kisses fell flat. We have done well with a couple of princes—but they were princes when purchased. At least our kisses didn't turn them into toads. And, finally, we have occasionally been quite successful in purchasing fractional interests in easily-identifiable princes at toad-like prices.

Berkshire and Blue Chip are considering merger in 1983. If it takes place, it will involve an exchange of stock based upon an identical valuation method applied to both companies. The one other significant issuance of shares by Berkshire or its affiliated companies that occurred during present management's tenure was in the 1978 merger of Berkshire with Diversified Retailing Company.

Our share issuances follow a simple basic rule: we will not issue shares unless we receive as much intrinsic business value as we give. Such a policy might seem axiomatic. Why, you might ask, would anyone issue dollar bills in exchange for fifty-cent pieces? Unfortunately, many corporate managers have been willing to do just that.

The first choice of these managers in making acquisitions may be to use cash or debt. But frequently the CEO's cravings outpace cash and credit resources (certainly mine always have). Frequently, also, these cravings occur when his own stock is selling far below intrinsic business value. This state of affairs produces a moment of truth. At that point, as Yogi Berra has said, "You can observe a lot just by watching." For shareholders then will find which objective the management truly prefers—expansion of domain or maintenance of owners' wealth.

The need to choose between these objectives occurs for some simple reasons. Companies often sell in the stock market below their intrinsic business value. But when a company wishes to sell out completely, in a negotiated transaction, it inevitably wants to— and usually can—receive full business value in whatever kind of currency the value is to be delivered. If cash is to be used in payment, the seller's calculation of value received couldn't be easier. If stock of the buyer is to be the currency, the seller's calculation is still relatively easy: just figure the market value in cash of what is to be received in stock.

Meanwhile, the buyer wishing to use his own stock as currency for the purchase has no problems if the stock is selling in the market at full intrinsic value.

But suppose it is selling at only half intrinsic value. In that case, the buyer is faced with the unhappy prospect of using a substantially undervalued currency to make its purchase.

Ironically, were the buyer to instead be a seller of its *entire* business, it too could negotiate for, and probably get, full intrinsic business value. But when the buyer makes a partial sale of itself—*and that is what the issuance of shares to make an acquisition amounts to*—it can customarily get no higher value set on its shares than the market chooses to grant it.

The acquirer who nevertheless barges ahead ends up using an undervalued (market value) currency to pay for a fully valued (negotiated value) property. In effect, the acquirer must give up $2 of value to receive $1 of value. Under such circumstances, a marvelous business purchased at a fair sales price becomes a terrible buy. For gold valued as gold cannot be purchased intelligently through the utilization of gold—or even silver—valued as lead.

If, however, the thirst for size and action is strong enough, the acquirer's manager will find ample rationalizations for such a value-destroying issuance of stock. Friendly investment bankers will reassure him as to the soundness of his actions. (Don't ask the barber whether you need a haircut.)

A few favorite rationalizations employed by stock-issuing managements follow:

(a) "The company we're buying is going to be worth a lot more in the future." (Presumably so is the interest in the old business that is being traded away; future prospects are implicit in the business valuation process. If 2X is issued for X, the imbalance still exists when both parts double in business value.)

(b) "We have to grow." (Who, it might be asked, is the "we"? For present shareholders, the reality is that all existing businesses shrink when shares are issued. Were Berkshire to issue shares tomorrow for an acquisition, Berkshire would own everything that it now owns plus the new business, but *your* interest in such hard-to-match businesses as See's Candy Shops, National Indemnity, etc. would automatically be reduced. If (1) your family owns a 120-acre farm and (2) you invite a neighbor with 60 acres of comparable land to merge his farm into an equal partnership— with you to be managing partner, then (3) your managerial domain will have grown to 180 acres but you will have permanently shrunk by 25% your family's ownership interest in both acreage and crops. Managers who want to expand their domain at the expense of owners might better consider a career in government.)

(c) "Our stock is undervalued and we've minimized its use in this deal—but we need to give the selling shareholder 51% in stock and 49% in cash so that certain of those shareholders can get the tax-free exchange they want." (This argument acknowledges that it is beneficial to the acquirer to hold down the issuance of shares, and we like that. But if it hurts old owners to utilize shares on a 100% basis, it very likely hurts on a 51% basis. After all, a man is not charmed if a spaniel defaces his lawn, just because it's a spaniel and not a St. Bernard. And the wishes of sellers can't be the determinant of the best interests of the buyer—what would happen if, heaven forbid, the seller insisted that as a condition of merger the CEO of the acquirer be replaced?)

There are three ways to avoid destruction of value for old owners when shares are issued for acquisitions. One is to have a true business-value-for-business-value merger, such as the Berkshire-Blue Chip combination is intended to be. Such a merger attempts to be fair to shareholders of *both* parties, with each receiving just as much as it gives in terms of intrinsic business value. The Dart Industries-Kraft and Nabisco-Standard Brands mergers appeared to be of this type, but they are the exceptions. It's not that acquirers wish to avoid such deals; it's just that they are very hard to do.

The second route presents itself when the acquirer's stock sells at or above its intrinsic business value. In that situation, the use of stock as currency actually may enhance the wealth of the acquiring company's owners. Many mergers were accomplished on this basis in the 1965-69 period. The results were the converse of most of the activity since 1970: the shareholders of the *acquired* company received very inflated currency (frequently pumped up by dubious accounting and promotional techniques) and were the losers of wealth through such transactions.

During recent years the second solution has been available to very few large companies. The exceptions have primarily been those companies in glamorous or promotional businesses to which the market temporarily attaches valuations at or above intrinsic business valuation.

The third solution is for the acquirer to go ahead with the acquisition, but then subsequently repurchase a quantity of shares equal to the number issued in the merger. In this manner, what originally was a stock-for-stock merger can be converted, effectively, into a cash-for-stock acquisition. Repurchases of this kind are damage-repair moves. Regular readers will correctly guess that we much prefer repurchases that directly enhance the wealth of owners instead of repurchases that merely repair previous damage. Scoring touchdowns is more exhilarating than recovering one's fumbles. But, when a fumble has occurred, recovery is important and we heartily recommend damage-repair repurchases that turn a bad stock deal into a fair cash deal.

The language utilized in mergers tends to confuse the issues and encourage irrational actions by managers. For example, "dilution" is usually carefully calculated on a pro forma basis for both book value and current earnings per share. Particular emphasis is given to the latter item. When that calculation is negative (dilutive) from the acquiring company's standpoint, a justifying explanation will be made (internally, if not elsewhere) that the lines will cross favorably at some point in the future. (While deals often fail in practice, they never fail in projections—if the CEO is visibly panting over a prospective acquisition, subordinates and consultants will supply the requisite projections to rationalize any price.) Should the calculation produce numbers that are immediately positive—that is, anti-dilutive—for the acquirer, no comment is thought to be necessary.

The attention given this form of dilution is overdone: current earnings per share (or even earnings per share of the next few years) are an important variable in most business valuations, but far from all-powerful.

There have been plenty of mergers, non-dilutive in this limited sense, that were instantly value-destroying for the acquirer. And some mergers that have diluted current and near-term earnings per share have in fact been value-enhancing. What really counts is whether a merger is dilutive or anti-dilutive in terms of intrinsic business value (a judgment involving consideration of many variables). We believe calculation of dilution from this viewpoint to be all-important (and too seldom made).

A second language problem relates to the equation of exchange. If Company A announces that it will issue shares to merge with Company B, the process is customarily described as "Company A to Acquire Company B", or "B Sells to A". Clearer thinking about the matter would result if a more awkward but more accurate description were used: "Part of A sold to acquire B", or "Owners of B to receive part of A in exchange for their properties". In a trade, what you are giving is just as important as what you are getting. This remains true even when the final tally on what is being given is delayed. Subsequent sales of common stock or convertible issues, either to complete the financing for a deal or to restore balance sheet strength, must be fully counted in evaluating the fundamental mathematics of the original acquisition. (If corporate pregnancy is going to be the consequence of corporate mating, the time to face that fact is before the moment of ecstasy.)

Managers and directors might sharpen their thinking by asking themselves if they would sell 100% of their business on the same basis they are being asked to sell part of it. And if it isn't smart to sell all on such a basis, they should ask themselves why it is smart to sell a portion. A cumulation of small managerial stupidities will produce a major stupidity—not a major triumph. (Las Vegas has been built upon the wealth transfers that occur when people engage in seemingly-small disadvantageous capital transactions.)

The "giving versus getting" factor can most easily be calculated in the case of registered investment companies. Assume Investment Company X, selling at 50% of asset value, wishes to merge with Investment Company Y. Assume, also, that Company X therefore decides to issue shares equal in market value to 100% of Y's asset value.

Such a share exchange would leave X trading $2 of its previous intrinsic value for $1 of Y's intrinsic value. Protests would promptly come forth from both X's shareholders and the SEC, which rules on the fairness of registered investment company mergers. Such a transaction simply would not be allowed.

In the case of manufacturing, service, financial companies, etc., values are not normally as precisely calculable as in the case of investment companies. But we have seen mergers in these industries that just as dramatically destroyed value for the owners of the acquiring company as was the case in the hypothetical illustration above. This destruction could not happen if management and directors would assess the fairness of any transaction by using the same yardstick in the measurement of both businesses.

Finally, a word should be said about the "double whammy" effect upon owners of the acquiring company when value-diluting stock issuances occur. Under such circumstances, the first blow is the loss of intrinsic business value that occurs through the merger itself. The second is the downward revision in market valuation that, quite rationally, is given to that now-diluted business value. For current and prospective owners understandably will not pay as much for assets lodged in the hands of a management that has a record of wealth-destruction through unintelligent share issuances as they will pay for assets entrusted to a management with precisely equal operating talents, but a known distaste for anti-owner actions. Once management shows itself insensitive to the interests of owners, shareholders will suffer a long time from the price/value ratio afforded their stock (relative to other stocks), no matter what assurances management gives that the value-diluting action taken was a one-of-a-kind event.

Those assurances are treated by the market much as one-bug-in-the-salad explanations are treated at restaurants. Such explanations, even when accompanied by a new waiter, do not eliminate a drop in the demand (and hence market value) for salads, both on the part of the offended customer and his neighbors pondering what to order. Other things being equal, the highest stock market prices relative to intrinsic business value are given to companies whose managers have demonstrated their unwillingness to issue shares at any time on terms unfavorable to the owners of the business.

———————

I've mentioned that we strongly prefer to use cash rather than Berkshire stock in acquisitions. A study of the record will tell you why: If you aggregate all of our stock-only mergers (excluding those we did with two affiliated companies, Diversified Retailing and Blue Chip Stamps), you will find that our shareholders are slightly worse off than they would have been had I not done the transactions. Though it hurts me to say it, when I've issued stock, I've cost you money.

Be clear about one thing: This cost has *not* occurred because we were misled in any way by sellers or because they thereafter failed to manage with diligence and skill. On the contrary, the sellers were completely candid when we were negotiating our deals and have been energetic and effective ever since.

Instead, our problem has been that we own a truly marvelous collection of businesses, which means that trading away a portion of them for something new almost never makes sense. When we issue shares in a merger, we reduce your ownership in all of our businesses—partly-owned companies such as Coca-Cola and American Express, and all of our terrific operating companies as well. An example from sports will illustrate the difficulty we face: For a baseball team, acquiring a player who can be expected to bat .350 is almost always a wonderful event—*except* when the team must trade a .380 hitter to make the deal.

Because our roster is filled with .380 hitters, we have tried to pay cash for acquisitions, and here our record has been far better. Starting with National Indemnity in 1967, and continuing with, among others, See's, Buffalo News, Scott Fetzer and GEICO, we have acquired—for cash—a number of large businesses that have performed incredibly well since we bought them. These acquisitions have delivered Berkshire tremendous value—indeed, far more than I anticipated when we made our purchases.

We believe that it is almost impossible for us to "trade up" from our present businesses and managements. Our situation is the opposite of Camelot's Mordred, of whom Guenevere commented, "The one thing I can say for him is that he is bound to marry well. Everybody is above him." Marrying well is extremely difficult for Berkshire.

[I]n contemplating business mergers and acquisitions, many managers tend to focus on whether the transaction is immediately dilutive or anti-dilutive to earnings per share (or, at financial institutions, to per-share book value). An emphasis of this sort carries great dangers. [I]magine that a 25-year-old first-year MBA student is considering merging his future economic interests with those of a 25-year-old day laborer. The MBA student, a non-earner, would find that a "share-for-share" merger of his equity interest in himself with that of the day laborer would enhance his near-term earnings (in a big way!). But what could be sillier for the student than a deal of this kind?

In corporate transactions, it's equally silly for the would-be purchaser to focus on current earnings when the prospective acquiree has either different prospects, a different mix of operating and non-operating assets, or a different capital structure. At Berkshire, we have rejected many merger and purchase opportunities that would have boosted current and near-term earnings but that would have reduced per-share intrinsic value. Our approach, rather, has been to follow Wayne Gretzky's advice: "Go to where the puck is going to be, not to where it is." As a result, our shareholders are now many billions of dollars richer than they would have been if we had used the standard catechism.

The sad fact is that most major acquisitions display an egregious imbalance: They are a bonanza for the shareholders of the acquiree; they increase the income and status of the acquirer's management; and they are a honey pot for the investment bankers and other professionals on both sides. But, alas, they usually reduce the wealth of the acquirer's shareholders, often to a substantial extent. That happens because the acquirer typically gives up more intrinsic value than it receives. Do that enough, says John Medlin, the retired head of Wachovia Corp., and "you are running a chain letter in reverse."

Over time, the skill with which a company's managers allocate capital has an enormous impact on the enterprise's value. Almost by definition, a really good business generates far more money (at least after its early years) than it can use internally. The company could, of course, distribute the money to shareholders by way of dividends or share repurchases. But often the CEO asks a strategic planning staff, consultants or investment bankers whether an acquisition or two might make sense. That's like asking your interior decorator whether you need a $50,000 rug.

The acquisition problem is often compounded by a biological bias: Many CEOs attain their positions in part because they possess an abundance of animal spirits and ego. If an executive is heavily endowed with these qualities—which, it should be acknowledged, sometimes have their advantages—they won't disappear when he reaches the top. When such a CEO is encouraged by his advisors to make deals, he responds much as would a teenage boy who is encouraged by his father to have a normal sex life. It's not a push he needs.

Some years back, a CEO friend of mine—in jest, it must be said—unintentionally described the pathology of many big deals. This friend, who ran a property-casualty insurer, was explaining to his directors why he wanted to acquire a certain life insurance company. After droning rather unpersuasively through the economics and strategic rationale for the acquisition, he abruptly abandoned the script. With an impish look, he simply said: "Aw, fellas, all the other kids have one."

At Berkshire, our managers will continue to earn extraordinary returns from what appear to be ordinary businesses. As a first step, these managers will look for ways to deploy their earnings advantageously in their businesses. What's left, they will send to Charlie and me. We then will try to use those funds in ways that build per-share intrinsic value. Our goal will be to acquire either part or all of businesses that we believe we understand, that have good, sustainable underlying economics, and that are run by managers whom we like, admire and trust.

B. *Sensible Share Repurchases Versus Greenmail*[50]

Our endorsement of repurchases is limited to those dictated by price/value relationships and does not extend to the "greenmail" repurchase—a practice we find odious and repugnant. In these transactions, two parties achieve their personal ends by exploitation of an innocent and unconsulted third party. The players are: (1) the "shareholder" extortionist who, even before the ink on his stock certificate dries, delivers his "your-money-or-your-life" message to managers; (2) the corporate insiders who quickly seek peace at any price—as long as the price is paid by someone else; and (3) the shareholders whose money is used by (2) to make (1) go away. As the dust settles, the mugging, transient shareholder gives his speech on "free enterprise", the muggee management gives its speech on "the best interests of the company", and the innocent shareholder standing by mutely funds the payoff.

C. *Leveraged Buyouts*[51]

If successful corporate business acquisition is so hard, how does one explain the widespread recent success of most of the leveraged-buy-out ("LBO") operators who have purchased corporations? A huge part of the answer comes from income-tax effects and other simple effects. When, in a typical LBO, the typical mostly equity corporate capitalization was replaced by 90% debt plus a new 10%-of-capitalization common stock position:

(1) the combined market value of all the new common stock plus all the new debt became much higher than the previous market value of all the older common stock, because the existing stream of pre-tax earnings was no longer shared with corporate income tax collectors who, in many cases, had previously received more cash each year than shareholders; and

(2) even after the value-enhancing effect of the corporate tax reduction was shared with former shareholders by paying them extra-high prices to leave, a retained residue of value-enhancing tax effect made the new common stock

---

[50] [1984.]

[51] [1989 Wesco Financial Corporation Letter to Shareholders, by Charles T. Munger. Reprinted with permission.]

(which now became much like a speculative warrant with good terms) worth considerably more than cost as the ink dried on acquisition papers; and

    (3) the new "owners" then resorted to strategies, difficult neither to conceive nor implement, including the following:

      (a) they eliminated many of the easily removable costs (largely personnel costs) and sub-par segments which in some mix (i) bedevil successful corporations (including ours) with sloth and folly and (ii) create their humane grace and, through present sacrifice, good long-term prospects, justifying sacrifice endured; and

      (b) they sold off a few operations at super-high prices, sometimes exercising the easiest microeconomic insight by selling to a direct competitor and sometimes selling to a surprisingly easy-to-find non-competitive corporate buyer, not owned by its managers, willing to pay almost as high a price as a competitor would; and

    (4) the new "owners" then profited, in due course, not only from the tax effect and other simple reshuffling activities described above, but also from the wonderful upside effects of extreme financial leverage during a long business boom accompanied by a rising stock market.

Whether the country wants a large number (or even any) of its large corporations to have extremely leveraged capitalizations, except through occasional adversity, presents interesting social questions. Is one social function of corporations to be financially strong so that they act as shock absorbers, protecting dependent employees, suppliers and customers from part of the volatility implicit in capitalism? Was Ben Franklin right when he included the following folk wisdom in *Poor Richard's Almanac*: "It is hard for an empty sack to stand upright." Is a weak corporation, borrowed to the hilt, the social equivalent of a bridge with an inadequate reserve of structural strength? Granting that leveraged buy outs have some favorable effects (as well as unfavorable effects) on long term efficiency, how many thousands of able people do we wish to attract into promotional corporate recapitalization activity which (1) reduces corporate income taxes, (2) often tests the limits of antitrust law, and (3) focuses business attention on short-term cash generation to pay down oppressive levels of debt? Finally, as Columbia Law School's Professor Lou Lowenstein puts it (more or less): "Do we really want entire corporate businesses, as important social institutions, continuously traded like pork belly contracts?"

However the social questions are answered, three aspects of the present situation are clear. First, the corporate tax effect is so large in LBO transactions that easy success in such transactions does not imply that success is easy in ordinary corporate acquisitions. Second, the hordes of leveraged-buy-out operators now with us raise the general level of acquisition prices to the detriment of other would-be acquirers, including Wesco, which are not willing to maximize tax benefits through maximized borrowing. And, third, the LBO operator will not go away so long as present permissive laws last. The operators have a real advantage under such laws, not just a fig leaf aiding promotion. Even though failure and disgrace will reduce their number, and prices paid in leveraged-buy-out transactions will fall, the capitalized value of reducing the corporate income tax will remain. Therefore, plenty of rational incentive will remain for transactions. The LBO genie will encounter reverses, but he is not going back in the bottle unless ordered to do so by new laws.

It should also be noted that the LBO operators' incentives to bid high do not end with real advantages derived from tax law and willingness to reshuffle businesses with much speed and few scruples. Additional incentives for high bids come from typical structures in which general partners of LBO partnerships risk little of their own money (often less than none after fees are taken into account), yet share significantly in gains. Such arrangements are similar to the system of the race track tout. And who has ever seen a tout who didn't want his backer to make a lot of bets?

To Wesco, as a non-LBO operator, the good-corporate-acquisition game was always tough. And that game in each recent year has become more like fishing for muskies at Leech Lake, in Minnesota, where the writer's earliest business partner, Ed Hoskins, had the following conversation with his Indian guide:

"Are any muskies caught in this lake?"

"More muskies are caught in this lake than in any other lake in Minnesota. This lake is famous for muskies."

"How long have you been fishing here?"

"19 years."

"And how many muskies have you caught?"

"None."

When a management has our point of view, infrequency of business acquisition may safely be predicted. Whether this happens, as we like to believe, because the game is hard for almost everyone, or merely because the game is hard for us, the result for Wesco shareholders is the same: less worthwhile activity than we all would like. But there may be one consolation: A series of big, incorrectable acquisition troubles, with no meaningful salvage, is seldom caused by people who think the acquisition game is like fishing for muskies at Leech Lake.

D. *Sound Acquisition Policies*[52]

It may seem strange that we exult over a year in which we made three acquisitions, given that we have regularly used these pages to question the acquisition activities of most managers. Rest assured, Charlie and I haven't lost our skepticism: We believe most deals do damage to the shareholders of the acquiring company. Too often, the words from *HMS Pinafore* apply: "Things are seldom what they seem, skim milk masquerades as cream." Specifically, sellers and their representatives invariably present financial projections having more entertainment value than educational value. In the production of rosy scenarios, Wall Street can hold its own against Washington.

In any case, why potential buyers even look at projections prepared by sellers baffles me. Charlie and I never give them a glance, but instead keep in mind the story of the man with an ailing horse. Visiting the vet, he said: "Can you help me? Sometimes my horse walks just fine and sometimes he limps." The vet's reply was pointed: "No problem—when he's walking fine, sell him." In the world of mergers and acquisitions, that horse would be peddled as Secretariat.

At Berkshire, we have all the difficulties in perceiving the future that other acquisition-minded companies do. Like [them] also, we face the inherent problem that the seller of a business practically always knows far more about it than the buyer and also picks the time of sale—a time when the business is likely to be walking "just fine."

Even so, we do have a few advantages, perhaps the greatest being that we *don't* have a strategic plan. Thus we feel no need to proceed in an ordained direction (a course leading almost invariably to silly purchase prices) but can instead simply decide what makes sense for our owners. In doing that, we always mentally

---

52 [Divided by hash lines: 1995; 1991 (the latter with similar versions beginning in 1982 and continuing thereafter).]

compare any move we are contemplating with dozens of other opportunities open to us, including the purchase of small pieces of the
best businesses in the world via the stock market. Our practice of
making this comparison—acquisitions against passive investments—is a discipline that managers focused simply on expansion
seldom use.

Talking to *Time* magazine a few years back, Peter Drucker got
to the heart of things: "I will tell you a secret: Dealmaking beats
working. Dealmaking is exciting and fun, and working is grubby.
Running anything is primarily an enormous amount of grubby detail work . . . dealmaking is romantic, sexy. That's why you have
deals that make no sense."

In making acquisitions, we have a further advantage: As payment, we can offer sellers a stock backed by an extraordinary collection of outstanding businesses. An individual or a family
wishing to dispose of a single fine business, but also wishing to defer personal taxes indefinitely, is apt to find Berkshire stock a particularly comfortable holding. I believe, in fact, that this calculus
played an important part in the two acquisitions for which we paid
shares in 1995.

Beyond that, sellers sometimes care about placing their companies in a corporate home that will both endure and provide
pleasant, productive working conditions for their managers. Here
again, Berkshire offers something special. Our managers operate
with extraordinary autonomy. Additionally, our ownership structure enables sellers to know that when I say we are buying to keep,
the promise means something. For our part, we like dealing with
owners who care what happens to their companies and people. A
buyer is likely to find fewer unpleasant surprises dealing with that
type of seller than with one simply auctioning off his business.

In addition to the foregoing being an explanation of our acquisition style, it is, of course, a not-so-subtle sales pitch. If you own
or represent a business earning $[75] million or more before tax,
and it fits the criteria [set forth below], just give me a call. Our
discussion will be confidential. And if you aren't interested now,
file our proposition in the back of your mind: We are never going
to lose our appetite for buying companies with good economics
and excellent management.

Concluding this little dissertation on acquisitions, I can't resist
repeating a tale told me last year by a corporate executive. The
business he grew up in was a fine one, with a long-time record of
leadership in its industry. Its main product, however, was distress-

ingly glamorless. So several decades ago, the company hired a management consultant who—naturally—advised diversification, the then-current fad. ("Focus" was not yet in style.) Before long, the company acquired a number of businesses, each after the consulting firm had gone through a long—and expensive—acquisition study. And the outcome? Said the executive sadly, "When we started, we were getting 100% of our earnings from the original business. After ten years, we were getting 150%."

It's discouraging to note that though we have on four occasions made major purchases of companies whose sellers were represented by prominent investment banks, we were in only one of these instances contacted by the investment bank. In the other three cases, I myself or a friend initiated the transaction at some point after the investment bank had solicited its own list of prospects. We would love to see an intermediary earn its fee by thinking of us—and therefore repeat here what we're looking for:

(1) Large purchases,

(2) Demonstrated consistent earning power (future projections are of no interest to us, nor are "turnaround" situations),

(3) Businesses earning good returns on equity while employing little or no debt,

(4) Management in place (we can't supply it),

(5) Simple businesses (if there's lots of technology, we won't understand it),

(6) An offering price (we don't want to waste our time or that of the seller by talking, even preliminarily, about a transaction when price is unknown).

We will not engage in unfriendly takeovers. We can promise complete confidentiality and a very fast answer—customarily within five minutes—as to whether we're interested. We prefer to buy for cash, but will consider issuing stock when we receive as much in intrinsic business value as we give.

Our favorite form of purchase is one [in which] the company's owner-managers wish to generate significant amounts of cash, sometimes for themselves, but often for their families or inactive shareholders. At the same time, these managers wish to remain significant owners who continue to run their companies just as they have in the past. We think we offer a particularly good fit for owners with such objectives, and we invite potential sellers to check us out by contacting people with whom we have done business in the past.

Charlie and I frequently get approached about acquisitions that don't come close to meeting our tests: We've found that if you advertise an interest in buying collies, a lot of people will call hoping to sell you their cocker spaniels. A line from a country song expresses our feeling about new ventures, turnarounds, or auction-like sales: "When the phone don't ring, you'll know it's me."[53]

E.   *On Selling One's Business*[54]

Most business owners spend the better part of their lifetimes building their businesses. By experience built upon endless repetition, they sharpen their skills in merchandising, purchasing, personnel selection, etc. It's a learning process, and mistakes made in one year often contribute to competence and success in succeeding years.

In contrast, owner-managers sell their business only once— frequently in an emotionally-charged atmosphere with a multitude of pressures coming from different directions. Often, much of the pressure comes from brokers whose compensation is contingent upon consummation of a sale, regardless of its consequences for both buyer and seller. The fact that the decision is so important, both financially and personally, to the owner can make the process more, rather than less, prone to error. And, mistakes made in the once-in-a-lifetime sale of a business are not reversible.

Price is very important, but often is not the most critical aspect of the sale. You and your family have an extraordinary business— one of a kind in your field—and any buyer is going to recognize that. It's also a business that is going to get more valuable as the years go by. So if you decide not to sell now, you are very likely to realize more money later on. With that knowledge you can deal from strength and take the time required to select the buyer you want.

If you should decide to sell, I think Berkshire Hathaway offers some advantages that most other buyers do not. Practically all of these buyers will fall into one of two categories:

---

[53] [In 1988 and 1989, the last sentence read: "Our interest in new ventures, turn-arounds, or auction-like sales can best be expressed by the Goldwynism: 'Please include me out.'"]

[54] [Divided by hash lines: 1990 Appendix B—form of letter sent to potential sellers of businesses; 1999.]

(1) A company located elsewhere but operating in your business or in a business somewhat akin to yours. Such a buyer—no matter what promises are made—will usually have managers who feel they know how to run your business operations and, sooner or later, will want to apply some hands-on "help." If the acquiring company is much larger, it often will have squads of managers, recruited over the years in part by promises that they will get to run future acquisitions. They will have their own way of doing things and, even though your business record undoubtedly will be far better than theirs, human nature will at some point cause them to believe that their methods of operating are superior. You and your family probably have friends who have sold their businesses to larger companies, and I suspect that their experiences will confirm the tendency of parent companies to take over the running of their subsidiaries, particularly when the parent knows the industry, or thinks it does.

(2) A financial maneuverer, invariably operating with large amounts of borrowed money, who plans to resell either to the public or to another corporation as soon as the time is favorable. Frequently, this buyer's major contribution will be to change accounting methods so that earnings can be presented in the most favorable light just prior to his bailing out. [T]his sort of transaction is becoming much more frequent because of a rising stock market and the great supply of funds available for such transactions.

If the sole motive of the present owners is to cash their chips and put the business behind them—and plenty of sellers fall in this category—either type of buyer that I've just described is satisfactory. But if the sellers' business represents the creative work of a lifetime and forms an integral part of their personality and sense of being, buyers of either type have serious flaws.

Berkshire is another kind of buyer—a rather unusual one. We buy to keep, but we don't have, and don't expect to have, operating people in our parent organization. All of the businesses we own are run autonomously to an extraordinary degree. In most cases, the managers of important businesses we have owned for many years have not been to Omaha or even met each other. When we buy a business, the sellers go on running it just as they did before the sale; we adapt to their methods rather than vice versa.

We have no one—family, recently recruited MBAs, etc.—to whom we have promised a chance to run businesses we have bought from owner-managers. And we won't have.

You know of some of our past purchases. I'm enclosing a list of everyone from whom we have ever bought a business, and I invite you to check with them as to our performance versus our promises. You should be particularly interested in checking with the few whose businesses did not do well in order to ascertain how we behaved under difficult conditions.

Any buyer will tell you that he needs you personally—and if he has any brains, he most certainly does need you. But a great many buyers, for the reasons mentioned above, don't match their subsequent actions to their earlier words. We will behave exactly as promised, both because we have so promised, and because we need to in order to achieve the best business results.

This need explains why we would want the operating members of your family to retain a 20% interest in the business. We need 80% to consolidate earnings for tax purposes, which is a step important to us. It is equally important to us that the family members who run the business remain as owners. Very simply, we would not want to buy unless we felt key members of present management would stay on as our partners. Contracts cannot guarantee your continued interest; we would simply rely on your word.

The areas I get involved in are capital allocation and selection and compensation of the top [managers]. Other personnel decisions, operating strategies, etc. are [their] bailiwick. Some Berkshire managers talk over some of their decisions with me; some don't. It depends upon their personalities and, to an extent, upon their own personal relationship with me.

If you should decide to do business with Berkshire, we would pay in cash. Your business would not be used as collateral for any loan by Berkshire. There would be no brokers involved.

Furthermore, there would be no chance that a deal would be announced and that the buyer would then back off or start suggesting adjustments (with apologies, of course, and with an explanation that banks, lawyers, boards of directors, etc. were to be blamed). And finally, you would know exactly with whom you are dealing. You would not have one executive negotiate the deal only to have someone else in charge a few years later, or have the president regretfully tell you that his board of directors required this change or that (or possibly required sale of your business to finance some new interest of the parent's).

It's only fair to tell you that you would be no richer after the sale than now. The ownership of your business already makes you wealthy and soundly invested. A sale would change the form of your wealth, but it wouldn't change its amount. If you sell, you will have exchanged a 100%-owned valuable asset that you understand for another valuable asset—cash—that will probably be invested in small pieces (stocks) of other businesses that you understand less well. There is often a sound reason to sell but, if the transaction is a fair one, the reason is not so that the seller can become wealthier.

I will not pester you; if you have any possible interest in selling, I would appreciate your call. I would be extraordinarily proud to have Berkshire, along with the key members of your family, own _____; I believe we would do very well financially; and I believe you would have just as much fun running the business over the next 20 years as you have had during the past 20.

Sincerely,

/s/ Warren E. Buffett

Our acquisitions usually develop [as referrals from other managers who have sold to us in the past]. At other companies, executives may devote themselves to pursuing acquisition possibilities with investment bankers, utilizing an auction process that has become standardized. In this exercise the bankers prepare a "book" that makes me think of the Superman comics of my youth. In the Wall Street version, a formerly mild-mannered company emerges from the investment banker's phone booth able to leap over competitors in a single bound and with earnings moving faster than a speeding bullet. Titillated by the book's description of the acquiree's powers, acquisition-hungry CEOs—Lois Lanes all, beneath their cool exteriors—promptly swoon.

What's particularly entertaining in these books is the precision with which earnings are projected for many years ahead. If you ask the author-banker, however, what his own firm will earn *next month*, he will go into a protective crouch and tell you that business and markets are far too uncertain for him to venture a forecast.

Here's one story I can't resist relating: In 1985, a major investment banking house undertook to sell Scott Fetzer, offering it widely—but with no success. Upon reading of this strikeout, I wrote Ralph Schey, Scott Fetzer's CEO, expressing an interest in buying the business. I had never met Ralph, but within a week we had a deal. Unfortunately, Scott Fetzer's letter of engagement with the banking firm provided it a $2.5 million fee upon sale, even if it had nothing to do with finding the buyer. I guess the lead banker felt he should do something for his payment, so he graciously offered us a copy of the book on Scott Fetzer that his firm had prepared. With his customary tact, Charlie responded: "I'll pay $2.5 million *not* to read it."

At Berkshire, our carefully-crafted acquisition strategy is simply to wait for the phone to ring. Happily, it sometimes does so, usually because a manager who sold to us earlier has recommended to a friend that he think about following suit.

F.   *The Buyer of Choice*[55]

Two economic factors probably contributed to the rush of acquisition activity we experienced last year. First, many managers and owners foresaw near-term slowdowns in their businesses—and, in fact, we purchased several companies whose earnings will almost certainly decline this year from peaks they reached in 1999 or 2000. The declines make no difference to us, given that we expect all of our businesses to now and then have ups and downs. (Only in the sales presentations of investment banks do earnings move forever upward.) We don't care about the bumps; what matters are the overall results. But the decisions of other people are sometimes affected by the near-term outlook, which can both spur sellers and temper the enthusiasm of purchasers who might otherwise compete with us.

A second factor that helped us in 2000 was that the market for junk bonds dried up as the year progressed. In the two preceding years, junk bond purchasers had relaxed their standards, buying the obligations of ever-weaker issuers at inappropriate prices. The effects of this laxity were felt last year in a ballooning of defaults. In this environment, "financial" buyers of businesses—those who wish to buy using only a sliver of equity—became unable to borrow all they thought they needed. What they could still borrow, moreover, came at a high price. Consequently, LBO operators became less aggressive in their bidding when businesses came up for sale last year. Because we analyze purchases on an all-equity basis, our evaluations did not change, which means we became considerably more competitive.

Aside from the economic factors that benefited us, we now enjoy a major and growing advantage in making acquisitions in that we are often the buyer of choice for the seller. That fact, of

---

[55] [2000; 2008.]

course, doesn't assure a deal—sellers have to like our price, and we have to like their business and management—but it does help.

We find it meaningful when an owner *cares* about whom he sells to. We like to do business with someone who loves his company, not just the money that a sale will bring him (though we certainly understand why he likes that as well). When this emotional attachment exists, it signals that important qualities will likely be found within the business: honest accounting, pride of product, respect for customers, and a loyal group of associates having a strong sense of direction. The reverse is apt to be true, also. When an owner auctions off his business, exhibiting a total lack of interest in what follows, you will frequently find that it has been dressed up for sale, particularly when the seller is a "financial owner." And if owners behave with little regard for their business and its people, their conduct will often contaminate attitudes and practices throughout the company.

When a business masterpiece has been created by a lifetime— or several lifetimes—of unstinting care and exceptional talent, it should be important to the owner what corporation is entrusted to carry on its history. Charlie and I believe Berkshire provides an almost unique home. We take our obligations to the people who created a business very seriously, and Berkshire's ownership structure ensures that we can fulfill our promises. When we tell John Justin that his business (Justin Industries) will remain headquartered in Fort Worth, or assure the Bridge family that its operation (Ben Bridge Jeweler) will not be merged with another jeweler, these sellers can take those promises to the bank.

How much better it is for the "painter" of a business Rembrandt to personally select its permanent home than to have a trust officer or uninterested heirs auction it off. Throughout the years we have had great experiences with those who recognize that truth and apply it to their business creations. We'll leave the auctions to others.

———————————

Our long-avowed goal is to be the "buyer of choice" for businesses—particularly those built and owned by families. The way to achieve this goal is to deserve it. That means we must keep our promises; avoid leveraging up acquired businesses; grant unusual autonomy to our managers; and hold the purchased companies through thick and thin (though we prefer thick and thicker).

Our record matches our rhetoric. Most buyers competing against us, however, follow a different path. For them, acquisitions are "merchandise." Before the ink dries on their purchase contracts, these operators are contemplating "exit strategies." We have a decided advantage, therefore, when we encounter sellers who truly care about the future of their businesses.

Some years back our competitors were known as "leveraged-buyout operators." But LBO became a bad name. So in Orwellian fashion, the buyout firms decided to change their moniker. What they did not change, though, were the essential ingredients of their previous operations, including their cherished fee structures and love of leverage.

Their new label became "private equity," a name that turns the facts upside-down: A purchase of a business by these firms almost invariably results in dramatic *reductions* in the equity portion of the acquiree's capital structure compared to that previously existing. A number of these acquirees, purchased only two to three years ago, are now in mortal danger because of the debt piled on them by their private-equity buyers. Much of the bank debt is selling below 70¢ on the dollar, and the public debt has taken a far greater beating. The private equity firms, it should be noted, are not rushing in to inject the equity their wards now desperately need. Instead, they're keeping their remaining funds *very* private.

In the regulated utility field there are no large family-owned businesses. Here, Berkshire hopes to be the "buyer of choice" of *regulators*. It is they, rather than selling shareholders, who judge the fitness of purchasers when transactions are proposed.

There is no hiding your history when you stand before these regulators. They can—and do—call their counterparts in other states where you operate and ask how you have behaved in respect to all aspects of the business, including a willingness to commit adequate equity capital.

When MidAmerican proposed its purchase of PacifiCorp in 2005, regulators in the six new states we would be serving immediately checked our record in Iowa. They also carefully evaluated our financing plans and capabilities. We passed this examination, just as we expect to pass future ones.

[W]e hope to buy more regulated utilities in the future—and we know that our business behavior in jurisdictions where we are operating today will determine how we are welcomed by new jurisdictions tomorrow.

VI.   VALUATION AND ACCOUNTING

To those of you who are uninterested in accounting, I apologize for this dissertation. I realize that many of you do not pore over our figures, but instead hold Berkshire primarily because you know that: (1) Charlie and I have the bulk of our money in Berkshire; (2) we intend to run things so that your gains or losses are in direct proportion to ours; (3) the record has so far been satisfactory. There is nothing necessarily wrong with this kind of "faith" approach to investing. Other shareholders, however, prefer an "analysis" approach and we want to supply the information they need. In our own investing, we search for situations in which both approaches give us the same answer.[56]

A.   *Aesop and Inefficient Bush Theory*[57]

The formula for valuing *all* assets that are purchased for financial gain has been unchanged since it was first laid out by a very smart man in about 600 B.C. (though he wasn't smart enough to know it was 600 B.C.).

The oracle was Aesop and his enduring, though somewhat incomplete, investment insight was "a bird in the hand is worth two in the bush." To flesh out this principle, you must answer only three questions. How certain are you that there are indeed birds in the bush? When will they emerge and how many will there be? What is the risk-free interest rate (which we consider to be the yield on long-term U.S. bonds)? If you can answer these three questions, you will know the maximum value of the bush—and the maximum number of the birds you now possess that should be offered for it. And, of course, don't literally think birds. Think dollars.

Aesop's investment axiom, thus expanded and converted into dollars, is immutable. It applies to outlays for farms, oil royalties, bonds, stocks, lottery tickets, and manufacturing plants. And neither the advent of the steam engine, the harnessing of electricity nor the creation of the automobile changed the formula one iota—nor will the Internet. Just insert the correct numbers, and you can rank the attractiveness of all possible uses of capital throughout the universe.

Common yardsticks such as dividend yield, the ratio of price to earnings or to book value, and even growth rates have *nothing*

---

56 [Introductory essay, 1988.]
57 [2000.]

to do with valuation except to the extent they provide clues to the amount and timing of cash flows into and from the business. Indeed, growth can destroy value if it requires cash inputs in the early years of a project or enterprise that exceed the discounted value of the cash that those assets will generate in later years. Market commentators and investment managers who glibly refer to "growth" and "value" styles as contrasting approaches to investment are displaying their ignorance, not their sophistication. Growth is simply a component—usually a plus, sometimes a minus—in the value equation.

Alas, though Aesop's proposition and the third variable—that is, interest rates—are simple, plugging in numbers for the other two variables is a difficult task. Using precise numbers is, in fact, foolish; working with a range of possibilities is the better approach.

Usually, the range must be so wide that no useful conclusion can be reached. Occasionally, though, even very conservative estimates about the future emergence of birds reveal that the price quoted is startingly low in relation to value. (Let's call this phenomenon the IBT—Inefficient Bush Theory.) To be sure, an investor needs some general understanding of business economics as well as the ability to think independently to reach a well-founded positive conclusion. But the investor does not need brilliance nor blinding insights.

At the other extreme, there are many times when the *most* brilliant of investors can't muster a conviction about the birds to emerge, not even when a very broad range of estimates is employed. This kind of uncertainty frequently occurs when new businesses and rapidly changing industries are under examination. In cases of this sort, any capital commitment must be labeled speculative.

Now, speculation—in which the focus is not on what an asset will produce but rather on what the next fellow will pay for it—is neither illegal, immoral nor un-American. But it is not a game in which Charlie and I wish to play. We bring nothing to the party, so why should we expect to take anything home?

The line separating investment and speculation, which is never bright and clear, becomes blurred still further when most market participants have recently enjoyed triumphs. Nothing sedates rationality like large doses of effortless money. After a heady experience of that kind, normally sensible people drift into behavior akin to that of Cinderella at the ball. They know that overstaying the festivities—that is, continuing to speculate in companies that have gigantic valuations relative to the cash they are likely to generate in the future—will eventually bring on pumpkins and mice. But they nevertheless hate to miss a single minute of what is one helluva party. Therefore, the giddy participants all plan to leave just seconds before midnight. There's a problem, though: They are dancing in a room in which the clocks have no hands.

Last year, we commented on the exuberance—and, yes, it was irrational—that prevailed, noting that investor expectations had grown to be several multiples of probable returns. One piece of evidence came from a Paine Webber-Gallup survey of investors conducted in December 1999, in which the participants were asked their opinion about the annual returns investors could expect to realize over the decade ahead. Their answers averaged 19%. That, for sure, was an irrational expectation: For American business as a whole, there couldn't possibly be enough birds in the 2009 bush to deliver such a return.

Far more irrational still were the huge valuations that market participants were then putting on businesses almost certain to end up being of modest or no value. Yet investors, mesmerized by soaring stock prices and ignoring all else, piled into these enterprises. It was as if some virus, racing wildly among investment professionals as well as amateurs, induced hallucinations in which the values of stocks in certain sectors became decoupled from the values of the businesses that underlay them.

This surreal scene was accompanied by much loose talk about "value creation." We readily acknowledge that there has been a huge amount of true value created in the past decade by new or young businesses, and that there is much more to come. But value is destroyed, not created, by any business that loses money over its lifetime, no matter how high its interim valuation may get.

What actually occurs in these cases is wealth *transfer*, often on a massive scale. By shamelessly merchandising birdless bushes, promoters have in recent years moved billions of dollars from the pockets of the public to their own purses (and to those of their friends and associates). The fact is that a bubble market has allowed the creation of bubble companies, entities designed more with an eye to making money *off* investors rather than *for* them. Too often, an IPO, not profits, was the primary goal of a company's promoters. At bottom, the "business model" for these companies has been the old-fashioned chain letter, for which many fee-hungry investment bankers acted as eager postmen.

But a pin lies in wait for every bubble. And when the two eventually meet, a new wave of investors learns some very old lessons: First, many in Wall Street—a community in which quality control is not prized—will sell investors anything they will buy. Second, speculation is most dangerous when it looks easiest.

At Berkshire, we make *no* attempt to pick the few winners that will emerge from an ocean of unproven enterprises. We're not smart enough to do that, and we know it. Instead, we try to apply Aesop's 2,600-year-old equation to opportunities in which we have reasonable confidence as to how many birds are in the bush and when they will emerge (a formulation that my grandsons would probably update to "A girl in a convertible is worth five in the phonebook."). Obviously, we can never precisely predict the timing of cash flows in and out of a business or their exact amount. We try, therefore, to keep our estimates conservative and to focus on industries where business surprises are unlikely to wreak havoc on owners. Even so, we make many mistakes: I'm the fellow, remember, who thought he understood the future economics of trading stamps, textiles, shoes and second-tier department stores.

Lately, the most promising "bushes" have been negotiated transactions for entire businesses, and that pleases us. You should clearly understand, however, that these acquisitions will at best provide us only reasonable returns. Really juicy results from negotiated deals can be anticipated only when capital markets are severely constrained and the whole business world is pessimistic. We are 180 degrees from that point.

B. *Intrinsic Value, Book Value, and Market Price*[58]

[Intrinsic value is] an all-important concept that offers the only logical approach to evaluating the relative attractiveness of investments and businesses. Intrinsic value can be defined simply: It is the discounted value of the cash that can be taken out of a business during its remaining life.

The calculation of intrinsic value, though, is not so simple. As our definition suggests, intrinsic value is an estimate rather than a precise figure, and it is additionally an estimate that must be changed if interest rates move or forecasts of future cash flows are revised. Two people looking at the same set of facts, moreover— and this would apply even to Charlie and me—will almost inevita-

---

[58] [Divided by hash lines: 1996 Owner's Manual; 1987; 1985; 1996; 2005, with condensed updated version in 2006.]

bly come up with at least slightly different intrinsic value figures. That is one reason we never give you our estimates of intrinsic value. What our annual reports do supply, though, are the facts that we ourselves use to calculate this value.

Meanwhile, we regularly report our per-share book value, an easily calculable number, though one of limited use. The limitations do not arise from our holdings of marketable securities, which are carried on our books at their current prices. Rather the inadequacies of book value have to do with the companies we control, whose values as stated on our books may be far different from their intrinsic values.

The disparity can go in either direction. For example, in 1964 we could state with certitude that Berkshire's per-share book value was $19.46. However, that figure considerably overstated the company's intrinsic value, since all of the company's resources were tied up in a sub-profitable textile business. Our textile assets had neither going-concern nor liquidation values equal to their carrying values. Today, however, Berkshire's situation is reversed: Our March 31, 1996 book value of $15,180 *far* understates Berkshire's intrinsic value, a point true because many of the businesses we control are worth much more than their carrying value.

Inadequate though they are in telling the story, we give you Berkshire's book-value figures because they today serve as a rough, albeit significantly understated, tracking measure for Berkshire's intrinsic value. In other words, the percentage change in book value in any given year is likely to be reasonably close to that year's change in intrinsic value.

You can gain some insight into the differences between book value and intrinsic value by looking at one form of investment, a college education. Think of the education's cost as its "book value." If this cost is to be accurate, it should include the earnings that were foregone by the student because he chose college rather than a job.

For this exercise, we will ignore the important non-economic benefits of an education and focus strictly on its economic value. First, we must estimate the earnings that the graduate will receive over his lifetime and subtract from that figure an estimate of what he would have earned had he lacked his education. That gives us an excess earnings figure, which must then be discounted, at an appropriate interest rate, back to graduation day. The dollar result equals the intrinsic economic value of the education.

Some graduates will find that the book value of their education exceeds its intrinsic value, which means that whoever paid for the education didn't get his money's worth. In other cases, the intrinsic value of an education will far exceed its book value, a result that proves capital was wisely deployed. In all cases, what is clear is that book value is meaningless as an indicator of intrinsic value.

———————

An interesting accounting irony overlays a comparison of the reported financial results of our controlled companies with those of the permanent minority holdings. [These holdings] have a market value of over $2 billion. Yet they produced only $11 million in reported after-tax earnings for Berkshire in 1987.

Accounting rules dictate that we take into income only the dividends these companies pay us—which are little more than nominal—rather than our share of their earnings, which in 1987 amounted to well over $100 million. On the other hand, accounting rules provide that the carrying value of these three holdings— owned, as they are, by insurance companies—must be recorded on our balance sheet at current market prices. The result: GAAP accounting lets us reflect in our net worth the up-to-date underlying values of the businesses we partially own, but does not let us reflect their underlying earnings in our income account.

In the case of our controlled companies, just the opposite is true. Here, we show full earnings in our income account but never change asset values on our balance sheet, no matter how much the value of a business might have increased since we purchased it.

Our mental approach to this accounting schizophrenia is to ignore GAAP figures and to focus solely on the future earning power of both our controlled and non-controlled businesses. Using this approach, we establish our own ideas of business value, keeping these independent from both the accounting values shown on our books for controlled companies and the values placed by a sometimes foolish market on our partially-owned companies. It is this business value that we hope to increase at a reasonable (or, preferably, unreasonable) rate in the years ahead.

———————

Historically, Berkshire shares have sold modestly below intrinsic business value. With the price there, purchasers could be certain (as long as they did not experience a widening of this discount) that their personal investment experience would at least equal the financial experience of the business. But recently the discount has disappeared, and occasionally a modest premium has prevailed.

The elimination of the discount means that Berkshire's market value increased even faster than business value (which, itself, grew at a pleasing pace). That was good news for any owner holding while that move took place, but it is bad news for the new or prospective owner. If the financial experience of new owners of Berkshire is merely to match the future financial experience of the company, any premium of market value over intrinsic business value that they pay must be maintained.

Over the long term there has been a more consistent relationship between Berkshire's market value and business value than has existed for any other publicly-traded equity with which I am familiar. This is a tribute to you. Because you have been rational, interested, and investment-oriented, the market price for Berkshire stock has almost always been sensible. This unusual result has been achieved by a shareholder group with unusual demographics: virtually all of our shareholders are individuals, not institutions. No other public company our size can claim the same.

Ben Graham told a story 40 years ago that illustrates why investment professionals behave as they do: An oil prospector, moving to his heavenly reward, was met by St. Peter with bad news. "You're qualified for residence", said St. Peter, "but, as you can see, the compound reserved for oil men is packed. There's no way to squeeze you in." After thinking a moment, the prospector asked if he might say just four words to the present occupants. That seemed harmless to St. Peter, so the prospector cupped his hands and yelled, "Oil discovered in hell." Immediately the gate to the compound opened and all of the oil men marched out to head for the nether regions. Impressed, St. Peter invited the prospector to move in and make himself comfortable. The prospector paused. "No," he said, "I think I'll go along with the rest of the boys. There might be some truth to that rumor after all."

In [the 1995] letter, with Berkshire shares selling at $36,000, I told you: (1) Berkshire's gain in market value in recent years had outstripped its gain in intrinsic value, even though the latter gain had been highly satisfactory; (2) that kind of overperformance could not continue indefinitely; (3) Charlie and I did not at that moment consider Berkshire to be undervalued.

Since I set down those cautions, Berkshire's intrinsic value has increased very significantly while the market price of our shares has changed little. This, of course, means that in 1996 Berkshire's stock underperformed the business. Consequently, today's price/

value relationship is both much different from what it was a year ago and, as Charlie and I see it, more appropriate.

Though our primary goal is to maximize the amount that our shareholders, in total, reap from their ownership of Berkshire, we wish also to minimize the benefits going to some shareholders at the expense of others. These are goals we would have were we managing a family partnership, and we believe they make equal sense for the manager of a public company. In a partnership, fairness requires that partnership interests be valued equitably when partners enter or exit; in a public company, fairness prevails when market price and intrinsic value are in sync. Obviously, they won't always meet that ideal, but a manager—by his policies and communications—can do much to foster equity.

Of course, the longer a shareholder holds his shares, the more bearing Berkshire's business results will have on his financial experience—and the less it will matter what premium or discount to intrinsic value prevails when he buys and sells his stock. That's one reason we hope to attract owners with long-term horizons. Overall, I think we have succeeded in that pursuit. Berkshire probably ranks number one among large American corporations in the percentage of its shares held by owners with a long-term view.

———————————

[C]alculations of intrinsic value, though all-important, are necessarily imprecise and often seriously wrong. The more uncertain the future of a business, the more possibility there is that the calculation will be wildly off-base. Here Berkshire has some advantages: a wide variety of relatively-stable earnings streams, combined with great liquidity and minimum debt. These factors mean that Berkshire's intrinsic value can be more precisely calculated than can the intrinsic value of most companies.

Yet if precision is aided by Berkshire's financial characteristics, the job of calculating intrinsic value has been made more complex by the mere presence of so many earnings streams. Back in 1965, when we owned only a small textile operation, the task of calculating intrinsic value was a snap. Now we own 68 distinct businesses with widely disparate operating and financial characteristics. This array of unrelated enterprises, coupled with our massive investment holdings, makes it impossible for you to simply examine our consolidated financial statements and arrive at an informed estimate of intrinsic value.

We have attempted to ease this problem by clustering our businesses into four logical groups. [These are: insurance (chiefly

GEICO, Gen Re and National Indemnity); regulated and capital intensive businesses (Berkshire Hathaway Energy and BNSF Railway); manufacturing, service and retailing operations (which cover the waterfront); and finance and financial products (especially XTRA, CORT, and Clayton Homes).] Of course, the value of Berkshire may be either greater or less than the sum of these four parts. The outcome depends on whether our many units function better or worse by being part of a larger enterprise and whether capital allocation improves or deteriorates when it is under the direction of a holding company. In other words, does Berkshire ownership bring anything to the party, or would our shareholders be better off if they directly owned shares in each of our 68 businesses? These are important questions but ones that you will have to answer for yourself.

[L]et's review two sets of figures that show where we've come from and where we are now. The first set is the amount of investments (including cash and cash-equivalents) we own on a per-share basis. In making this calculation, we exclude investments held in our finance operation because these are largely offset by borrowings:

Year	Per-Share Investments*
1965	$ 4
1975	159
1985	2,407
1995	21,817
2005	74,129
Compound Growth Rate 1965-2005	28.0%
Compound Growth Rate 1995-2005	13.0%

*Net of minority interests

In addition to these marketable securities, which with minor exceptions are held in our insurance companies, we own a wide variety of non-insurance businesses. Below, we show the pre-tax earnings (excluding goodwill amortization) of these businesses, again on a per-share basis:

Year	Per-Share Earnings*
1965	$ 4
1975	4
1985	52
1995	175
2005	2,441
Compound Growth Rate 1965-2005	17.2%
Compound Growth Rate 1995-2005	30.2%

*Pre-tax and net of minority interests

When growth rates are under discussion, it will pay you to be suspicious as to why the beginning and terminal years have been selected. If either year was aberrational, any calculation of growth will be distorted. In particular, a base year in which earnings were poor can produce a breathtaking, but meaningless, growth rate. In the table above, however, the base year of 1965 was abnormally *good*; Berkshire earned more money in that year than it did in all but one of the previous ten.

As you can see from the two tables, the comparative growth rates of Berkshire's two elements of value have changed in the last decade, a result reflecting our ever-increasing emphasis on business acquisitions. Nevertheless, Charlie and I want to increase the figures in *both* tables.

C. Look-Through Earnings[59]

When one company owns part of another company, appropriate accounting procedures pertaining to that ownership interest must be selected from one of three major categories. The percentage of voting stock that is owned, in large part, determines which category of accounting principles should be utilized.

Generally accepted accounting principles require (subject to exceptions, naturally . . .) full consolidation of sales, expenses, taxes, and earnings of business holdings more than 50% owned. Blue Chip Stamps, 60% owned by Berkshire Hathaway Inc., falls into this category. Therefore, all Blue Chip income and expense items are included in full in Berkshire's Consolidated Statement of Earnings, with the 40% ownership interest of others in Blue Chip's net earnings reflected in the Statement as a deduction for "minority interest".

Full inclusion of underlying earnings from another class of holdings, companies owned 20% to 50% (usually called "investees"), also normally occurs. Earnings from such companies—for example, Wesco Financial, controlled by Berkshire but only 48% owned—are included via a one-line entry in the owner's Statement of Earnings. Unlike the over-50% category, all items of revenue and expense are omitted; just the proportional share of net income is included. Thus, if Corporation A owns one-third of Corporation B, one-third of B's earnings, whether or not distributed by B, will end up in A's earnings. There are some modifications, both in this and the over-50% category, for intercorporate taxes and purchase

---

[59] [Divided by hash lines: 1980; 1990; 1982; 1991, 1979.]

price adjustments, the explanation of which we will save for a later day. (We know you can hardly wait.)

Finally come holdings representing less than 20% ownership of another corporation's voting securities. In these cases, accounting rules dictate that the owning companies include in their earnings only dividends received from such holdings. Undistributed earnings are ignored. Thus, should we own 10% of Corporation X with earnings of $10 million in 1980, we would report in our earnings (ignoring relatively minor taxes on intercorporate dividends) either (a) $1 million if X declared the full $10 million in dividends; (b) $500,000 if X paid out 50%, or $5 million, in dividends; or (c) zero if X reinvested all earnings.

We impose this short—and over-simplified—course in accounting upon you because Berkshire's concentration of resources in the insurance field produces a corresponding concentration of its assets in companies in that third (less than 20% owned) category. Many of these companies pay out relatively small proportions of their earnings in dividends. This means that only a small proportion of their current earning power is recorded in our own current operating earnings. But, while our reported operating earnings reflect only the dividends received from such companies, our economic well-being is determined by their earnings, not their dividends.

Our holdings in this third category of companies have increased dramatically in recent years as our insurance business has prospered and as securities markets have presented particularly attractive opportunities in the common stock area. The large increase in such holdings, plus the growth of earnings experienced by those partially-owned companies, has produced an unusual result; the part of "our" earnings that these companies retained last year (the part not paid to us in dividends) exceeded the total reported annual operating earnings of Berkshire Hathaway. Thus, conventional accounting only allows less than half of our earnings "iceberg" to appear above the surface, in plain view. Within the corporate world such a result is quite rare; in our case it is likely to be recurring.

Our own analysis of earnings reality differs somewhat from generally accepted accounting principles, particularly when those principles must be applied in a world of high and uncertain rates of inflation. (But it's much easier to criticize than to improve such accounting rules. The inherent problems are monumental.) We have owned 100% of businesses whose reported earnings were not worth close to 100 cents on the dollar to us even though, in an accounting sense, we totally controlled their disposition. (The "control" was theoretical. Unless we reinvested all earnings, massive deterioration in the value of assets already in place would occur. But those reinvested earnings had no prospect of earning anything close to a market return on capital.) We have also owned small fractions of businesses with extraordinary reinvestment possibilities whose retained earnings had an economic value to us far in excess of 100 cents on the dollar.

The value to Berkshire Hathaway of retained earnings is not determined by whether we own 100%, 50%, 20% or 1% of the businesses in which they reside. Rather, the value of those retained earnings is determined by the use to which they are put and the subsequent level of earnings produced by that usage. This is true whether we determine the usage, or whether managers we did not hire—but did elect to join—determine that usage. (It's the act that counts, not the actors.) And the value is in no way affected by the inclusion or non-inclusion of those retained earnings in our own reported operating earnings. If a tree grows in a forest partially owned by us, but we don't record the growth in our financial statements, we still own part of the tree.

Our view, we warn you, is non-conventional. But we would rather have earnings for which we did not get accounting credit put to good use in a 10%-owned company by a management we did not personally hire, than have earnings for which we did get credit put into projects of more dubious potential by another management—even if we are that management.

The term "earnings" has a precise ring to it. And when an earnings figure is accompanied by an unqualified auditor's certificate, a naive reader might think it comparable in certitude to π, calculated to dozens of decimal places.

In reality, however, earnings can be as pliable as putty when a charlatan heads the company reporting them. Eventually truth will surface, but in the meantime a lot of money can change hands. Indeed, some important American fortunes have been created by the monetization of accounting mirages.

Berkshire's own reported earnings are misleading in a different, but important, way: We have huge investments in companies ("investees") whose earnings far exceed their dividends and in which we record our share of earnings only to the extent of the dividends we receive. The extreme case is Capital Cities/ABC, Inc.

Our 17% share of the company's earnings amounted to more than $83 million last year. Yet only about $530,000 ($600,000 of dividends it paid us less some $70,000 of tax) is counted in Berkshire's GAAP earnings. The residual $82 million-plus stayed with Cap Cities as retained earnings, which work for our benefit but go unrecorded on our books.

Our perspective on such "forgotten-but-not-gone" earnings is simple: The way they are accounted for is of no importance, but their ownership and subsequent utilization is all-important. We care not whether the auditors hear a tree fall in the forest; we do care who owns the tree and what's next done with it.

When Coca-Cola uses retained earnings to repurchase its shares, the company increases our percentage ownership in what I regard to be the most valuable franchise in the world. (Coke also, of course, uses retained earnings in many other value-enhancing ways.) Instead of repurchasing stock, Coca-Cola could pay those funds to us in dividends, which we could then use to purchase more Coke shares. That would be a less efficient scenario: Because of taxes we would pay on dividend income, we would not be able to increase our proportionate ownership to the degree that Coke can, acting for us. If this less efficient procedure were followed, however, Berkshire would report far greater "earnings."

I believe the best way to think about our earnings is in terms of "look-through" results, calculated as follows: Take $250 million, which is roughly our share of the 1990 operating earnings retained by our investees; subtract $30 million, for the incremental taxes we would have owed had that $250 million been paid to us in dividends; and add the remainder, $220 million, to our reported operating earnings of $371 million. Thus our 1990 "look-through earnings" were about $590 million.

In our view, the value to all owners of the retained earnings of a business enterprise is determined by the effectiveness with which those earnings are used—and not by the size of one's ownership percentage. If you have owned .01 of 1% of Berkshire during the past decade, you have benefited economically in full measure from your share of our retained earnings, no matter what your accounting system. Proportionately, you have done just as well as if you had owned the magic 20%. But if you have owned 100% of a great many capital-intensive businesses during the decade, retained earnings that were credited fully and with painstaking precision to you under standard accounting methods have resulted in minor or zero economic value. This is not a criticism of accounting procedures. We would not like to have the job of designing a better system. It's simply to say that managers and investors alike must understand that accounting numbers are the beginning, not the end, of business valuation.

In most corporations, less-than-20% ownership positions are unimportant (perhaps, in part, because they prevent maximization of cherished reported earnings) and the distinction between accounting and economic results we have just discussed matters little. But in our own case, such positions are of very large and growing importance. Their magnitude, we believe, is what makes our reported operating earnings figure of limited significance.

Within [the] gigantic auction arena [composed of the entire array of major American corporations], it is our job to select businesses with economic characteristics allowing each dollar of retained earnings to be translated eventually into at least a dollar of market value. Despite a lot of mistakes, we have so far achieved this goal. In doing so, we have been greatly assisted by Arthur Okun's patron saint for economists—St. Offset. In some cases, that is, retained earnings attributable to our ownership position have had insignificant or even negative impact on market value, while in other major positions a dollar retained by an investee corporation has been translated into two or more dollars of market value. To date, our corporate over-achievers have more than offset the laggards. If we can continue this record, it will validate our efforts to maximize "economic" earnings, regardless of the impact upon "accounting" earnings.

We also believe that investors can benefit by focusing on their own look-through earnings. To calculate these, they should determine the underlying earnings attributable to the shares they hold in their portfolio and total these. The goal of each investor should be to create a portfolio (in effect, a "company") that will deliver him or her the highest possible look-through earnings a decade or so from now.

An approach of this kind will force the investor to think about long-term business prospects rather than short-term stock market prospects, a perspective likely to improve results. It's true, of course, that, in the long run, the scoreboard for investment decisions is market price. But prices will be determined by future earnings. In investing, just as in baseball, to put runs on the scoreboard one must watch the playing field, not the scoreboard.

The primary test of managerial economic performance is the achievement of a high earnings rate on equity capital employed (without undue leverage, accounting gimmickry, etc.) and not the achievement of consistent gains in earnings per share. In our view, many businesses would be better understood by their shareholder owners, as well as the general public, if managements and financial analysts modified the primary emphasis they place upon earnings per share, and upon yearly changes in that figure.

D. *Economic versus Accounting Goodwill*[60]

[O]ur intrinsic business value considerably exceeds book value. There are two major reasons:

(1) Standard accounting principles require that common stocks held by our insurance subsidiaries be stated on our books at market value, but that other stocks we own be carried at the lower of aggregate cost or market. At the end of 1983, the market value of this latter group exceeded carrying value by $70 million pre-tax, or about $50 million after tax. This excess belongs in our intrinsic business value, but is not included in the calculation of book value;

(2) More important, we own several businesses that possess economic Goodwill (which is properly includable in intrinsic business value) far larger than the accounting Goodwill that is carried on our balance sheet and reflected in book value.

You can live a full and rewarding life without ever thinking about Goodwill and its amortization. But students of investment and management should understand the nuances of the subject. My own thinking has changed drastically from 35 years ago when I was taught to favor tangible assets and to shun businesses whose value depended largely upon economic Goodwill. This bias caused me to make many important business mistakes of omission, although relatively few of commission.

Keynes identified my problem: "The difficulty lies not in the new ideas but in escaping from the old ones." My escape was long delayed, in part because most of what I had been taught by the same teacher had been (and continues to be) so extraordinarily valuable. Ultimately, business experience, direct and vicarious,

---

[60] [Divided by hash lines: 1983; 1983 Appendix; 1996 Owner's Manual; 1999.]

produced my present strong preference for businesses that possess large amounts of enduring Goodwill and that utilize a minimum of tangible assets.

I recommend the [following essay] to those who are comfortable with accounting terminology and who have an interest in understanding the business aspects of Goodwill. Whether or not you wish to tackle the [essay] you should be aware that Charlie and I believe that Berkshire possesses very significant economic Goodwill value above that reflected in our book value.

[The following discussion] deals only with economic and accounting Goodwill—not the goodwill of everyday usage. For example, a business may be well liked, even loved, by most of its customers but possess no economic goodwill. (AT&T, before the breakup, was generally well thought of, but possessed not a dime of economic Goodwill.) And, regrettably, a business may be disliked by its customers but possess substantial, and growing economic Goodwill. So, just for the moment, forget emotions and focus only on economics and accounting.

When a business is purchased, accounting principles require that the purchase price first be assigned to the fair value of the identifiable assets that are acquired. Frequently the sum of the fair values put on the assets (after the deduction of liabilities) is less than the total purchase price of the business. In that case, the difference is assigned to an asset entitled "excess of cost over equity in net assets acquired". To avoid constant repetition of this mouthful, we will substitute "Goodwill."

Accounting Goodwill arising from businesses purchased before November 1970 has a special standing. Except under rare circumstances, it can remain an asset on the balance sheet as long as the business bought is retained. That means no amortization charges to gradually extinguish that asset need be made against earnings.

The case is different, however, with purchases made from November 1970 on. When these create Goodwill, it must be amortized over not more than 40 years through charges—of equal amount in every year—to the earnings account. Since 40 years is the maximum period allowed, 40 years is what managements (including us) usually elect.

That's how accounting Goodwill works. To see how it differs from economic reality, let's look at an example close at hand. We'll round some figures, and greatly oversimplify, to make the example easier to follow. We'll also mention some implications for investor and manager.

Blue Chip Stamps bought See's early in 1972 for $25 million, at which time See's had about $8 million of net tangible assets. (Throughout this discussion, accounts receivable will be classified as tangible assets, a definition proper for business analysis.) This level of tangible assets was adequate to conduct the business without use of debt, except for short periods seasonally. See's was earning about $2 million after tax at the time, and such earnings seemed conservatively representative of future earning power in constant 1972 dollars.

Thus our first lesson: businesses logically are worth far more than net tangible assets when they can be expected to produce earnings on such assets considerably in excess of market rates of return. The capitalized value of this excess return is economic Goodwill.

In 1972 (and now) relatively few businesses could be expected to consistently earn the 25% after tax on net tangible assets that was earned by See's—doing it, furthermore, with conservative accounting and no financial leverage. It was not the fair market value of the inventories, receivables or fixed assets that produced the premium rates of return. Rather it was a combination of intangible assets, particularly a pervasive favorable reputation with consumers based upon countless pleasant experiences they have had with both product and personnel.

Such a reputation creates a consumer franchise that allows the value of the product to the purchaser, rather than its production cost, to be the major determinant of selling price. Consumer franchises are a prime source of economic Goodwill. Other sources include governmental franchises not subject to profit regulation, such as television stations, and an enduring position as the low cost producer in an industry.

Let's return to the accounting in the See's example. Blue Chip's purchase of See's at $17 million over net tangible assets required that a Goodwill account of this amount be established as an asset on Blue Chip's books and that $425,000 be charged to income annually for 40 years to amortize that asset. By 1983, after 11 years of such charges, the $17 million had been reduced to about $12.5 million. Berkshire, meanwhile, owned 60% of Blue Chip and, therefore, also 60% of See's. This ownership meant that Berkshire's balance sheet reflected 60% of See's Goodwill, or about $7.5 million.

In 1983 Berkshire acquired the rest of Blue Chip in a merger that required purchase accounting as contrasted to the "pooling" treatment allowed for some mergers. Under purchase accounting, the "fair value" of the shares we gave to (or "paid") Blue Chip holders had to be spread over the net assets acquired from Blue Chip. This "fair value" was measured, as it almost always is when public companies use their shares to make acquisitions, by the market value of the shares given up.

The assets "purchased" consisted of 40% of everything owned by Blue Chip (as noted, Berkshire already owned the other 60%). What Berkshire "paid" was more than the net identifiable assets we received by $51.7 million, and was assigned to two pieces of Goodwill: $28.4 million to See's and $23.3 million to Buffalo Evening News.

After the merger, therefore, Berkshire was left with a Goodwill asset for See's that had two components: the $7.5 million remaining from the 1971 purchase, and $28.4 million newly created by the 40% "purchased" in 1983. Our amortization charge now will be about $1.0 million for the next 28 years, and $.7 million for the following 12 years, 2002 through 2013.

In other words, different purchase dates and prices have given us vastly different asset values and amortization charges for two pieces of the same asset. (We repeat our usual disclaimer: we have no better accounting system to suggest. The problems to be dealt with are mind boggling and require arbitrary rules.)

But what are the economic realities? One reality is that the amortization charges that have been deducted as costs in the earnings statement each year since acquisition of See's were not true economic costs. We know that because See's last year earned $13 million after taxes on about $20 million of net tangible assets—a performance indicating the existence of economic Goodwill far larger than the total original cost of our accounting Goodwill. In other words, while accounting Goodwill regularly decreased from the moment of purchase, economic Goodwill increased in irregular but very substantial fashion.

Another reality is that annual amortization charges in the future will not correspond to economic costs. It is possible, of course, that See's economic Goodwill will disappear. But it won't shrink in even decrements or anything remotely resembling them. What is more likely is that the Goodwill will increase—in current, if not in constant, dollars—because of inflation.

That probability exists because true economic Goodwill tends to rise in nominal value proportionally with inflation. To illustrate how this works, let's contrast a See's kind of business with a more mundane business. When we purchased See's in 1972, it will be recalled, it was earning about $2 million on $8 million of net tangible assets. Let us assume that our hypothetical mundane business then had $2 million of earnings also, but needed $18 million in net tangible assets for normal operations. Earning only 11% on required tangible assets, that mundane business would possess little or no economic Goodwill.

A business like that, therefore, might well have sold for the value of its net tangible assets, or for $18 million. In contrast, we paid $25 million for See's, even though it had no more in earnings and less than half as much in "honest-to-God" assets. Could less really have been more, as our purchase price implied? The answer is "yes"—*even if both businesses were expected to have flat unit volume*—as long as you anticipated, as we did in 1972, a world of continuous inflation.

To understand why, imagine the effect that a doubling of the price level would subsequently have on the two businesses. Both would need to double their nominal earnings to $4 million to keep themselves even with inflation. This would seem to be no great trick: just sell the same number of units at double earlier prices and, assuming profit margins remain unchanged, profits also must double.

But, crucially, to bring that about, both businesses probably would have to double their nominal investment in net tangible assets, since that is the kind of economic requirement that inflation usually imposes on businesses, both good and bad. A doubling of dollar sales means correspondingly more dollars must be employed immediately in receivables and inventories. Dollars employed in fixed assets will respond more slowly to inflation, but probably just as surely. And all of this inflation-required investment will produce no improvement in rate of return. The motivation for this investment is the survival of the business, not the prosperity of the owner.

Remember, however, that See's had net tangible assets of only $8 million. So it would only have had to commit an additional $8 million to finance the capital needs imposed by inflation. The mundane business, meanwhile, had a burden over twice as large—a need for $18 million of additional capital.

After the dust had settled, the mundane business, now earning $4 million annually, might still be worth the value of its tangible assets, or $36 million. That means its owners would have gained only a dollar of nominal value for every new dollar invested. (This is the same dollar-for-dollar result they would have achieved if they had added money to a savings account.)

See's, however, also earning $4 million, might be worth $50 million if valued (as it logically would be) on the same basis as it was at the time of our purchase. So it would have gained $25 million in nominal value while the owners were putting up only $8 million in additional capital—over $3 of nominal value gained for each $1 invested.

Remember, even so, that the owners of the See's kind of business were forced by inflation to ante up $8 million in additional capital just to stay even in real profits. Any unleveraged business that requires some net tangible assets to operate (and almost all do) is hurt by inflation. Businesses needing little in the way of tangible assets simply are hurt the least.

And that fact, of course, has been hard for many people to grasp. For years the traditional wisdom—long on tradition, short on wisdom—held that inflation protection was best provided by businesses laden with natural resources, plants and machinery, or other tangible assets ("In Goods We Trust"). It doesn't work that way. Asset-heavy businesses generally earn low rates of return—rates that often barely provide enough capital to fund the inflationary needs of the existing business, with nothing left over for real growth, for distribution to owners, or for acquisition of new businesses.

In contrast, a disproportionate number of the great business fortunes built up during the inflationary years arose from ownership of operations that combined intangibles of lasting value with relatively minor requirements for tangible assets. In such cases earnings have bounded upward in nominal dollars, and these dollars have been largely available for the acquisition of additional businesses. This phenomenon has been particularly evident in the communications business. That business has required little in the way of tangible investment—yet its franchises have endured. During inflation, Goodwill is the gift that keeps giving.

But that statement applies, naturally, only to true economic Goodwill. Spurious accounting Goodwill—and there is plenty of it around—is another matter. When an overexcited management purchases a business at a silly price, the same accounting niceties described earlier are observed. Because it can't go anywhere else, the silliness ends up in the Goodwill account. Considering the lack of managerial discipline that created the account, under such circumstances it might better be labeled "No-Will". Whatever the term, the 40-year ritual typically is observed and the adrenalin so capitalized remains on the books as an "asset" just as if the acquisition had been a sensible one.

* * * * *

If you cling to any belief that accounting treatment of Goodwill is the best measure of economic reality, I suggest one final item to ponder.

Assume a company with $20 per share of net worth, all tangible assets. Further assume the company has internally developed some magnificent consumer franchise, or that it was fortunate enough to obtain some important television stations by original FCC grant. Therefore, it earns a great deal on tangible assets, say $5 per share, or 25%.

With such economics, it might sell for $100 per share or more, and it might well also bring that price in a negotiated sale of the entire business.

Assume an investor buys the stock at $100 per share, paying in effect $80 per share for Goodwill (just as would a corporate purchaser buying the whole company). Should the investor impute a $2 per share amortization charge annually ($80 divided by 40 years) to calculate "true" earnings per share? And, if so, should the new "true" earnings of $3 per share cause him to rethink his purchase price?

* * * * *

We believe managers and investors alike should view intangible assets from two perspectives:

(1) In analysis of operating results—that is, in evaluating the underlying economics of a business unit—amortization charges should be ignored. What a business can be expected to earn on unleveraged net tangible assets, excluding any charges against earnings for amortization of Goodwill, is the best guide to the economic attractiveness of the operation. It is also the best guide to the current value of the operation's economic Goodwill.

(2) In evaluating the wisdom of business acquisitions, amortization charges should be ignored also. They should be de-

ducted neither from earnings nor from the cost of the business. This means forever viewing purchased Goodwill at its full cost, before any amortization. Furthermore, cost should be defined as including the full intrinsic business value—not just the recorded accounting value—of all consideration given, irrespective of market prices of the securities involved at the time of merger and irrespective of whether pooling treatment was allowed. For example, what we truly paid in the Blue Chip merger for 40% of the Goodwill of See's and the News was considerably more than the $51.7 million entered on our books. This disparity exists because the market value of the Berkshire shares given up in the merger was less than their intrinsic business value, which is the value that defines the true cost to us.

Operations that appear to be winners based upon perspective (1) may pale when viewed from perspective (2). A good business is not always a good purchase—although it's a good place to look for one.

When Berkshire buys a business for a premium over the GAAP net worth of the acquiree—as will usually be the case, since most companies we'd want to buy don't come at a discount—that premium has to be entered on the asset side of our balance sheet. There are loads of rules about just how a company should record the premium. But to simplify this discussion, we will focus on "Goodwill," the asset item to which almost all of Berkshire's acquisition premiums have been allocated. For example, when we recently acquired the half of GEICO we didn't previously own, we recorded goodwill of about $1.6 billion.

GAAP requires Goodwill to be amortized—that is, written off—over a period no longer than 40 years. Therefore, to extinguish our $1.6 billion in GEICO Goodwill, we will annually take charges of about $40 million against our earnings.

In an accounting sense, consequently, our GEICO Goodwill will disappear gradually in even-sized bites. But the one thing I can guarantee you is that the *economic* Goodwill we have purchased at GEICO will not decline in the same measured way. In fact, my best guess is that the economic goodwill assignable to GEICO will not decline at all, but rather will increase—and probably in a very substantial way.

I made a similar statement in our 1983 Annual Report about the Goodwill attributed to See's Candy, when I used that company as an example in a discussion of Goodwill accounting. At that time, our balance sheet carried about $36 million of See's Goodwill. We have since been charging about $1 million against earnings every year in order to amortize the asset, and the See's Goodwill on our balance sheet is now down to about $23 million. In other words, from an accounting standpoint, See's is now presented as having lost a good deal of goodwill since 1983.

The economic facts could not be more different. In 1983, See's earned about $27 million pre-tax on $11 million of net operating assets; in 1995 it earned $50 million on only $5 million of net operating assets. Clearly See's economic Goodwill has increased dramatically during the interval rather than decreased. Just as clearly, See's is worth many hundreds of millions of dollars more than its stated value on our books.

We could, of course, be wrong, but we expect GEICO's gradual loss of accounting value to be paired with increases in its economic value. Certainly that has been the pattern at most of our subsidiaries, not just See's. That is why we regularly present our operating earnings in a way that allows you to ignore all purchase-accounting adjustments.

In the future, also, we will adopt a similar policy for look-through earnings, moving to a form of presentation that rids these earnings of the major purchase-accounting adjustments of investees. We will not apply this policy to companies that have only small amounts of goodwill on their books, such as Coca-Cola. We will extend it, however, to Wells Fargo, which recently made huge acquisitions and consequently dealing with exceptionally large goodwill charges.

Before leaving this subject, we should issue an important warning: Investors are often led astray by CEOs and Wall Street analysts who equate depreciation charges with the amortization charges we have just discussed. In no way are the two the same: With rare exceptions, depreciation is an economic cost every bit as real as wages, materials, or taxes. Certainly that is true at Berkshire and at virtually all the other businesses we have studied. Furthermore, we do *not* think so-called EBITDA (earnings before interest, taxes, depreciation and amortization) is a meaningful measure of performance. Managements that dismiss the importance of depreciation—and emphasize "cash flow" or EBITDA—

are apt to make faulty decisions, and you should keep that in mind as you make your own investment decisions.

[The application of accounting to acquisitions] is currently a very contentious topic and, before the dust settles, Congress may even intervene (a truly terrible idea).

When a company is acquired, generally accepted accounting principles ("GAAP") currently condone two very different ways of recording the transaction: "purchase" and "pooling." In a pooling, stock must be the currency; in a purchase, payment can be made in either cash or stock. Whatever the currency, managements usually detest purchase accounting because it almost always requires that a "goodwill" account be established and subsequently written off—a process that saddles earnings with a large annual charge that normally persists for decades. In contrast, pooling avoids a goodwill account, which is why managements love it.

Now, the Financial Accounting Standards Board ("FASB") has proposed an end to pooling, and many CEOs are girding for battle. It will be an important fight, so we'll venture some opinions. To begin with, we agree with the many managers who argue that goodwill amortization charges are usually spurious.

For accounting rules to mandate amortization that will, in the usual case, conflict with reality is deeply troublesome: Most accounting charges *relate* to what's going on, even if they don't precisely measure it. As an example, depreciation charges can't with precision calibrate the decline in value that physical assets suffer, but these charges do at least describe something that is truly occurring: Physical assets invariably deteriorate. Correspondingly, obsolescence charges for inventories, bad debt charges for receivables and accruals for warranties are among the charges that reflect true costs. The annual charges for these expenses can't be exactly measured, but the necessity for estimating them is obvious.

In contrast, economic goodwill does not, in many cases, diminish. Indeed, in a great many instances—perhaps most—it actually grows in value over time. In character, economic goodwill is much like land: The value of both assets is sure to fluctuate, but the direction in which value is going to go is in no way ordained. At See's, for example, economic goodwill has grown, in an irregular but very substantial manner, for 78 years. And, if we run the business right, growth of that kind will probably continue for at least another 78 years.

To escape from the fiction of goodwill charges, managers embrace the fiction of pooling. This accounting convention is grounded in the poetic notion that when two rivers merge their streams become indistinguishable. Under this concept, a company that has been merged into a larger enterprise has not been "purchased" (even though it will often have received a large "sell-out" premium). Consequently, no goodwill is created, and those pesky subsequent charges to earnings are eliminated. Instead, the accounting for the ongoing entity is handled as if the businesses had forever been one unit.

So much for poetry. The reality of merging is usually far different: There is indisputably an acquirer and an acquiree, and the latter has been "purchased," no matter how the deal has been structured. If you think otherwise, just ask employees severed from their jobs which company was the conqueror and which was the conquered. You will find no confusion. So on this point the FASB is correct: In most mergers, a purchase has been made. Yes, there are some true "mergers of equals," but they are few and far between.

Charlie and I believe there's a reality-based approach that should both satisfy the FASB, which correctly wishes to record a purchase, and meet the objections of managements to nonsensical charges for diminution of goodwill. We would first have the acquiring company record its purchase price—whether paid in stock or cash—at fair value. In most cases, this procedure would create a large asset representing economic goodwill. We would then leave this asset on the books, not requiring its amortization. Later, if the economic goodwill became impaired, as it sometimes would, it would be written down just as would any other asset judged to be impaired.

If our proposed rule were to be adopted, it should be applied retroactively so that acquisition accounting would be consistent throughout America—a far cry from what exists today. One prediction: If this plan were to take effect, managements would structure acquisitions more sensibly, deciding whether to use cash or stock based on the real consequences for their shareholders rather than on the unreal consequences for their reported earnings.

E.   *Owner Earnings and the Cash Flow Fallacy*[61]

[Many business acquisitions require] major purchase-price accounting adjustments, as prescribed by generally accepted accounting principles (GAAP). The GAAP figures, of course, are the ones used in our consolidated financial statements. But, in our view, the GAAP figures are not necessarily the most useful ones for investors or managers. Therefore, the figures shown for specific operating units are earnings before purchase-price adjustments are taken into account. In effect, these are the earnings that would have been reported by the businesses if we had not purchased them.

A discussion of our reasons for preferring this form of presentation [follows. It] will never substitute for a steamy novel and definitely is not required reading. However, I know that among our shareholders there are those who are thrilled by my essays on accounting—and I hope that both of you enjoy [it].

First a short quiz: below are abbreviated 1986 statements of earnings for two companies. Which business is the more valuable?

	Company O		Company N
		(000s Omitted)	
Revenues		$677,240	$677,240
Cost of Goods Sold:			
Historical costs, excluding depreciation	$341,170		$341,170
Special non-cash inventory costs			4,979[(1)]
Depreciation of plant and equipment	8,301		13,355[(2)]
		349,471	359,504
Gross Profit		$327,769	$317,736
Selling & Admin. Expense	$260,286		$260,286
Amortization of Goodwill			595[(3)]
		260,286	260,881
Operating Profit		$ 67,483	$ 56,855
Other Income, Net		4,135	4,135
Pre-Tax Income		$ 71,618	$ 60,990
Applicable Income Tax:			
Historical deferred and current tax	$ 31,387		$ 31,387
Non-Cash Inter-period Allocation Adjustment			998[(4)]
		31,387	32,385
Net Income		$ 40,231	$ 28,605

(Numbers (1) through (4) designate items discussed later in this section.)

---

[61] [Divided by hash lines: 1986; 1986 Appendix]

As you've probably guessed, Companies O and N are the same business—Scott Fetzer. In the "O" (for "old") column we have shown what the company's 1986 GAAP earnings would have been if we had not purchased it; in the "N" (for "new") column we have shown Scott Fetzer's GAAP earnings as actually reported by Berkshire.

It should be emphasized that the two columns depict identical economics—i.e., the same sales, wages, taxes, etc. And both "companies" generate the same amount of cash for owners. Only the accounting is different.

So, fellow philosophers, which column presents truth? Upon which set of numbers should managers and investors focus?

Before we tackle those questions, let's look at what produces the disparity between O and N. We will simplify our discussion in some respects, but the simplification should not produce any inaccuracies in analysis or conclusions.

The contrast between O and N comes about because we paid an amount for Scott Fetzer that was different from its stated net worth. Under GAAP, such differences—such premiums or discounts—must be accounted for by "purchase-price adjustments." In Scott Fetzer's case, we paid $315 million for net assets that were carried on its books at $172.4 million. So we paid a premium of $142.6 million.

The first step in accounting for any premium paid is to adjust the carrying value of current assets to current values. In practice, this requirement usually does not affect receivables, which are routinely carried at current value, but often affects inventories. Because of a $22.9 million LIFO reserve and other accounting intricacies,[62] Scott Fetzer's inventory account was carried at a $37.3 million discount from current value. So, making our first accounting move, we used $37.3 million of our $142.6 million premium to increase the carrying value of the inventory.

Assuming any premium is left after current assets are adjusted, the next step is to adjust fixed assets to current value. In our case, this adjustment also required a few accounting acrobatics relating to deferred taxes. Since this has been billed as a simplified discussion, I will skip the details and give you the bottom line: $68.0 million was added to fixed assets and $13.0 million was elimi-

---

[62] [A LIFO reserve is the difference between the current cost to replace inventory and the amount shown as the cost of inventory on a balance sheet. This difference can grow significantly, especially during inflationary periods.]

nated from deferred tax liabilities. After making this $81.0 million adjustment, we were left with $24.3 million of premium to allocate.

Had our situation called for them, two steps would next have been required: the adjustment of intangible assets other than Goodwill to current fair values, and the restatement of liabilities to current fair values, a requirement that typically affects only long-term debt and unfunded pension liabilities. In Scott Fetzer's case, however, neither of these steps was necessary.

The final accounting adjustment we needed to make, after recording fair market values for all assets and liabilities, was the assignment of the residual premium to Goodwill (technically known as "excess of cost over the fair value of net assets acquired"). This residual amounted to $24.3 million. Thus, the balance sheet of Scott Fetzer immediately before the acquisition, which is summarized below in column O, was transformed by the purchase into the balance sheet shown in column N. In real terms, both balance sheets depict the same assets and liabilities—but, as you can see, certain figures differ significantly.

	Company O	Company N
	(000s Omitted)	
Assets		
Cash and Cash Equivalents...........	$ 3,593	$ 3,593
Receivables, net	90,919	90,919
Inventories	77,489	114,764
Other	5,954	5,954
Total Current Assets	177,955	215,230
Property, Plant, and Equipment, net ..	80,967	148,960
Investments in the Advances to Unconsolidated Subsidiaries and Joint Ventures	93,589	93,589
Other Assets, including Goodwill	9,836	34,210
	$362,347	$491,989
Liabilities		
Notes Payable and Current Portion of Long-term Debt	$ 4,650	$ 4,650
Accounts Payable....................	39,003	39,003
Accrued Liabilities...................	84,939	84,939
Total Current Liabilities	128,592	128,592
Long-term Debt and Capitalized Leases	34,669	34,669
Deferred Income Taxes	17,052	4,075
Other Deferred Credits	9,657	9,657
Total Liabilities	189,970	176,993
Shareholder's Equity.................	172,377	314,996
	$362,347	$491,989

The higher balance sheet figures shown in column N produce the lower income figures shown in column N of the earnings statement presented earlier. This is the result of the asset write-ups and of the fact that some of the written-up assets must be depreciated or amortized. The higher the asset figure, the higher the annual depreciation or amortization charge to earnings must be. The charges that flowed to the earnings statement because of the balance sheet write-ups were numbered in the statement of earnings shown earlier:

1. $4,979,000 for non-cash inventory costs resulting, primarily, from reductions that Scott Fetzer made in its inventories during 1986; charges of this kind are apt to be small or non-existent in future years.

2. $5,054,000 for extra depreciation attributable to the write-up of fixed assets; a charge approximating this amount will probably be made annually for 12 more years.

3. $595,000 for amortization of Goodwill; this charge will be made annually for 39 more years in a slightly larger amount because our purchase was made on January 6 and, therefore, the 1986 figure applies to only 98% of the year.

4. $998,000 for deferred-tax acrobatics that are beyond my ability to explain briefly (or perhaps even non-briefly); a charge approximating this amount will probably be made annually for 12 more years.

By the end of 1986 the difference between the net worth of the "old" and "new" Scott Fetzer had been reduced from $142.6 million to $131.0 million by means of the extra $11.6 million that was charged to earnings of the new entity. As the years go by, similar charges to earnings will cause most of the premium to disappear, and the two balance sheets will converge. However, the higher land values and most of the higher inventory values that were established on the new balance sheet will remain unless land is disposed of or inventory levels are further reduced.

*   *   *   *   *

What does all this mean for owners? Did the shareholders of Berkshire buy a business that earned $40.2 million in 1986 or did they buy one earning $28.6 million? Were those $11.6 million of new charges a real economic cost to us? Should investors pay more for the stock of Company O than of Company N? And, if a business is worth some given multiple of earnings, was Scott Fetzer worth considerably more the day before we bought it than it was worth the following day?

If we think through these questions, we can gain some insights about what may be called "owner earnings." These represent (a) reported earnings plus (b) depreciation, depletion, amortization, and certain other non-cash charges such as Company N's items (1) and (4) less (c) the average annual amount of capitalized expenditures for plant and equipment, etc. that the business requires to fully maintain its long-term competitive position and its unit volume. (If the business requires additional working capital to maintain its competitive position and unit volume, the increment also should be included in (c). However, businesses following the LIFO inventory method usually do not require additional working capital if unit volume does not change.)

Our owner-earnings equation does not yield the deceptively precise figures provided by GAAP, since (c) must be a guess—and one sometimes very difficult to make. Despite this problem, we consider the owner earnings figure, not the GAAP figure, to be the relevant item for valuation purposes—both for investors in buying stocks and for managers in buying entire businesses.

The approach we have outlined produces "owner earnings" for Company O and Company N that are identical, which means valuations are also identical, just as common sense would tell you should be the case. This result is reached because the sum of (a) and (b) is the same in both columns O and N, and because (c) is necessarily the same in both cases.

And what do Charlie and I, as owners and managers, believe is the correct figure for the owner earnings of Scott Fetzer? Under current circumstances, we believe (c) is very close to the "old" company's (b) number of $8.3 million and much below the "new" company's (b) number of $19.9 million. Therefore, we believe that owner earnings are far better depicted by the reported earnings in the O column than by those in the N column. In other words, we feel owner earnings of Scott Fetzer are considerably larger than the GAAP figures that we report.

That is obviously a happy state of affairs. But calculations of this sort usually do not provide such pleasant news. Most managers probably will acknowledge that they need to spend something more than (b) on their businesses over the longer term just to hold their ground in terms of both unit volume and competitive position. When this imperative exists—that is, when (c) exceeds (b)— GAAP earnings overstate owner earnings. Frequently this overstatement is substantial. The oil industry has in recent years provided a conspicuous example of this phenomenon. Had most major oil companies spent only (b) each year, they would have guaranteed their shrinkage in real terms.

All of this points up the absurdity of the "cash flow" numbers that are often set forth in Wall Street reports. These numbers routinely include (a) plus (b)—but do not subtract (c). Most sales brochures of investment bankers also feature deceptive presentations of this kind. These imply that the business being offered is the commercial counterpart of the Pyramids—forever state-of-the-art, never needing to be replaced, improved or refurbished. Indeed, if all U.S. corporations were to be offered simultaneously for sale through our leading investment bankers—and if the sales brochures describing them were to be believed—governmental projections of national plant and equipment spending would have to be slashed by 90%.

"Cash Flow," true, may serve as a shorthand of some utility in descriptions of certain real estate businesses or other enterprises that make huge initial outlays and only tiny outlays thereafter. A company whose only holding is a bridge or an extremely long-lived gas field would be an example. But "cash flow" is meaningless in such businesses as manufacturing, retailing, extractive companies, and utilities because, for them, (c) is always significant. To be sure, businesses of this kind may in a given year be able to defer capital spending. But over a five- or ten-year period, they must make the investment—or the business decays.

Why, then, are "cash flow" numbers so popular today? In answer, we confess our cynicism: we believe these numbers are frequently used by marketers of businesses and securities in attempts to justify the unjustifiable (and thereby to sell what should be the unsaleable). When (a)—that is, GAAP earnings—looks by itself inadequate to service debt of a junk bond or justify a foolish stock price, how convenient it becomes for salesmen to focus on (a) + (b). But you shouldn't add (b) without subtracting (c): though dentists correctly claim that if you ignore your teeth they'll go away, the same is not true for (c). The company or investor believing that the debt-servicing ability or the equity valuation of an enterprise can be measured by totalling (a) and (b) while ignoring (c) is headed for certain trouble.

*   *   *   *   *

To sum up: in the case of both Scott Fetzer and our other businesses, we feel that (b) on an historical-cost basis—i.e., with both amortization of intangibles and other purchase-price adjustments excluded—is quite close in amount to (c). (The two items are not identical, of course. For example, at See's we annually make capitalized expenditures that exceed depreciation by $500,000 to $1 million, simply to hold our ground competitively.) Our conviction about this point is the reason we show our amortization and other purchase-price adjustment items separately . . . and is also our reason for viewing the earnings of the individual businesses . . . as much more closely approximating owner earnings than the GAAP figures.

Questioning GAAP figures may seem impious to some. After all, what are we paying the accountants for if it is not to deliver us the "truth" about our business. But the accountants' job is to record, not to evaluate. The evaluation job falls to investors and managers.

Accounting numbers of course, are the language of business and as such are of enormous help to anyone evaluating the worth of a business and tracking its progress. Charlie and I would be lost without these numbers: they invariably are the starting point for us in evaluating our own businesses and those of others. Managers and owners need to remember, however, that accounting is but an aid to business thinking, never a substitute for it.

F.   *Option Valuation*[63]

The Black-Scholes formula has approached the status of holy writ in finance, and we use it when valuing our equity put options for financial statement purposes. Key inputs to the calculation include a contract's maturity and strike price, as well as the analyst's expectations for volatility, interest rates and dividends.

If the formula is applied to extended time periods, however, it can produce absurd results. In fairness, Black and Scholes almost certainly understood this point well. But their devoted followers may be ignoring whatever caveats the two men attached when they first unveiled the formula.

It's often useful in testing a theory to push it to extremes. So let's postulate that we sell a 100-year $1 billion put option on the S&P 500 at a strike price of 903 (the index's level on 12/31/08).

---

[63] [2008; 2010.]

Using the implied volatility assumption for long-dated contracts that we do, and combining that with appropriate interest and dividend assumptions, we would find the "proper" Black-Scholes premium for this contract to be $2.5 million.

To judge the rationality of that premium, we need to assess whether the S&P will be valued a century from now at less than today. Certainly the dollar will then be worth a small fraction of its present value (at only 2% inflation it will be worth roughly 14¢). So that will be a factor pushing the stated value of the index higher. Far more important, however, is that one hundred years of retained earnings will hugely increase the value of most of the companies in the index. In the 20th Century, the Dow-Jones Industrial Average increased by about 175-fold, mainly because of this retained-earnings factor.

Considering everything, I believe the probability of a decline in the index over a one-hundred-year period to be *far* less than 1%. But let's use that figure and also assume that the most likely decline—should one occur—is 50%. Under these assumptions, the mathematical expectation of loss on our contract would be $5 million ($1 billion X 1% X 50%).

But if we had received our theoretical premium of $2.5 million up front, we would have only had to invest it at 0.7% compounded annually to cover this loss expectancy. Everything earned above that would have been profit. Would you like to borrow money for 100 years at a 0.7% rate?

Let's look at my example from a worst-case standpoint. Remember that 99% of the time we would pay nothing if my assumptions are correct. But even in the worst case among the remaining 1% of possibilities—that is, one assuming a *total* loss of $1 billion—our borrowing cost would come to only 6.2%. Clearly, either my assumptions are crazy or the formula is inappropriate.

The ridiculous premium that Black-Scholes dictates in my extreme example is caused by the inclusion of volatility in the formula and by the fact that volatility is determined by how much stocks have moved around in some past period of days, months or years. This metric is simply irrelevant in estimating the probability weighted range of values of American business 100 years from now. (Imagine, if you will, getting a quote every day on a farm from a manic-depressive neighbor and then using the volatility calculated from these changing quotes as an important ingredient in an equation that predicts a probability-weighted range of values for the farm a century from now.)

Though historical volatility is a useful—but far from fool-proof—concept in valuing short-term options, its utility diminishes rapidly as the duration of the option lengthens. In my opinion, the valuations that the Black-Scholes formula now place on our long-term put options overstate our liability, though the overstatement will diminish as the contracts approach maturity.

Even so, we will continue to use Black-Scholes when we are estimating our financial-statement liability for long-term equity puts. The formula represents conventional wisdom and any substitute that I might offer would engender extreme skepticism. That would be perfectly understandable: CEOs who have concocted their own valuations for esoteric financial instruments have seldom erred on the side of conservatism. That club of optimists is one that Charlie and I have no desire to join.

Both Charlie and I believe that Black-Scholes produces wildly inappropriate values when applied to long-dated options. [Besides the hypothetical example given above,] we put our money where our mouth was by entering into our equity put contracts. By doing so, we implicitly asserted that the Black-Scholes calculations used by our counterparties or their customers were faulty.

We continue, nevertheless, to use that formula in presenting our financial statements. Black-Scholes is the accepted standard for option valuation—almost all leading business schools teach it—and we would be accused of shoddy accounting if we deviated from it. Moreover, we would present our auditors with an insurmountable problem were we to do that: They have clients who are our counterparties and who use Black-Scholes values for the same contracts we hold. It would be impossible for our auditors to attest to the accuracy of both their values and ours were the two far apart.

Part of the appeal of Black-Scholes to auditors and regulators is that it produces a precise number. Charlie and I can't supply one of those. We believe the true liability of our contracts to be far lower than that calculated by Black-Scholes, but we can't come up with an exact figure—anymore than we can come up with a *precise* value for GEICO, BNSF, or for Berkshire Hathaway itself. Our inability to pinpoint a number doesn't bother us: We would rather be approximately right than precisely wrong.

John Kenneth Galbraith once slyly observed that economists were most economical with ideas: They made the ones learned in graduate school last a lifetime. University finance departments often behave similarly. Witness the tenacity with which almost all clung to the theory of efficient markets throughout the 1970s and 1980s, dismissively calling powerful facts that refuted it "anomalies." (I always love explanations of that kind: The Flat Earth Society probably views a ship's circling of the globe as an annoying, but inconsequential, anomaly.)

VII. Accounting Shenanigans

Despite the shortcomings of generally accepted accounting principles (GAAP), I would hate to have the job of devising a better set of rules. The limitations of the existing set, however, need not be inhibiting: CEOs are free to treat GAAP statements as a beginning rather than an end to their obligation to inform owners and creditors—and indeed they should. After all, any manager of a subsidiary company would find himself in hot water if he reported barebones GAAP numbers that omitted key information needed by his boss, the parent corporation's CEO. Why, then, should the CEO himself withhold information vitally useful to *his* bosses—the shareholder-owners of the corporation?

What needs to be reported is data—whether GAAP, non-GAAP, or extra-GAAP—that helps financially-literate readers answer three key questions: (1) Approximately how much is this company worth? (2) What is the likelihood that it can meet its future obligations? and (3) How good a job are its managers doing, given the hand they have been dealt?

In most cases, answers to one or more of these questions are somewhere between difficult and impossible to glean from the minimum GAAP presentation. The business world is simply too complex for a single set of rules to effectively describe economic reality for all enterprises, particularly those operating in a wide variety of businesses, such as Berkshire.

Further complicating the problem is the fact that many managements view GAAP not as a standard to be met, but as an obstacle to overcome. Too often their accountants willingly assist them. ("How much," says the client, "is two plus two?" Replies the co-operative accountant, "What number did you have in mind?") Even honest and well-intentioned managements sometimes stretch GAAP a bit in order to present figures they think will more appropriately describe their performance. Both the smoothing of earnings and the "big bath" quarter are "white lie" techniques employed by otherwise upright managements.

Then there are managers who actively use GAAP to deceive and defraud. They know that many investors and creditors accept GAAP results as gospel. So these charlatans interpret the rules "imaginatively" and record business transactions in ways that technically comply with GAAP but actually display an economic illusion to the world.

As long as investors—including supposedly sophisticated institutions—place fancy valuations on reported "earnings" that march steadily upward, you can be sure that some managers and promoters will exploit GAAP to produce such numbers, no matter what the truth may be. Over the years, Charlie and I have observed many accounting-based frauds of staggering size. Few of the perpetrators have been punished; many have not even been censured. It has been far safer to steal large sums with a pen than small sums with a gun.[64]

A. *Satire*[65]

U.S. STEEL ANNOUNCES
SWEEPING MODERNIZATION SCHEME*

Myron C. Taylor, Chairman of U.S. Steel Corporation, today announced the long awaited plan for completely modernizing the world's largest industrial enterprise. Contrary to expectations, no changes will be made in the company's manufacturing or selling policies. Instead, the bookkeeping system is to be entirely revamped. By adopting and further improving a number of modern accounting and financial devices the corporation's earning power will be amazingly transformed. Even under the subnormal conditions of 1935, it is estimated that the new bookkeeping methods would have yielded a reported profit of close to $50 per share on the common stock. The scheme of improvement is the result of a comprehensive survey made by Messrs. Price, Bacon, Guthrie & Colpitts; it includes the following six points:

1. Writing down of Plant Account to Minus $1,000,000,000.
2. Par Value of Common Stock to be reduced to 1¢.
3. Payment of all wages and salaries in option warrants.
4. Inventories to be carried at $1.
5. Preferred Stock to be replaced by non-interest bearing bonds redeemable at 50% discount.
6. A $1,000,000,000 Contingency Reserve to be established.

The official statement of this extraordinary Modernization Plan follows in full:

The Board of Directors of U.S. Steel Corporation is pleased to announce that after intensive study of the problems arising from changed conditions in the industry, it has approved a comprehensive plan for remodeling the Corporation's accounting methods. A

---

[64] [Introductory essay, 1988.]
[65] [1990 Appendix A.]
* An unpublished satire by Ben Graham, written in 1936 and given by the author to Warren Buffett in 1954.

survey by a Special Committee, aided and abetted by Messrs. Price, Bacon, Guthrie & Colpitts, revealed that our company has lagged somewhat behind other American business enterprises in utilizing certain advanced bookkeeping methods, by means of which the earning power may be phenomenally enhanced without requiring any cash outlay or any changes in operating or sales conditions. It has been decided not only to adopt these newer methods, but to develop them to a still higher stage of perfection. The changes adopted by the Board may be summarized under six heads, as follows:

1.   Fixed Assets to be written down to *Minus $1,000,000,000*.

Many representative companies have relieved their income accounts of all charges for depreciation by writing down their plant account to $1. The Special Committee points out that if their plants are worth only $1, the fixed assets of U.S. Steel Corporation are worth a good deal less than that sum. It is now a well-recognized fact that many plants are in reality a liability rather than an asset, entailing not only depreciation charges, but taxes, maintenance, and other expenditures. Accordingly, the Board has decided to extend the write-down policy initiated in the 1935 report, and to mark down the Fixed Assets from $1,338,522,858.96 to a round *Minus $1,000,000,000*.

The advantages of this move should be evident. As the plant wears out, the liability becomes correspondingly reduced. Hence, instead of the present depreciation charge of some $47,000,000 yearly there will be an annual *appreciation credit* of 5%, or $50,000,000. This will increase earnings by no less than $97,000,000 per annum.

2.   Reduction of Par Value of Common Stock to 1¢, and

3.   Payment of Salaries and Wages in Option Warrants.

Many corporations have been able to reduce their overhead expenses substantially by paying a large part of their executive salaries in the form of options to buy stock, which carry no charge against earnings. The full possibilities of this modern device have apparently not been adequately realized. The Board of Directors have adopted the following advanced form of this idea:

The entire personnel of the Corporation are to receive their compensation in the form of rights to buy common stock at $50 per share, at the rate of one purchase right for each $50 of salary and/ or wages in their present amounts. The par value of the common stock is to be reduced to 1¢.

The almost incredible advantages of this new plan are evident from the following:

A.   The payroll of the Corporation will be entirely eliminated, a saving of $250,000,000 per annum, based on 1935 operations.

B.   At the same time, the effective compensation of all our employees will be increased severalfold. Because of the large earnings per share to be shown on our common stock under the new methods, it is certain that the shares will command a price in the market far above the option level of $50 per share, making the readily realizable value of these option warrants greatly in excess of the present cash wages that they will replace.

C.   The Corporation will realize an additional large annual profit through the exercise of these warrants. Since the par value of the common stock will be fixed at 1¢, there will be a gain of $49.99 on each share subscribed for. In the interest of conservative accounting, however, this profit will not be included in the income account, but will be shown separately as a credit to Capital Surplus.

D.   The Corporation's cash position will be enormously strengthened. In place of the present annual cash *outgo* of $250,000,000 for wages (1935 basis), there will be annual cash *inflow* of $250,000,000 through exercise of the subscription warrants for 5,000,000 shares of common stock. The Company's large earnings and strong cash position will permit the payment of a liberal dividend which, in turn, will result in the exercise of these option warrants immediately after issuance which, in turn, will further improve the cash position which, in turn, will permit a higher dividend rate—and so on, indefinitely.

4.   Inventories to be carried at $1.

Serious losses have been taken during the depression due to the necessity of adjusting inventory value to market. Various enterprises—notably in the metal and cotton-textile fields—have successfully dealt with this problem by carrying all or part of their inventories at extremely low unit prices. The U.S. Steel Corporation has decided to adopt a still more progressive policy, and to carry its entire inventory at $1. This will be effected by an appropriate write-down at the end of each year, the amount of said write-down to be charged to the Contingency Reserve hereinafter referred to.

The benefits to be derived from this new method are very great. Not only will it obviate all possibility of inventory depreciation, but it will substantially enhance the annual earnings of the Corporation. The inventory on hand at the beginning of the year, valued at $1, will be sold during the year at an excellent profit. It is estimated that our income will be increased by means of this method to the extent of at least $150,000,000 per annum which, by a coincidence, will about equal the amount of the write-down to be made each year against Contingency Reserve.

A minority report of the Special Committee recommends that Accounts Receivable and Cash also be written down to $1, in the interest of consistency and to gain additional advantages similar to those just discussed. This proposal has been rejected for the time being because our auditors still require that any recoveries of receivables and cash so charged off be credited to surplus instead of to the year's income. It is expected, however, that this auditing rule—which is rather reminiscent of the horse-and-buggy days—will soon be changed in line with modern tendencies. Should this occur, the minority report will be given further and favorable consideration.

5. Replacement of Preferred Stock by Non-Interest Bearing Bonds Redeemable at 50% Discount.

During the recent depression many companies have been able to offset their operating losses by including in income profits arising from repurchases of their own bonds at a substantial discount from par. Unfortunately the credit of U.S. Steel Corporation has always stood so high that this lucrative source of revenue has not hitherto been available to it. The Modernization Scheme will remedy this condition.

It is proposed that each share of preferred stock be exchanged for $300 face value of non-interest-bearing sinking-fund notes, redeemable by lot at 50% of face value in 10 equal annual installments. This will require the issuance of $1,080,000,000 of new notes, of which $108,000,000 will be retired each year at a cost to the Corporation of only $54,000,000, thus creating an annual profit of the same amount.

Like the wage-and/or-salary plan described under 3. above, this arrangement will benefit both the Corporation and its preferred stockholders. The latter are assured payment for their present shares at 150% of par value over an average period of five years. Since short-term securities yield practically no return at present, the non-interest-bearing feature is of no real importance. The Corporation will convert its present annual *charge* of $25,000,000 for preferred dividends into an annual bond-retirement *profit* of $54,000,000—an aggregate yearly gain of $79,000,000.

6.   Establishment of a Contingency Reserve of $1,000,000,000.

The Directors are confident that the improvements hereinbefore described will assure the Corporation of a satisfactory earning power under all conditions in the future. Under modern accounting methods, however, it is unnecessary to incur the slightest risk of loss through adverse business developments of any sort, since all these may be provided for in advance by means of a Contingency Reserve.

The Special Committee has recommended that the Corporation create such a Contingency Reserve in the fairly substantial amount of $1,000,000,000. As previously set forth, the annual write-down of inventory of $1 will be absorbed by this reserve. To prevent eventual exhaustion of the Contingency Reserve, it has been further decided that it be replenished each year by transfer of an appropriate sum from Capital Surplus. Since the latter is expected to increase each year by not less than $250,000,000 through the exercise of the Stock Option Warrants (see 3. above), it will readily make good any drains on the Contingency Reserve.

In setting up this arrangement, the Board of Directors must confess regretfully that they have been unable to improve upon the devices already employed by important corporations in transferring large sums between Capital, Capital Surplus, Contingency Reserves and other Balance Sheet Accounts. In fact, it must be admitted that our entries will be somewhat too simple, and will lack that element of extreme mystification that characterizes the most advanced procedure in this field. The Board of Directors, however, have insisted upon clarity and simplicity in framing their Modernization Plan, even at the sacrifice of possible advantage to the Corporation's earning power.

In order to show the combined effect of the new proposals upon the Corporation's earning power, we submit herewith a condensed Income Account for 1935 on two bases, viz:

	A. As Reported	B. Pro-Forma Giving Effect to Changes Proposed Herewith
Gross Receipts from all Sources (Including Inter Company)	$765,000,000	$765,000,000
Salaries and Wages	251,000,000	—
Other Operating Expenses and Taxes	461,000,000	311,000,000
Depreciation	47,000,000	(50,000,000)
Interest	5,000,000	5,000,000
Discount on Bonds Retired...............	—	(54,000,000)
Preferred Dividends......................	25,000,000	—
Balance for Common	(24,000,000)	553,000,000
Average Shares Outstanding...............	8,703,252	11,203,252
Earned Per Share........................	($2.76)	$49.80

In accordance with a somewhat antiquated custom there is appended herewith a condensed pro-forma Balance Sheet of the U.S. Steel Corporation as of December 31, 1935, after giving effect to proposed changes in asset and liability accounts.

ASSETS

Fixed Assets, net	($1,000,000,000)
Cash Assets	142,000,000
Receivables....................................	56,000,000
Inventory......................................	1
Miscellaneous Assets	27,000,000
Total.......................................	($774,999,999)

LIABILITIES

Common Stock Par 1¢ (Par Value $87,032.52) Stated Value*	($3,500,000,000)
Subsidiaries' Bonds and Stocks	113,000,000
New Sinking Fund Notes	1,080,000,000
Current Liabilities	69,000,000
Contingency Reserve	1,000,000,000
Other Reserves................................	74,000,000
Initial Surplus	389,000,001
Total.......................................	($774,999,999)

*Given a Stated Value differing from Par Value, in accordance with the laws of the State of Virginia, where the company will be re-incorporated.

It is perhaps unnecessary to point out to our stockholders that modern accounting methods give rise to balance sheets differing somewhat in appearance from those of a less advanced period. In view of the very large earning power that will result from these changes in the Corporation's Balance Sheet, it is not expected that undue attention will be paid to the details of assets and liabilities.

In conclusion, the Board desires to point out that the combined procedure, whereby plant will be carried at a minus figure, our wage bill will be eliminated, and inventory will stand on our books at virtually nothing, will give U.S. Steel Corporation an enormous competitive advantage in the industry. We shall be able to sell our products at exceedingly low prices and still show a handsome margin of profit. It is the considered view of the Board of Directors that under the Modernization Scheme we shall be able to undersell all competitors to such a point that the anti-trust laws will constitute the only barrier to 100% domination of the industry.

In making this statement, the Board is not unmindful of the possibility that some of our competitors may seek to offset our new advantages by adopting similar accounting improvements. We are confident, however, that U.S. Steel will be able to retain the loyalty of its customers, old and new, through the unique prestige that will accrue to it as the originator and pioneer in these new fields of service to the user of steel. Should necessity arise, moreover, we believe we shall be able to maintain our deserved superiority by introducing still more advanced bookkeeping methods, which are even now under development in our Experimental Accounting Laboratory.

B. *Standard Setting*[66]

A few decades ago, an Arthur Andersen audit opinion was the gold standard of the profession. Within the firm, an elite Professional Standards Group (PSG) insisted on honest reporting, no matter what pressures were applied by the client. Sticking to these principles, the PSG took a stand in 1992 that the cost of stock options should be recorded as the expense it clearly was. The PSG's position was reversed, however, by the "rainmaking" partners of Andersen who knew what their clients wanted—higher reported earnings no matter what the reality. Many CEOs also fought expensing because they knew that the obscene mega-grants of options they craved would be slashed if the true costs of these had to be recorded.

Soon after the Andersen reversal, the independent accounting standards board (FASB) voted 7-0 for expensing options. Predictably, the major auditing firms and an army of CEOs stormed

---

[66] [2002.]

Washington to pressure the Senate—what better institution to decide accounting questions?—into castrating the FASB. The voices of the protesters were amplified by their large political contributions, usually made with corporate money belonging to the very owners about to be bamboozled. It was not a sight for a civics class.

To its shame, the Senate voted 88-9 against expensing. Several prominent Senators even called for the demise of the FASB if it didn't abandon its position. (So much for independence.) Arthur Levitt, Jr., then Chairman of the SEC—and generally a vigilant champion of shareholders—has since described his reluctant bowing to Congressional and corporate pressures as the act of his chairmanship that he most regrets. (The details of this sordid affair are related in Levitt's excellent book, *Take on the Street*.)

With the Senate in its pocket and the SEC outgunned, corporate America knew that it was now boss when it came to accounting. With that, a new era of anything-goes earnings reports— blessed and, in some cases, encouraged by big-name auditors—was launched. The licentious behavior that followed quickly became an air pump for The Great Bubble.

After being threatened by the Senate, FASB backed off its original position and adopted an "honor system" approach, declaring expensing to be preferable but also allowing companies to ignore the cost if they wished. The disheartening result: Of the 500 companies in the S&P, 498 adopted the method deemed less desirable, which of course let them report higher "earnings." Compensation-hungry CEOs loved this outcome: Let FASB have the honor; *they* had the system.

C. *Stock Options*[67]

The most egregious case of let's-not-face-up-to-reality behavior by executives and accountants has occurred in the world of stock options. In Berkshire's 1985 annual report, I laid out my opinions about the use and misuse of options.[68] But even when options are structured properly, they are accounted for in ways that make no sense. The lack of logic is not accidental: For decades, much of the business world has waged war against accounting rulemakers, trying to keep the costs of stock options from being reflected in the profits of the corporations that issue them.

---

[67] [Divided by hash lines: 1992; 1998; 2004.]

[68] [*See* the essay A Principled Approach to Executive Pay in Part I.F.]

Typically, executives have argued that options are hard to value and that therefore their costs should be ignored. At other times managers have said that assigning a cost to options would injure small start-up businesses. Sometimes they have even solemnly declared that "out-of-the-money" options (those with an exercise price equal to or above the current market price) have no value when they are issued.

Oddly, the Council of Institutional Investors has chimed in with a variation on that theme, opining that options should not be viewed as a cost because they "aren't dollars out of a company's coffers." I see this line of reasoning as offering exciting possibilities to American corporations for instantly improving their reported profits. For example, they could eliminate the cost of insurance by paying for it with options. So if you're a CEO and subscribe to this "no cash-no cost" theory of accounting, I'll make you an offer you can't refuse: Give us a call at Berkshire and we will happily sell you insurance in exchange for a bundle of long-term options on your company's stock.

Shareholders should understand that companies incur costs when they deliver something of value to another party and not just when cash changes hands. Moreover, it is both silly and cynical to say that an important item of cost should not be recognized simply because it can't be quantified with pinpoint precision. Right now, accounting abounds with imprecision. After all, no manager or auditor knows how long a 747 is going to last, which means he also does not know what the yearly depreciation charge for the plane should be. No one knows with any certainty what a bank's annual loan loss charge ought to be. And the estimates of losses that property casualty companies make are notoriously inaccurate.

Does this mean that these important items of cost should be ignored simply because they can't be quantified with absolute accuracy? Of course not. Rather, these costs should be estimated by honest and experienced people and then recorded. When you get right down to it, what other item of major but hard-to-precisely-calculate cost—other, that is, than stock options—does the accounting profession say should be ignored in the calculation of earnings?

Moreover, options are just not that difficult to value. Admittedly, the difficulty is increased by the fact that the options given to executives are restricted in various ways. These restrictions affect value. They do not, however, eliminate it. In fact, since I'm in the mood for offers, I'll make one to any executive who is granted a restricted option, even though it may be out of the money: On the day of issue, Berkshire will pay him or her a substantial sum for the right to any future gain he or she realizes on the option. So if you find a CEO who says his newly-issued options have little or no value, tell him to try us out. In truth, we have far more confidence in our ability to determine an appropriate price to pay for an option than we have in our ability to determine the proper depreciation rate for [a] corporate jet.

The accounting profession and the SEC should be shamed by the fact that they have long let themselves be muscled by business executives on the option-accounting issue. Additionally, the lobbying that executives engage in may have an unfortunate by-product: In my opinion, the business elite risks losing its credibility on issues of significance to society—about which it may have much of value to say—when it advocates the incredible on issues of significance to itself.

Our General Re acquisition put a spotlight on an egregious flaw in accounting procedure. Sharp-eyed shareholders reading our proxy statement probably noticed an unusual item on page 60. In the pro-forma statement of income—which detailed how the combined 1997 earnings of the two entities would have been affected by the merger—there was an item stating that compensation expense would have been increased by $63 million.

This item, we hasten to add, does not signal that either Charlie or I have experienced a major personality change. (He still travels coach and quotes Ben Franklin.) Nor does it indicate any shortcoming in General Re's accounting practices, which have followed GAAP to the letter. Instead, the pro-forma adjustment came about because we are replacing General Re's longstanding stock option plan with a cash plan that ties the incentive compensation of General Re managers to their operating achievements. Formerly what counted for these managers was General Re's stock price; now their payoff will come from the business performance they deliver.

The new plan and the terminated option arrangement have matching economics, which means that the rewards they deliver to employees should, for a given level of performance, be the same. But what these people could have formerly anticipated earning from new option grants will now be paid in cash. (Options granted in past years remain outstanding.)

Though the two plans are an economic wash, the cash plan we are putting in will produce a vastly different accounting result. This Alice-in-Wonderland outcome occurs because existing accounting principles ignore the cost of stock options when earnings are being calculated, even though options are a huge and increasing expense at a great many corporations. In effect, accounting principles offer management a choice: Pay employees in one form and count the cost, or pay them in another form and ignore the cost. Small wonder then that the use of options has mushroomed. This lop-sided choice has a big downside for owners, however: Though options, if properly structured, can be an appropriate, *and even ideal*, way to compensate and motivate top managers, they are more often wildly capricious in their distribution of rewards, inefficient as motivators, and inordinately expensive for shareholders.

Whatever the merits of options may be, their accounting treatment is outrageous. Think for a moment of [the hundreds of millions] we spend for advertising at GEICO [each] year. Suppose that instead of paying cash for our ads, we paid the media in ten-year, at-the-market Berkshire options. Would anyone then care to argue that Berkshire had not borne a cost for advertising, or should not be charged this cost on its books?

Perhaps Bishop Berkeley—you may remember him as the philosopher who mused about trees falling in a forest when no one was around—would believe that an expense unseen by an accountant does not exist. Charlie and I, however, have trouble being philosophical about unrecorded costs. When we consider investing in an option-issuing company, we make an appropriate downward adjustment to reported earnings, simply subtracting an amount equal to what the company could have realized by publicly selling options of like quantity and structure. Similarly, if we contemplate an acquisition, we include in our evaluation the cost of replacing any option plan. Then, if we make a deal, we promptly take that cost out of hiding.

Readers who disagree with me about options will by this time be mentally quarreling with my equating the cost of options issued to employees with those that might theoretically be sold and traded publicly. It is true, to state one of these arguments, that employee options are sometimes forfeited—that lessens the damage done to shareholders—whereas publicly-offered options would not be. It is true, also, that companies receive a tax deduction when employee options are exercised; publicly-traded options deliver no such benefit. But there's an offset to these points: Options issued to employees are often repriced, a transformation that makes them much more costly than the public variety.

It's sometimes argued that a non-transferable option given to an employee is less valuable to him than would be a publicly-traded option that he could freely sell. That fact, however, does not reduce the *cost* of the non-transferable option: Giving an employee a company car that can only be used for certain purposes diminishes its value to the employee, but does not in the least diminish its cost to the employer.

The earning revisions that Charlie and I have made for options in recent years have frequently cut the reported per-share figures by 5%, with 10% not all that uncommon. On occasion, the downward adjustment has been so great that it has affected our portfolio decisions, causing us either to make a sale or to pass on a stock purchase we might otherwise have made.

A few years ago we asked three questions to which we have not yet received an answer: "If options aren't a form of compensation, what are they? If compensation isn't an expense, what is it? And, if expenses shouldn't go into the calculation of earnings, where in the world should they go?"

Because the attempts to obfuscate the stock-option issue continue, it's worth pointing out that no one—neither the FASB, nor investors generally, nor I—are talking about restricting the use of options in any way. Indeed, my successor at Berkshire may well receive much pay via options, albeit logically-structured ones in respect to (1) an appropriate strike price, (2) an escalation in price that reflects the retention of earnings, and (3) a ban on his quickly disposing of any shares purchased through options. We cheer arrangements that motivate managers, whether these be cash bonuses or options. And if a company is truly receiving value for the options it issues, we see no reason why recording their cost should cut down on their use.[69]

D. *"Restructuring" Charges*[70]

The role that managements have played in stock-option accounting has hardly been benign: A distressing number of both CEOs and auditors have in recent years bitterly fought FASB's attempts to replace option fiction with truth and virtually none have

---

[69] [Option-expensing became mandatory in 2005.]
[70] [1998.]

spoken out in support of FASB. Its opponents even enlisted Congress in the fight, pushing the case that inflated figures were in the national interest.

Still, I believe that the behavior of managements has been even worse when it comes to restructurings and merger accounting. Here, many managements purposefully work at manipulating numbers and deceiving investors. And, as Michael Kinsley has said about Washington: "The scandal isn't in what's done that's *illegal* but rather in what's *legal*."

It was once relatively easy to tell the good guys in accounting from the bad: The late 1960's, for example, brought on an orgy of what one charlatan dubbed "bold, imaginative accounting" (the practice of which, incidentally, made him loved for a time by Wall Street because he never missed expectations). But most investors of that period knew who was playing games. And, to their credit, virtually all of America's most-admired companies then shunned deception.

In recent years, probity has eroded. Many major corporations still play things straight, but a significant and growing number of otherwise high-grade managers—CEOs you would be happy to have as spouses for your children or as trustees under your will—have come to the view that it's okay to manipulate earnings to satisfy what they believe are Wall Street's desires. Indeed, many CEOs think this kind of manipulation is not only okay, but actually their *duty*.

These managers start with the assumption, all too common, that their job at all times is to encourage the highest stock price possible (a premise with which we adamantly disagree). To pump the price, they strive, admirably, for operational excellence. But when operations don't produce the result hoped for, these CEOs resort to unadmirable accounting stratagems. These either manufacture the desired "earnings" or set the stage for them in the future.

Rationalizing this behavior, these managers often say that their shareholders will be hurt if their currency for doing deals—that is, their stock—is not fully-priced, and they also argue that in using accounting shenanigans to get the figures they want, they are only doing what everybody else does. Once such an everybody's-doing-it attitude takes hold, ethical misgivings vanish. Call this behavior Son of Gresham: Bad accounting drives out good.

The distortion *du jour* is the "restructuring charge," an accounting entry that can, of course, be legitimate but that too often is a device for manipulating earnings. In this bit of legerdemain, a large chunk of costs that should properly be attributed to a number of years is dumped into a single quarter, typically one already fated to disappoint investors. In some cases, the purpose of the charge is to clean up earnings misrepresentations of the past, and in others it is to prepare the ground for future misrepresentations. In either case, the size and timing of these charges is dictated by the cynical proposition that Wall Street will not mind if earnings fall short by $5 per share in a given quarter, just as long as this deficiency ensures that quarterly earnings in the future will consistently exceed expectations by five cents per share.

This dump-everything-into-one-quarter behavior suggests a corresponding "bold, imaginative" approach to—golf scores. In his first round of the season, a golfer should ignore his actual performance and simply fill his card with atrocious numbers—double, triple, quadruple bogeys—and then turn in a score of, say, 140. Having established this "reserve," he should go to the golf shop and tell his pro that he wishes to "restructure" his imperfect swing. Next, as he takes his new swing onto the course, he should count his good holes, but not the bad ones. These remnants from his old swing should be charged instead to the reserve established earlier. At the end of five rounds, then, his record will be 140, 80, 80, 80, 80 rather than 91, 94, 89, 94, 92. On Wall Street, they will ignore the 140—which, after all, came from a "discontinued" swing—and will classify our hero as an 80 shooter (and one who *never* disappoints).

For those who prefer to cheat up front, there would be a variant of this strategy. The golfer, playing alone with a cooperative caddy-auditor, should defer the recording of bad holes, take four 80s, accept the plaudits he gets for such athleticism and consistency, and then turn in a fifth card carrying a 140 score. After rectifying his earlier scorekeeping sins with this "big bath," he may mumble a few apologies but will refrain from returning the sums he has previously collected from comparing scorecards in the clubhouse. (The caddy, need we add, will have acquired a loyal patron.)

Unfortunately, CEOs who use variations of these scoring schemes in real life tend to become addicted to the games they're playing—after all, it's easier to fiddle with the scorecard than to spend hours on the practice tee—and never muster the will to give them up. Their behavior brings to mind Voltaire's comment on sexual experimentation: "Once a philosopher, twice a pervert."

In the acquisition arena, restructuring has been raised to an art form: Managements now frequently use mergers to dishonestly rearrange the value of assets and liabilities in ways that will allow them to both smooth and swell future earnings. Indeed, at deal time, major auditing firms sometimes point out the possibilities for a little accounting magic (or for a lot). Getting this push from the pulpit, first-class people will frequently stoop to third-class tactics. CEOs understandably do not find it easy to reject auditor-blessed strategies that lead to increased future "earnings."

An example from the property-casualty insurance industry will illuminate the possibilities. When a p-c company is acquired, the buyer sometimes simultaneously increases its loss reserves, often substantially. This boost may merely reflect the previous inadequacy of reserves—though it is uncanny how often an actuarial "revelation" of this kind coincides with the inking of a deal. In any case, the move sets up the possibility of "earnings" flowing into income at some later date, as reserves are released.

Berkshire has kept entirely clear of these practices: If we are to disappoint you, we would rather it be with our earnings than with our accounting. In all of our acquisitions, we have left the loss reserve figures exactly as we found them. After all, we have consistently joined with insurance managers knowledgeable about their business and honest in their financial reporting. When deals occur in which liabilities are increased immediately and substantially, simple logic says that at least one of those virtues must have been lacking—or, alternatively, that the acquirer is laying the groundwork for future infusions of "earnings."

Here's a true story that illustrates an all-too-common view in corporate America. The CEOs of two large banks, one of them a man who'd made many acquisitions, were involved not long ago in a friendly merger discussion (which in the end didn't produce a deal). The veteran acquirer was expounding on the merits of the possible combination, only to be skeptically interrupted by the other CEO: "But won't that mean a huge charge," he asked, "perhaps as much as $1 billion?" The "sophisticate" wasted no words: "We'll make it bigger than that—that's why we're doing the deal."

A preliminary tally by R.G. Associates, of Baltimore, of special charges taken or announced during 1998—that is, charges for restructuring, in-process R&D, merger-related items, and write-downs—identified no less than 1,369 of these, totaling $72.1 billion. That is a staggering amount as evidenced by this bit of perspective:

The 1997 earnings of the 500 companies in *Fortune's* famous list totaled $324 billion.

Clearly the attitude of disrespect that many executives have today for accurate reporting is a business disgrace. And auditors, as we have already suggested, have done little on the positive side. Though auditors *should* regard the investing public as their client, they tend to kowtow instead to the managers who choose them and dole out their pay. ("Whose bread I eat, his song I sing.")

E.   *Pension Estimates and Retiree Benefits*[71]

[Shenanigans often result from the inherent discretion that accounting standards grant managers. Consider] the investment-return assumption a company uses in calculating pension expense. It will come as no surprise that many companies continue to choose an assumption that allows them to report less-than-solid "earnings." For the 363 companies in the S&P that have pension plans, this assumption in 2006 averaged 8%. Let's look at the chances of that being achieved.

The average holdings of bonds and cash for all pension funds is about 28%, and on these assets returns can be expected to be no more than 5%. Higher yields, of course, are obtainable but they carry with them a risk of commensurate (or greater) loss.

This means that the remaining 72% of assets—which are mostly in equities, either held directly or through vehicles such as hedge funds or private-equity investments—must earn 9.2% in order for the fund overall to achieve the postulated 8%. And that return must be delivered *after* all fees, which are now far higher than they have ever been.

How realistic is this expectation? During the 20th Century, the Dow advanced from 66 to 11,497. This gain, though it appears huge, shrinks to 5.3% when compounded annually. An investor who owned the Dow throughout the century would also have received generous dividends for much of the period, but only about 2% or so in the final years. It was a wonderful century.

Think now about *this* century. For investors to merely match that 5.3% market-value gain, the Dow—recently below 13,000— would need to close at about *2,000,000* on December 31, 2099. We are now eight years into this century, and we have racked up less than 2,000 of the 1,988,000 Dow points the market needed to travel in this hundred years to equal the 5.3% of the last.

---

[71] [2007; 1992.]

It's amusing that commentators regularly hyperventilate at the prospect of the Dow crossing an even number of thousands, such as 14,000 or 15,000. If they keep reacting that way, a 5.3% annual gain for the century will mean they experience at least 1,986 seizures during the next 92 years. While anything is possible, does anyone really believe this is the most likely outcome?

Dividends continue to run about 2%. Even if stocks were to average the 5.3% annual appreciation of the 1900s, the equity portion of plan assets—allowing for expenses of .5%—would produce no more than 7% or so. And .5% may well understate costs, given the presence of layers of consultants and high priced managers ("helpers").[72]

Naturally, everyone expects to be above average. And those helpers—bless their hearts—will certainly encourage their clients in this belief. But, as a class, the helper-aided group must be *below* average. The reason is simple: 1) Investors, overall, will necessarily earn an average return, minus costs they incur; 2) Passive and index investors, through their very inactivity, will earn that average minus costs that are very low; 3) With that group earning average returns, so must the remaining group—the active investors. But this group will incur high transaction, management, and advisory costs. Therefore, the active investors will have their returns diminished by a far greater percentage than will their inactive brethren. That means that the passive group—the "know-nothings"—must win.

I should mention that people who expect to earn 10% annually from equities during this century—envisioning that 2% of that will come from dividends and 8% from price appreciation—are implicitly forecasting a level of about *24,000,000* on the Dow by 2100. If your adviser talks to you about double digit returns from equities, explain this math to him—not that it will faze him. Many helpers are apparently direct descendants of the queen in Alice in Wonderland, who said: "Why, sometimes I've believed as many as six impossible things before breakfast." Beware the glib helper who fills your head with fantasies while he fills his pockets with fees.

Some companies have pension plans in Europe as well as in the U.S. and, in their accounting, almost all assume that the U.S. plans will earn more than the non-U.S. plans. This discrepancy is puzzling: Why should these companies not put their U.S. managers

---

[72] [*See* the essay The Bane of Trading: Transaction Costs in Part IV.A.]

in charge of the non-U.S. pension assets and let them work their magic on these assets as well? I've never seen this puzzle explained. But the auditors and actuaries who are charged with vetting the return assumptions seem to have no problem with it.

An accounting change [that took effect in 1993] mandates that businesses recognize their present-value liability for post-retirement health benefits. Though GAAP has previously required recognition of pensions to be paid in the future, it has illogically ignored the costs that companies will then have to bear for health benefits. The new rule will force many companies to record a huge balance-sheet liability (and a consequent reduction in net worth) and also henceforth to recognize substantially higher costs when they are calculating annual profits.

In recent decades, no CEO would have dreamed of going to his board with the proposition that his company become an insurer of uncapped post-retirement health benefits that other corporations chose to install. A CEO didn't need to be a medical expert to know that lengthening life expectancies and soaring health costs would guarantee an insurer a financial battering from such a business. Nevertheless, many a manager blithely committed his own company to a self-insurance plan embodying precisely the same promises—and thereby doomed his shareholders to suffer the inevitable consequences. In health-care, open-ended promises have created open-ended liabilities that in a few cases loom so large as to threaten the global competitiveness of major American industries.

I believe part of the reason for this reckless behavior was that accounting rules did not, for so long, require the booking of post-retirement health costs as they were incurred. Instead, the rules allowed cash-basis accounting, which vastly understated the liabilities that were building up. In effect, the attitude of both managements and their accountants toward these liabilities was "out-of-sight, out-of-mind." Ironically, some of these same managers would be quick to criticize Congress for employing "cash-basis" thinking in respect to Social Security promises or other programs creating future liabilities of size.

Managers thinking about accounting issues should never forget one of Abraham Lincoln's favorite riddles: "How many legs does a dog have if you call his tail a leg?" The answer: "Four, because calling a tail a leg does not make it a leg." It behooves managers to remember that Abe's right even if an auditor is willing to certify that the tail is a leg.

F. *Realization Events*[73]

Let's focus on a number [that] many in the media feature above all others: net income. Important though that number may be at most companies, it is almost always *meaningless* at Berkshire. Regardless of how our businesses might be doing, Charlie and I could—quite legally—cause net income in any given period to be almost any number we would like.

We have that flexibility because *realized* gains or losses on investments go into the net income figure, whereas *unrealized* gains (and, in most cases, losses) are excluded. For example, imagine that Berkshire had a $10 billion increase in unrealized gains in a given year and concurrently had $1 billion of realized losses. Our net income—which would count only the loss—would be reported as *less* than our operating income. If we had meanwhile realized gains in the *previous* year, headlines might proclaim that our earnings were down X% when in reality our business might be much improved.

If we really thought net income important, we could regularly feed realized gains into it simply because we have a huge amount of unrealized gains upon which to draw. Rest assured, though, that Charlie and I have *never* sold a security because of the effect a sale would have on the net income we were soon to report. We both have a deep disgust for "game playing" with numbers, a practice that was rampant throughout corporate America in the 1990s and still persists, though it occurs less frequently and less blatantly than it used to.

Operating earnings, despite having some shortcomings, are in general a reasonable guide as to how our businesses are doing. Ignore our net income figure, however. Regulations require that we report it to you. But if you find reporters focusing on it, that will speak more to their performance than ours.

Both realized and unrealized gains and losses are fully reflected in the calculation of our book value. Pay attention to the changes in that metric and to the course of our operating earnings, and you will be on the right track.

---

[73] [2010.]

VIII. TAXATION

[W]e would owe taxes of [many billions] were we to sell all of our securities at year-end market values. Is this liability equal, or even similar, to a liability payable to a trade creditor 15 days after the end of the year? Obviously not—despite the fact that both items have exactly the same effect on audited net worth.

On the other hand, is this liability for deferred taxes a meaningless accounting fiction because its payment can be triggered only by the sale of stocks that, in very large part, we have no intention of selling? Again, the answer is no.

In economic terms, the liability resembles an interest-free loan from the U.S. Treasury that comes due only at our election (unless, of course, Congress moves to tax gains before they are realized). This "loan" is peculiar in other respects as well: It can be used only to finance the ownership of the particular, appreciated stocks and it fluctuates in size—daily as market prices change and periodically if tax rates change. In effect, this deferred tax liability is equivalent to a very large transfer tax that is payable only if we elect to move from one asset to another.

Because of the way the tax law works, the Rip Van Winkle style of investing that we favor—if successful—has an important mathematical edge over a more frenzied approach. We have not, we should stress, adopted our strategy favoring long-term investment commitments because of these mathematics. Indeed, it is possible we could earn greater after-tax returns by moving rather frequently from one investment to another. Many years ago, that's exactly what Charlie and I did.

Now we would rather stay put, even if that means slightly lower returns. Our reason is simple: We have found splendid business relationships to be so rare and so enjoyable that we want to retain all we develop. This decision is particularly easy for us because we feel that these relationships will produce good—though perhaps not optimal—financial results. Considering that, we think it makes little sense for us to give up time with people we know to be interesting and admirable for time with others we do not know and who are likely to have human qualities far closer to average.[74]

---

[74] [Divided by hash lines: 1986; 1998.]

A. *Distribution of the Corporate Tax Burden*[75]

[O]ver the years there has been a lot of fuzzy and often partisan commentary about who really pays corporate taxes—businesses or their customers. The argument, of course, has usually turned around tax increases, not decreases. Those people resisting increases in corporate rates frequently argue that corporations in reality pay none of the taxes levied on them but, instead, act as a sort of economic pipeline, passing all taxes through to consumers. According to these advocates, any corporate-tax increase will simply lead to higher prices that, for the corporation, offset the increase. Having taken this position, proponents of the "pipeline" theory must also conclude that a tax decrease for corporations will not help profits but will instead flow through, leading to correspondingly lower prices for consumers.

Conversely, others argue that corporations not only pay the taxes levied upon them, but absorb them also. Consumers, this school says, will be unaffected by changes in corporate rates.

What really happens? When the corporate rate is cut, do Berkshire, The Washington Post, Cap Cities, etc., themselves soak up the benefits, or do these companies pass the benefits along to their customers in the form of lower prices? This is an important question for investors and managers, as well as for policymakers.

Our conclusion is that in some cases the benefits of lower corporate taxes fall exclusively, or almost exclusively, upon the corporation and its shareholders, and that in other cases the benefits are entirely, or almost entirely, passed through to the customer. What determines the outcome is the strength of the corporation's business franchise and whether the profitability of the franchise is regulated.

For example, when the franchise is strong and after-tax profits are regulated in a relatively precise manner, as is the case with electric utilities, changes in corporate tax rates are largely reflected in prices, not in profits. When taxes are cut, prices will usually be reduced in short order. When taxes are increased, prices will rise, though often not as promptly.

A similar result occurs in a second arena—in the price-competitive industry, whose companies typically operate with very weak business franchises. In such industries, the free market "regulates" after-tax profits in a delayed and irregular, but generally effective, manner. The marketplace, in effect, performs much the

---

[75] [Introductory essay, 1989.]

same function in dealing with the price-competitive industry as the Public Utilities Commission does in dealing with electric utilities. In these industries, therefore, tax changes eventually affect prices more than profits.

In the case of unregulated businesses blessed with strong franchises, however, it's a different story: the corporation and its shareholders are then the major beneficiaries of tax cuts. These companies benefit from a tax cut much as the electric company would if it lacked a regulator to force down prices.

Many of our businesses, both those we own in whole and in part, possess such franchises. Consequently, reductions in their taxes largely end up in our pockets rather than the pockets of our customers. While this may be impolitic to state, it is impossible to deny. If you are tempted to believe otherwise, think for a moment of the most able brain surgeon or lawyer in your area. Do you really expect the fees of this expert (the local "franchise-holder" in his or her specialty) to be reduced now that the top personal tax rate is being cut from 50% to 28%?

But tax increases will affect profits of Berkshire's property/ casualty companies even though they operate in an intensely price-competitive industry. The reason this industry is likely to be an exception to our general rule is that not all major insurers will be working with identical tax equations. Important differences will exist for several reasons: a new alternative minimum tax will materially affect some companies but not others; certain major insurers have huge loss carry-forwards that will largely shield their income from significant taxes for at least a few years; and the results of some large insurers will be folded into the consolidated returns of companies with non-insurance businesses. These disparate conditions will produce widely-varying marginal tax rates in the property/casualty industry. That will not be the case, however, in most other price-competitive industries, such as aluminum, autos and department stores, in which the major players will generally contend with similar tax equations.

The absence of a common tax calculus for property/casualty companies means that the increased taxes falling on the industry will probably not be passed along to customers to the degree that they would in a typical price-competitive industry. Insurers, in other words, will themselves bear much of the new tax burdens.

Berkshire's tax situation is sometimes misunderstood. First, capital gains have no special attraction for us: A corporation pays a

35% rate on taxable income, whether it comes from capital gains or from ordinary operations. This means that Berkshire's tax on a long-term capital gain is fully 75% higher than what an individual would pay on an identical gain.

Some people harbor another misconception, believing that we can exclude 70% of all dividends we receive from our taxable income. Indeed, the 70% rate applies to most corporations and also applies to Berkshire in cases where we hold stocks in non-insurance subsidiaries. However, almost all of our equity investments are owned by our insurance companies, and in that case the exclusion is 59.5%. That still means a dollar of dividends is considerably more valuable to us than a dollar of ordinary income, but not to the degree often assumed.

B.   Taxation and Investment Philosophy[76]

Berkshire is a substantial payer of federal income taxes. In aggregate, we will pay 1993 federal income taxes of $390 million, about $200 million of that attributable to operating earnings and $190 million to realized capital gains.

Speaking for our own shares, Charlie and I have absolutely no complaint about these taxes. We know we work in a market-based economy that rewards our efforts far more bountifully than it does the efforts of others whose output is of equal or greater benefit to society. Taxation should, and does, partially redress this inequity. But we still remain extraordinarily well-treated.

Berkshire and its shareholders, in combination, would pay a much smaller tax if Berkshire operated a partnership or "S" corporation, two structures often used for business activities. For a variety of reasons, that's not feasible for Berkshire to do. However, the penalty our corporate form imposes is mitigated—though far from eliminated—by our strategy of investing for the long term. Charlie and I would follow a buy-and-hold policy even if we ran a tax-exempt institution. We think it the soundest way to invest, and it also goes down the grain of our personalities. A third reason to favor this policy, however, is the fact that taxes are due only when gains are realized.

Through my favorite comic strip, Li'l Abner, I got a chance during my youth to see the benefits of delayed taxes, though I missed the lesson at the time. Making his readers feel superior, Li'l Abner bungled happily, but moronically, through life in Dogpatch.

---

[76] [Divided by hash lines: 1993; 2000; 2003.]

At one point he became infatuated with a New York temptress, Appassionatta Van Climax, but despaired of marrying her because he had only a single silver dollar and she was interested solely in millionaires. Dejected, Abner took his problem to Old Man Mose, the font of all knowledge in Dogpatch. Said the sage: Double your money 20 times and Appassionatta will be yours (1, 2, 4, 8 . . . . 1,048,576).

My last memory of the strip is Abner entering a roadhouse, dropping his dollar into a slot machine, and hitting a jackpot that spilled money all over the floor. Meticulously following Mose's advice, Abner picked up two dollars and went off to find his next double. Whereupon I dumped Abner and began reading Ben Graham.

Mose clearly was overrated as a guru: Besides failing to anticipate Abner's slavish obedience to instructions, he also forgot about taxes. Had Abner been subject, say, to the 35% federal tax rate that Berkshire pays, and had he managed one double annually, he would after 20 years only have accumulated $22,370. Indeed, had he kept on both getting his annual doubles and paying a 35% tax on each, he would have needed 7½ years more to reach the $1 million required to win Appassionatta.

But what if Abner had instead put his dollar in a single investment and held it until it doubled the same 27½ times? In that case, he would have realized about $200 million pre-tax or, after paying a $70 million tax in the final year, about $130 million after-tax. For that, Appassionatta would have crawled to Dogpatch. Of course, with 27½ years having passed, how Appassionatta would have looked to a fellow sitting on $130 million is another question.

What this little tale tells us is that tax-paying investors will realize a far, far greater sum from a single investment that compounds internally at a given rate than from a succession of investments compounding at the same rate. But I suspect many Berkshire shareholders figured that out long ago.

———————————

There's a powerful financial reason behind Berkshire's preference [to acquire 100% of a business rather than a small fraction], and that has to do with taxes. The tax code makes Berkshire's owning 80% or more of a business far more profitable for us, proportionately, than our owning a smaller share. When a company we own all of earns $1 million after tax, the entire amount inures to our benefit. If the $1 million is upstreamed to Berkshire, we owe no tax on the dividend. And, if the earnings are retained and we were to sell the subsidiary—not likely at Berkshire!—for $1 million more than we paid for it, we would owe no capital gains tax. That's because our "tax cost" upon sale would include both what we paid for the business and all earnings it subsequently retained.

Contrast that sitution to what happens when we own an investment in a marketable security. There, if we own a 10% stake in a business earning $10 million after tax, our $1 million share of the earnings is subject to additional state and federal taxes of (1) about $140,000 if it is distributed to us (our tax rate on most dividends is 14%); or (2) no less than $350,000 if the $1 million is retained and subsequently captured by us in the form of a capital gain (on which our tax rate is usually about 35%, though it sometimes approaches 40%). We may defer paying the $350,000 by not immediately realizing our gain, but eventually we must pay the tax. In effect, the government is our "partner" twice when we own part of a business through a stock investment, but only once when we own at least 80%.

———————

On May 20, 2003, *The Washington Post* ran an op-ed piece by me that was critical of the Bush tax proposals. Thirteen days later, Pamela Olson, Assistant Secretary for Tax Policy at the U.S. Treasury, delivered a speech about the new tax legislation saying, "That means a certain mid-western oracle, who, it must be noted, has played the tax code like a fiddle, is still safe retaining all his earnings." I think she was talking about me.

Alas, my "fiddle playing" will not get me to Carnegie Hall—or even to a high school recital. Berkshire, on your behalf and mine, will send the Treasury $3.3 billion for tax on its 2003 income, a sum equaling 2½% of the total income tax paid by all U.S. corporations in fiscal 2003. (In contrast, Berkshire's market valuation is about 1% of the value of all American corporations.)

Our payment will almost certainly place us among our country's top ten taxpayers. Indeed, if only 540 taxpayers paid the amount Berkshire will pay, no other individual or corporation would have to pay anything to Uncle Sam. That's right: 290 million Americans and all other businesses would not have to pay a dime in income, social security, excise or estate taxes to the federal government. (Here's the math: Federal tax receipts, including social security receipts, in fiscal 2003 totaled $1.782 trillion and 540 "Berkshires," each paying $3.3 billion, would deliver the same $1.782 trillion.)

Our federal tax return for 2002, when we paid $1.75 billion, covered a mere 8,905 pages. As is required, we dutifully filed two copies of this return, creating a pile of paper seven feet tall. At World Headquarters, our small band of 15.8 [personnel], though exhausted, momentarily flushed with pride: Berkshire, we felt, was surely pulling its share of our country's fiscal load.

I can understand why the Treasury is now frustrated with Corporate America and prone to outbursts. But it should look to Congress and the Administration for redress, not to Berkshire. Corporate income taxes in fiscal 2003 accounted for 7.4% of all federal tax receipts, down from a post-war peak of 32% in 1952. With one exception (1983), last year's percentage is the lowest recorded since data was first published in 1934.

Even so, tax breaks for corporations (and their investors, particularly large ones) were a major part of the Administration's 2002 and 2003 initiatives. If class warfare is being waged in America, my class is clearly winning. Today, many large corporations—run by CEOs whose fiddle-playing talents make your Chairman look like he is all thumbs—pay nothing close to the stated federal tax rate of 35%.

In 1985, Berkshire paid $132 million in federal income taxes, and all corporations paid $61 billion. The comparable amounts in 1995 were $286 million and $157 billion respectively. And, as mentioned, we will pay about $3.3 billion for 2003, a year when all corporations paid $132 billion. We hope our taxes continue to rise in the future—it will mean we are prospering—but we also hope that the rest of Corporate America antes up along with us. This might be a project for Ms. Olson to work on.

IX. Berkshire at Fifty and Beyond

Berkshire is now a sprawling conglomerate, constantly trying to sprawl further. Conglomerates, it should be acknowledged, have a terrible reputation with investors. And they richly deserve it. Let me first explain why they are in the doghouse, and then I will go on to describe why the conglomerate form brings huge and enduring advantages to Berkshire.[77]

A. *Conglomerates and Succession*[78]

Since I entered the business world, conglomerates have enjoyed several periods of extreme popularity, the silliest of which occurred in the late 1960s. The drill for conglomerate CEOs then was simple: By personality, promotion or dubious accounting—and often by all three—these managers drove a fledgling conglomerate's stock to, say, 20 times earnings and then issued shares as fast as possible to acquire another business selling at ten-or-so times earnings. They immediately applied "pooling" accounting to the acquisition, which—with not a dime's worth of change in the underlying businesses—automatically increased per-share earnings, and used the rise as proof of managerial genius. They next explained to investors that this sort of talent justified the maintenance, or even the enhancement, of the acquirer's p/e multiple. And, finally, they promised to endlessly repeat this procedure and thereby create ever-increasing per-share earnings.

Wall Street's love affair with this hocus-pocus intensified as the 1960s rolled by. The Street's denizens are always ready to suspend disbelief when dubious maneuvers are used to manufacture rising per-share earnings, particularly if these acrobatics produce mergers that generate huge fees for investment bankers. Auditors willingly sprinkled their holy water on the conglomerates' accounting and sometimes even made suggestions as to how to further juice the numbers. For many, gushers of easy money washed away ethical sensitivities.

Since the per-share earnings gains of an expanding conglomerate came from exploiting p/e differences, its CEO had to search for businesses selling at low multiples of earnings. These, of course, were characteristically mediocre businesses with poor long-term prospects. This incentive to bottom-fish usually led to a conglomerate's collection of underlying businesses becoming [ever junkier].

---

[77] [Introductory paragraph, 2014, 50th Anniversary section.]
[78] [2015, 50th Anniversary section.]

287

That mattered little to investors: It was deal velocity and pooling accounting they looked to for increased earnings.

The resulting firestorm of merger activity was fanned by an adoring press. Companies such as ITT, Litton Industries, Gulf & Western, and LTV were lionized, and their CEOs became celebrities. (These once-famous conglomerates are now long gone. As Yogi Berra said, "Every Napoleon meets his Watergate.") Back then, accounting shenanigans of all sorts—many of them ridiculously transparent—were excused or overlooked. Indeed, having an accounting wizard at the helm of an expanding conglomerate was viewed as a huge plus: Shareholders in those instances could be sure that *reported* earnings would never disappoint, no matter how bad the operating realities of the business might become.

In the late 1960s, I attended a meeting at which an acquisitive CEO bragged of his "bold, imaginative accounting." Most of the analysts listening responded with approving nods, seeing themselves as having found a manager whose forecasts were certain to be met, whatever the business results might be. Eventually, however, the clock struck twelve, and everything turned to pumpkins and mice. Once again, it became evident that business models based on the serial issuances of overpriced shares—just like chain-letter models—most assuredly redistribute wealth, but in no way create it. Both phenomena, nevertheless, periodically blossom in our country—they are every promoter's dream—though often they appear in a carefully-crafted disguise. The ending is always the same: Money flows from the gullible to the fraudster. And with stocks, unlike chain letters, the sums hijacked can be staggering.

So what do Charlie and I find so attractive about Berkshire's conglomerate structure? To put the case simply: If the conglomerate form is used judiciously, it is an ideal structure for maximizing long-term capital growth. One of the heralded virtues of capitalism is that it efficiently allocates funds. The argument is that markets will direct investment to promising businesses and deny it to those destined to wither. That is true: With all its excesses, market-driven allocation of capital is usually far superior to any alternative.

Nevertheless, there are often obstacles to the rational movement of capital. A CEO with capital employed in a declining operation seldom elects to massively redeploy that capital into unrelated activities. A move of that kind would usually require that long-time associates be fired and mistakes be admitted. Moreover, it's unlikely *that* CEO would be the manager you would wish to handle the redeployment job even if he or she was inclined to undertake it.

At the shareholder level, taxes and frictional costs weigh heavily on individual investors when they attempt to reallocate capital among businesses and industries. Even tax-free institutional investors face major costs as they move capital because they usually need intermediaries to do this job. A lot of mouths with expensive tastes then clamor to be fed—among them investment bankers, accountants, consultants, lawyers and such capital-reallocators as leveraged buyout operators. Money-shufflers don't come cheap.

In contrast, a conglomerate such as Berkshire is perfectly positioned to allocate capital rationally and at minimal cost. Of course, form itself is no guarantee of success: We have made plenty of mistakes, and we will make more. Our structural advantages, however, are formidable.

At Berkshire, we can—without incurring taxes or much in the way of other costs—move huge sums from businesses that have limited opportunities for incremental investment to other sectors with greater promise. Moreover, we are free of historical biases created by lifelong association with a given industry and are not subject to pressures from colleagues having a vested interest in maintaining the status quo. That's important: If horses had controlled investment decisions, there would have been no auto industry.

Another major advantage we possess is the ability to buy *pieces* of wonderful businesses—a.k.a. common stocks. That's not a course of action open to most managements. Over our history, this strategic alternative has proved to be very helpful; a broad range of options sharpens decision-making. The businesses we are offered by the stock market every day—in small pieces, to be sure—are often far more attractive than the businesses we are concurrently being offered in their entirety. Additionally, the gains we've realized from marketable securities have helped us make certain large acquisitions that would otherwise have been beyond our financial capabilities.

In effect, the world is Berkshire's oyster—a world offering us a range of opportunities far beyond those realistically open to most companies. We are limited, of course, to businesses whose economic prospects we can evaluate. And that's a serious limitation: Charlie and I have no idea what a great many companies will look like ten years from now. But that limitation is much smaller than that borne by an executive whose experience has been confined to a single industry. On top of that, we can profitably scale to a *far* larger size than the many businesses that are constrained by the limited potential of the single industry in which they operate.

Berkshire has one further advantage that has become increasingly important over the years: We are now the home of choice for the owners and managers of many outstanding businesses. Families that own successful businesses have multiple options when they contemplate sale. Frequently, the best decision is to do nothing. There are worse things in life than having a prosperous business that one understands well. But sitting tight is seldom recommended by Wall Street. (Don't ask the barber whether you need a haircut.)

When one part of a family wishes to sell while others wish to continue, a public offering often makes sense. But, when owners wish to cash out entirely, they usually consider one of two paths. The first is sale to a competitor who is salivating at the possibility of wringing "synergies" from the combining of the two companies. This buyer invariably contemplates getting rid of large numbers of the seller's associates, the very people who have helped the owner build his business. A caring owner, however—and there are plenty of them—usually does not want to leave his long-time associates sadly singing the old country song: "*She got the goldmine, I got the shaft.*"

The second choice for sellers is the Wall Street buyer. For some years, these purchasers accurately called themselves "leveraged buyout firms." When that term got a bad name in the early 1990s—remember RJR and *Barbarians at the Gate*?—these buyers hastily relabeled themselves "private-equity." The name may have changed but that was all: Equity is dramatically *reduced* and debt is piled on in virtually all private-equity purchases. Indeed, the amount that a private-equity purchaser offers to the seller is in part determined by the buyer assessing the *maximum* amount of debt that can be placed on the acquired company.

Later, if things go well and equity begins to build, leveraged buy-out shops will often seek to re-leverage with new borrowings. They then typically use part of the proceeds to pay a huge dividend that drives equity sharply downward, sometimes even to a negative figure. In truth, "equity" is a dirty word for many private-equity buyers; what they love is debt. And, [when interest rates are very low], these buyers can frequently pay top dollar. Later, the business will be resold, often to another leveraged buyer. In effect, the business becomes a piece of merchandise.

Berkshire offers a third choice to the business owner who wishes to sell: a permanent home, in which the company's people and culture will be retained (though, occasionally, management changes will be needed). Beyond that, any business we acquire dramatically increases its financial strength and ability to grow. Its days of dealing with banks and Wall Street analysts are also forever ended. Some sellers don't care about these matters. But, when sellers do, Berkshire does not have a lot of competition.

Sometimes pundits propose that Berkshire spin-off certain of its businesses. These suggestions make no sense. Our companies are worth more as part of Berkshire than as separate entities. One reason is our ability to move funds between businesses or into new ventures instantly and without tax. In addition, certain costs duplicate themselves, in full or part, if operations are separated. Here's the most obvious example: Berkshire incurs nominal costs for its single board of directors; were our dozens of subsidiaries to be split off, the overall cost for directors would soar. So, too, would regulatory and administration expenditures.

Finally, there are sometimes important tax efficiencies for Subsidiary A because we own Subsidiary B. For example, certain tax credits that are available to our utilities are currently realizable only because we generate huge amounts of taxable income at other Berkshire operations. That gives Berkshire Hathaway Energy a major advantage over most public-utility companies in developing wind and solar projects.

Investment bankers, being paid as they are for action, constantly urge acquirers to pay 20% to 50% premiums over market price for publicly-held businesses. The bankers tell the buyer that the premium is justified for "control value" and for the wonderful things that are going to happen once the acquirer's CEO takes charge. (What acquisition-hungry manager will challenge *that* assertion?)

A few years later, bankers—bearing straight faces—again appear and just as earnestly urge spinning off the earlier acquisition in order to "unlock shareholder value." Spin-offs, of course, strip the owning company of its purported "control value" without any compensating payment. The bankers explain that the spun-off company will flourish because its management will be more entrepreneurial, having been freed from the smothering bureaucracy of the parent company. (So much for that talented CEO we met earlier.)

If the divesting company later wishes to reacquire the spun-off operation, it presumably would again be urged by its bankers to pay a hefty "control" premium for the privilege. (Mental "flexibility" of this sort by the banking fraternity has prompted the saying that fees too often lead to transactions rather than transactions leading to fees.)

It's possible, of course, that someday a spin-off or sale at Berkshire would be required by regulators. Berkshire carried out such a spin-off in 1979, when new regulations for bank holding companies forced us to divest a bank we owned in Rockford, Illinois.

Voluntary spin-offs, though, make no sense for us: We would lose control value, capital-allocation flexibility and, in some cases, important tax advantages. The CEOs who brilliantly run our subsidiaries now would have difficulty in being as effective if running a spun-off operation, given the operating and financial advantages derived from Berkshire's ownership. Moreover, the parent and the spun-off operations, once separated, would likely incur moderately greater costs than existed when they were combined.

* * * * *

Today Berkshire possesses (1) an unmatched collection of businesses, most of them now enjoying favorable economic prospects; (2) a cadre of outstanding managers who, with few exceptions, are unusually devoted to both the subsidiary they operate *and* to Berkshire; (3) an extraordinary diversity of earnings, premier financial strength and oceans of liquidity that we will maintain under *all* circumstances; (4) a first-choice ranking among many owners and managers who are contemplating sale of their businesses; and (5) in a point related to the preceding item, a culture, distinctive in many ways from that of most large companies, that we have worked 50 years to develop and that is now rock-solid. These strengths provide us a wonderful foundation on which to build.

Now let's take a look at the road ahead. Bear in mind that if I had attempted 50 years ago to gauge what was coming, certain of my predictions would have been far off the mark. With that warning, I will tell you what I would say to my family today if they asked me about Berkshire's future.

• First and definitely foremost, I believe that the chance of permanent capital loss for patient Berkshire shareholders is as low as can be found among single-company investments. That's because our per-share *intrinsic business value* is almost certain to advance over time.

This cheery prediction comes, however, with an important caution: If an investor's entry point into Berkshire stock is unusually high—at a price, say, approaching double book value, which Berkshire shares have occasionally reached—it may well be many years before the investor can realize a profit. In other words, a sound investment can morph into a rash speculation if it is bought at an elevated price. Berkshire is not exempt from this truth.

Purchases of Berkshire that investors make at a price modestly above the level at which the company would repurchase its shares, however, should produce gains within a reasonable period of time. Berkshire's directors will only authorize repurchases at a price they believe to be well below intrinsic value. (In our view, that is an essential criterion for repurchases that is often ignored by other managements.)

For those investors who plan to sell within a year or two after their purchase, I can offer *no* assurances, whatever the entry price. Movements of the general stock market during such abbreviated periods will likely be far more important in determining your results than the concomitant change in the intrinsic value of your Berkshire shares. Since I know of no way to reliably predict market movements, I recommend that you purchase Berkshire shares *only* if you expect to hold them for at least five years. Those who seek short-term profits should look elsewhere.

Another warning: Berkshire shares should not be purchased with borrowed money. There have been three times since 1965 when our stock has fallen about 50% from its high point. Someday, something close to this kind of drop will happen again, and no one knows when. Berkshire will almost certainly be a satisfactory holding for *investors*. But it could well be a disastrous choice for speculators employing leverage.

• I believe the chance of any event causing Berkshire to experience financial problems is essentially zero. We will always be prepared for the thousand-year flood; in fact, if it occurs we will be selling life jackets to the unprepared. Berkshire played an important role as a "first responder" during the 2008-2009 meltdown, and we have since more than doubled the strength of our balance sheet and our earnings potential. Your company is the Gibraltar of American business and will remain so.

Financial staying power requires a company to maintain three strengths under *all* circumstances: (1) a large and reliable stream of earnings; (2) massive liquid assets; and (3) *no* significant near-term cash requirements. Ignoring that last necessity is what usually leads companies to experience unexpected problems: Too often, CEOs of profitable companies feel they will always be able to refund maturing obligations, however large these are. In 2008-2009, many managements learned how perilous that mindset can be.

Here's how we will *always* stand on the three essentials. First, our earnings stream is huge and comes from a vast array of businesses. Our shareholders now own many large companies that have durable competitive advantages, and we will acquire more of those in the future. Our diversification assures Berkshire's continued profitability, even if a catastrophe causes insurance losses that far exceed any previously experienced.

Next up is cash. At a healthy business, cash is sometimes thought of as something to be minimized—as an unproductive asset that acts as a drag on such markers as return on equity. Cash, though, is to a business as oxygen is to an individual: never thought about when it is present, the only thing in mind when it is absent.

American business provided a case study of that in 2008. In September of that year, many long-prosperous companies suddenly wondered whether their checks would bounce in the days ahead. Overnight, their financial oxygen disappeared. At Berkshire, our "breathing" went uninterrupted. Indeed, in a three-week period spanning late September and early October, we supplied $15.6 *billion* of fresh money to American businesses. We could do that because we always maintain at least $20 billion—and usually far more—in cash equivalents. And by that we mean U.S. Treasury bills, not other substitutes for cash that are claimed to deliver liquidity and actually do so, *except* when it is truly needed. When bills come due, only cash is legal tender. Don't leave home without it.

Finally—getting to our third point—we will never engage in operating or investment practices that can result in sudden demands for large sums. That means we will not expose Berkshire to short-term debt maturities of size nor enter into derivative contracts or other business arrangements that could require large collateral calls.

Some years ago, we became a party to certain derivative contracts that we believed were significantly mispriced and that had only minor collateral requirements. These have proved to be quite profitable. Recently, however, newly-written derivative contracts have required full collateralization. And that ended our interest in derivatives, regardless of what profit potential they might offer. We have not, for some years, written these contracts, except for a few needed for operational purposes at our utility businesses.

Moreover, we will not write insurance contracts that give policyholders the right to cash out at their option. Many *life* insurance products contain redemption features that make them susceptible to a "run" in times of extreme panic. Contracts of that sort, however, do not exist in the property-casualty world that we inhabit. If our premium volume should shrink, our float would decline—but only at a very slow pace.

The reason for our conservatism, which may impress some people as extreme, is that it is entirely predictable that people will occasionally panic, but not at all predictable when this will happen. Though practically all days are relatively uneventful, tomorrow is *always* uncertain. (I felt no special apprehension on December 6, 1941 or September 10, 2001.) And if you can't predict what tomorrow will bring, you must be prepared for whatever it does.

A CEO who is 64 and plans to retire at 65 may have his own special calculus in evaluating risks that have only a tiny chance of happening in a given year. He may, in fact, be "right" 99% of the time. Those odds, however, hold no appeal for us. We will never play financial Russian roulette with the funds you've entrusted to us, even if the metaphorical gun has 100 chambers and only one bullet. In our view, it is madness to risk losing what you *need* in pursuing what you simply *desire*.

• Despite our conservatism, I think we will be able *every* year to build the underlying per-share earning power of Berkshire. That does *not* mean operating earnings will increase each year—far from it. The U.S. economy will ebb and flow—though mostly flow—and, when it weakens, so will our current earnings. But we will continue to achieve organic gains, make bolt-on acquisitions and enter new fields. I believe, therefore, that Berkshire will annually add to its *underlying* earning power.

In some years the gains will be substantial, and at other times they will be minor. Markets, competition, and chance will determine when opportunities come our way. Through it all, Berkshire will keep moving forward, powered by the array of solid businesses we now possess and the new companies we will purchase. In most years, moreover, our country's economy will provide a strong tailwind for business. We are blessed to have the United States as our home field.

• The bad news is that Berkshire's long-term gains—measured by percentages, not by dollars—cannot be dramatic and *will not come close* to those achieved in the past 50 years. The numbers have become too big. I think Berkshire will outperform the average American company, but our advantage, if any, won't be great.

Eventually—probably between ten and twenty years from now—Berkshire's earnings and capital resources will reach a level that will not allow management to intelligently reinvest all of the company's earnings. At that time our directors will need to determine whether the best method to distribute the excess earnings is through dividends, share repurchases or both. If Berkshire shares are selling below intrinsic business value, massive repurchases will almost certainly be the best choice. You can be comfortable that your directors will make the right decision.

• No company will be more shareholder-minded than Berkshire. For more than 30 years, we have annually reaffirmed our Shareholder Principles (reprinted in the Prologue), always leading off with: "Although our form is corporate, our attitude is partnership." This covenant with you is etched in stone. We have an extraordinarily knowledgeable and business-oriented board of directors ready to carry out that promise of partnership.

To further ensure continuation of our culture, I have suggested that my son, Howard, succeed me as a *non-executive* Chairman. My only reason for this wish is to make change easier if the wrong CEO should ever be employed and there occurs a need for the Chairman to move forcefully. I can assure you that this problem has a *very* low probability of arising at Berkshire—likely as low as at any public company. In my service on the boards of nineteen public companies, however, I've seen how hard it is to replace a mediocre CEO if that person is also Chairman. (The deed usually gets done, but almost always very late.)

If elected, Howard will receive no pay and will spend no time at the job other than that required of all directors. He will simply be a safety valve to whom any director can go if he or she has concerns about the CEO and wishes to learn if other directors are expressing doubts as well. Should multiple directors be apprehensive, Howard's chairmanship will allow the matter to be promptly and properly addressed.

• Choosing the right CEO is all-important and is a subject that commands much time at Berkshire board meetings. Managing Berkshire is primarily a job of capital allocation, coupled with the selection and retention of outstanding managers to captain our operating subsidiaries. Obviously, the job also requires the replacement of a subsidiary's CEO when that is called for. These duties require Berkshire's CEO to be a rational, calm and decisive individual who has a broad understanding of business and good insights into human behavior. It's important as well that he knows his limits.

Character is crucial: A Berkshire CEO must be "all in" for the company, not for himself. (I'm using male pronouns to avoid awkward wording, but gender should never decide who becomes CEO.) He can't help but earn money far in excess of any possible need for it. But it's important that neither ego nor avarice motivate him to reach for pay matching his most lavishly-compensated peers, even if his achievements far exceed theirs. A CEO's behavior has a huge impact on managers down the line: If it's clear to them that shareholders' interests are paramount to him, they will, with few exceptions, also embrace that way of thinking.

My successor will need one other particular strength: the ability to fight off the ABCs of business decay, which are arrogance, bureaucracy and complacency. When these corporate cancers metastasize, even the strongest of companies can falter. The examples available to prove the point are legion, but to maintain friendships I will exhume only cases from the distant past.

In their glory days, General Motors, IBM, Sears Roebuck and U.S. Steel sat atop huge industries. Their strengths seemed unassailable. But the destructive behavior I deplored above eventually led each of them to fall to depths that their CEOs and directors had not long before thought impossible. Their one-time financial strength and their historical earning power proved no defense.

Only a vigilant and determined CEO can ward off such debilitating forces as Berkshire grows ever larger. He must never forget Charlie's plea: "Tell me where I'm going to die, so I'll never go there." If our non-economic values were to be lost, much of Berkshire's economic value would collapse as well. "Tone at the top" will be key to maintaining Berkshire's special culture.

Fortunately, the structure our future CEOs will need to be successful is firmly in place. The extraordinary delegation of authority now existing at Berkshire is the ideal antidote to bureaucracy. In an operating sense, Berkshire is not a giant company but rather a collection of large companies. At headquarters, we have never had a committee nor have we ever required our subsidiaries to submit budgets (though many use them as an important internal tool). We don't have a legal office nor departments that other companies take for granted: human relations, public relations, investor relations, strategy, acquisitions, you name it.

We do, of course, have an active audit function; no sense being a damned fool. To an unusual degree, however, we trust our managers to run their operations with a keen sense of stewardship. After all, they were doing exactly that before we acquired their businesses. With only occasional exceptions, furthermore, our trust produces better results than would be achieved by streams of directives, endless reviews and layers of bureaucracy. Charlie and I try to interact with our managers in a manner consistent with what we would wish for, if the positions were reversed.

• Our directors believe that our future CEOs should come from internal candidates whom the Berkshire board has grown to know well. Our directors also believe that an incoming CEO should be relatively young, so that he or she can have a long run in the job. Berkshire will operate best if its CEOs average well over ten years at the helm. (It's hard to teach a new dog old tricks.) And they are not likely to retire at 65 either (or have you noticed?).

In both Berkshire's business acquisitions and large, tailored investment moves, it is important that our counterparties be both familiar with and feel comfortable with Berkshire's CEO. Developing confidence of that sort and cementing relationships takes time. The payoff, though, can be huge. Both the board and I believe we now have the right person to succeed me as CEO—a successor ready to assume the job the day after I die or step down. In certain important respects, this person will do a better job than I am doing.

• Investments will always be of great importance to Berkshire and will be handled by several specialists. They will report to the CEO because their investment decisions, in a broad way, will need to be coordinated with Berkshire's operating and acquisition programs. Overall, though, our investment managers will enjoy great autonomy. In this area, too, we are in fine shape for decades to come.

All told, Berkshire is ideally positioned for life after Charlie and I leave the scene. We have the right people in place—the right directors, managers and prospective successors to those managers. Our culture, furthermore, is embedded throughout their ranks. Our system is also regenerative. To a large degree, both good and bad cultures self-select to perpetuate themselves. For very good reasons, business owners and operating managers with values similar to ours will continue to be attracted to Berkshire as a one-of-a-kind and *permanent* home.

B. *Munger on "The Berkshire System"*[79]

The management system and policies of Berkshire under Buffett (the "Berkshire system") were fixed early: Berkshire would be a diffuse conglomerate, averse only to activities about which it could not make useful predictions; the parent company would do almost all business through separately incorporated subsidiaries whose CEOs would operate with extreme autonomy; there would be almost nothing at conglomerate headquarters except a tiny office suite containing a Chairman, a CFO, and a few assistants; Berkshire subsidiaries would always prominently include casualty insurers (which as a group would be expected to produce dependable underwriting gains while also producing substantial "float" for investment); there would be no significant system-wide personnel system, stock option system, other incentive system, retirement system, or the like, because the subsidiaries would have their own systems, often different.

Berkshire's Chairman would reserve only a few activities for himself: (i) manage almost all security investments, with these normally residing in Berkshire's casualty insurers; (ii) choose all CEOs of important subsidiaries, and fix their compensation and obtain from each a private recommendation for a successor; (iii) deploy most cash not needed in subsidiaries after they had increased their competitive advantage, with the ideal deployment being to acquire new subsidiaries; (iv) make himself promptly available for almost any contact wanted by any subsidiary's CEO, and require almost no additional contact; (v) write a long, logical, and useful letter for inclusion in his annual report, designed as he would wish it to be if he were only a passive shareholder, and be available for hours of answering questions at annual shareholders' meetings; (vi) try to be an exemplar in a culture that would work well for customers, shareholders, and other [constituents] for a long time, both before and after his departure; (vii) [reserve] much time for quiet reading and thinking, particularly that which might advance his determined learning, no matter how old he became; and (viii) spend much time in enthusiastically admiring what others were accomplishing.

---

[79] [This essay was written by Charles T. Munger to Berkshire Hathaway shareholders for the 50th Anniversary section of the company's 2014 annual report. The format of what follows is edited slightly, to conserve space and make reading easier, principally by omitting tabulation and numerals assigned to various lists.]

New subsidiaries would usually be bought with cash, not newly issued stock; Berkshire would not pay dividends so long as more than one dollar of market value for shareholders was being created by each dollar of retained earnings; in buying a new subsidiary, Berkshire would seek to pay a fair price for a good business that the Chairman could understand. Berkshire would also want a good CEO in place, one expected to remain for a long time and to manage well without need for help from headquarters; in choosing CEOs of subsidiaries, Berkshire would try to secure trustworthiness, skill, energy, and love for the business and circumstances the CEO was in.

As an important matter of preferred conduct, Berkshire would almost never sell a subsidiary; Berkshire would almost never transfer a subsidiary's CEO to another unrelated subsidiary; Berkshire would never force the CEO of a subsidiary to retire on account of mere age; Berkshire would have little debt outstanding as it tried to maintain virtually perfect creditworthiness under all conditions and easy availability of cash and credit for deployment in times presenting unusual opportunities; and Berkshire would always be user-friendly to a prospective seller of a large business. An offer of such a business would get prompt attention. No one but the Chairman and one or two others at Berkshire would ever know about the offer if it did not lead to a transaction. And they would never tell outsiders about it.

Both the elements of the Berkshire system and their collected size are quite unusual. No other large corporation I know of has half of such elements in place. How did Berkshire happen to get a corporate personality so different from the norm? Buffett, even when only 34 years old, controlled about 45% of Berkshire's shares and was completely trusted by all the other big shareholders. He could install whatever system he wanted. And he did so, creating the Berkshire system. Almost every element was chosen because Buffett believed that, under him, it would help maximize Berkshire's achievement. He was not trying to create a one-type-fits-all system for other corporations. Indeed, Berkshire's subsidiaries were not required to use the Berkshire system in their own operations. And some flourished while using different systems.

What was Buffett aiming at as he designed the Berkshire system? Over the years I diagnosed several important themes. [He wanted]: continuous maximization of the rationality, skills, and devotion of the most important people in the system, starting with himself; win/win results everywhere—in gaining loyalty by giving it, for instance; decisions that maximized long-term results, seeking these from decision makers who usually stayed long enough in place to bear the consequences of decisions; to minimize the bad effects that would almost inevitably come from a large bureaucracy at headquarters; to personally contribute, like Professor Ben Graham, to the spread of wisdom attained.

When Buffett developed the Berkshire system, did he foresee all the benefits that followed? No. Buffett stumbled into some benefits through practice evolution. But, when he saw useful consequences, he strengthened their causes. Why did Berkshire under Buffett do so well? Only four large factors occur to me: the constructive peculiarities of Buffett; the constructive peculiarities of the Berkshire system; good luck, and the weirdly intense, contagious devotion of some shareholders and other admirers, including some in the press. I believe all four factors were present and helpful. But the heavy freight was carried by the constructive peculiarities, the weird devotion, and their interactions.

Buffett's decision to limit his activities to a few kinds and to maximize his attention to them, and to keep doing so for 50 years, was a lollapalooza. Buffett was, in effect, using the winning method of the famous basketball coach, John Wooden, who won most regularly after he had learned to assign virtually all playing time to his seven best players. That way, opponents always faced his best players, instead of his second best. And, with the extra playing time, the best players improved more than was normal.

Buffett much out-Woodened Wooden, because in his case the exercise of skill was concentrated in one person, not seven, and his skill improved and improved as he got older and older during 50 years, instead of deteriorating like the skill of a basketball player does. Moreover, by concentrating so much power and authority in the often-long-serving CEOs of important subsidiaries, Buffett was also creating strong Wooden-type effects there. And such effects enhanced the skills of the CEOs and the achievements of the subsidiaries.

Then, as the Berkshire system bestowed much-desired autonomy on many subsidiaries and their CEOs, and Berkshire became successful and well known, these outcomes attracted both more and better subsidiaries into Berkshire, and better CEOs as well. And the better subsidiaries and CEOs then required less attention from headquarters, creating what is often called a "virtuous circle."

How well did it work out for Berkshire to always include casualty insurers as important subsidiaries? Marvelously well. Berkshire's ambitions were unreasonably extreme and, even so, it got what it wanted. Casualty insurers often invest in common stocks with a value amounting roughly to their shareholders' equity, as did Berkshire's insurance subsidiaries. And the S&P 500 Index produced about 10% per annum, pre-tax, during the last 50 years, creating a significant tailwind.

In the early decades of the Buffett era, common stocks within Berkshire's insurance subsidiaries greatly outperformed the index, exactly as Buffett expected; later, when both the large size of Berkshire's stockholdings and income tax considerations caused the index-beating part of returns to fade to insignificance (perhaps not forever), other and better advantage came. Ajit Jain created out of nothing an immense reinsurance business that produced both a huge "float" and a large underwriting gain. All of GEICO came into Berkshire, followed by a quadrupling of GEICO's market share. The rest of Berkshire's insurance operations hugely improved, largely by dint of reputational advantage, underwriting discipline, finding and staying within good niches, and recruiting and holding outstanding people.

Later, as Berkshire's nearly unique and quite dependable corporate personality and large size became well known, its insurance subsidiaries got and seized many attractive opportunities, not available to others, to buy privately issued securities. Most of these securities had fixed maturities and produced outstanding results. Berkshire's marvelous outcome in insurance was not a natural result. Ordinarily, a casualty insurance business is a producer of mediocre results, even when very well managed. And such results are of little use. Berkshire's better outcome was so astoundingly large that I believe that Buffett would now fail to recreate it if he returned to a small base while retaining his smarts and regaining his youth.

Did Berkshire suffer from being a diffuse conglomerate? No, its opportunities were usefully enlarged by a widened area for operation. And bad effects, common elsewhere, were prevented by Buffett's skills. Why did Berkshire prefer to buy companies with cash, instead of its own stock? It was hard to get anything in exchange for Berkshire stock that was as valuable as what was given up. Why did Berkshire's acquisition of companies outside the insurance business work out so well for Berkshire shareholders when the normal result in such acquisitions is bad for shareholders of the acquirer?

Berkshire, by design, had methodological advantages to supplement its better opportunities. It never had the equivalent of a "department of acquisitions" under pressure to buy. And it never relied on advice from "helpers" sure to be prejudiced in favor of transactions. And Buffett held self-delusion at bay as he underclaimed expertise while he knew better than most corporate executives what worked and what didn't in business, aided by his long experience as a passive investor. And, finally, even when Berkshire was getting much better opportunities than most others, Buffett often displayed almost inhuman patience and seldom bought. For instance, during his first ten years in control of Berkshire, Buffett saw one business (textiles) move close to death and two new businesses come in, for a net gain of one.

What were the big mistakes made by Berkshire under Buffett? While mistakes of commission were common, almost all huge errors were in not making a purchase, including not purchasing Walmart stock when that was sure to work out enormously well. The errors of omission were of much importance. Berkshire's net worth would now be at least $50 billion higher if it had seized several opportunities it was not quite smart enough to recognize as virtually sure things.

[Would] abnormally good results continue at Berkshire if Buffett were soon to depart? The answer is yes. Berkshire has in place in its subsidiaries much business momentum grounded in much durable competitive advantage. Moreover, its railroad and utility subsidiaries now provide much desirable opportunity to invest large sums in new fixed assets. And many subsidiaries are now engaged in making wise "bolt-on" acquisitions. Provided that most of the Berkshire system remains in place, the combined momentum and opportunity now present is so great that Berkshire [will] almost surely remain a better-than-normal company for a very long time.

[Finally,] consider whether Berkshire's great results over the last 50 years have implications that may prove useful elsewhere. The answer is plainly yes. In its early Buffett years, Berkshire had a big task ahead: turning a tiny stash into a large and useful company. And it solved that problem by avoiding bureaucracy and relying much on one thoughtful leader for a long, long time as he kept improving and brought in more people like himself.

Compare this to a typical big-corporation system with much bureaucracy at headquarters and a long succession of CEOs who come in at about age 59, pause little thereafter for quiet thought, and are soon forced out by a fixed retirement age. I believe that versions of the Berkshire system should be tried more often elsewhere and that the worst attributes of bureaucracy should much more often be treated like the cancers they so much resemble.

C.   Methuselah's Estate[80]

A fat wallet is the enemy of superior investment results. And Berkshire now has a [massive] net worth compared to when Charlie and I began to manage the company. Though there are as many good businesses as ever, it is useless for us to make purchases that are inconsequential in relation to Berkshire's capital. Given that, Berkshire's investment universe has shrunk dramatically.

Nevertheless, we will stick with the approach that got us here and try not to relax our standards. Ted Williams, in *The Story of My Life*, explains why: "My argument is, to be a good hitter, you've got to get a good ball to hit. It's the first rule in the book. If I have to bite at stuff that is out of my happy zone, I'm not a .344 hitter. I might only be a .250 hitter." Charlie and I agree and will try to wait for opportunities that are well within our own "happy zone."

We will continue to ignore political and economic forecasts, which are an expensive distraction for many investors and businessmen. Thirty years ago, no one could have foreseen the huge expansion of the Vietnam War, wage and price controls, two oil shocks, the resignation of a president, the dissolution of the Soviet Union, a one-day drop in the Dow of 508 points, or treasury bill yields fluctuating between 2.8% and 17.4%.

But, surprise—none of these blockbuster events made the slightest dent in Ben Graham's investment principles. Nor did they render unsound the negotiated purchases of fine businesses at sensible prices. Imagine the cost to us, then, if we had let a fear of unknowns cause us to defer or alter the deployment of capital. Indeed, we have usually made our best purchases when apprehensions about some macro event were at a peak. Fear is the foe of the faddist, but the friend of the fundamentalist.

A different set of major shocks is sure to occur in the next 30 years. We will neither try to predict these nor to profit from them. If we can identify businesses similar to those we have purchased in the past, external surprises will have little effect on our long-term results.

---

[80] [Divided by hash lines: 1994; 2005; 2006; 1996 Owner's Manual updated annually.]

We achieved our gains through the efforts of a superb corps of operating managers who get extraordinary results from some ordinary-appearing businesses. Casey Stengel described managing a baseball team as "getting paid for home runs other fellows hit." That's my formula at Berkshire, also.

It's far better to own a significant portion of the Hope diamond than 100% of a rhinestone, and the companies just mentioned easily qualify as rare gems. Best of all, we aren't limited to simply a few of this breed, but instead possess a growing collection.

Stock prices will continue to fluctuate—sometimes sharply—and the economy will have its ups and downs. Over time, however, we believe it is highly probable that the sort of businesses we own will continue to increase in value at a satisfactory rate.

As owners, you are naturally concerned about whether I will insist on continuing as CEO after I begin to fade and, if so, how the board will handle that problem. That problem would not be unique to me. Charlie and I have faced this situation from time to time at Berkshire's subsidiaries.

Humans age at greatly varying rates—but sooner or later their talents and vigor decline. Some managers remain effective well into their 80s and others noticeably fade in their 60s. When their abilities ebb, so usually do their powers of self-assessment. Someone else often needs to blow the whistle. When that time comes for me, our board will have to step up to the job. From a financial standpoint, its members are unusually motivated to do so. I know of no other board in the country in which the financial interests of directors are so completely aligned with those of shareholders. Few boards even come close. On a personal level, however, it is extraordinarily difficult for most people to tell someone, particularly a friend, that he or she is no longer capable.

If I become a candidate for that message, however, our board will be doing me a favor by delivering it. Every share of Berkshire that I own is destined to go to philanthropies, and I want society to reap the maximum good from these gifts and bequests. It would be a tragedy if the philanthropic potential of my holdings was diminished because my associates shirked their responsibility to (tenderly, I hope) show me the door. But don't worry about this. We have an outstanding group of directors, and they will always do what's right for shareholders.

I [have] arranged for the bulk of my Berkshire holdings to go to five charitable foundations, thus carrying out part of my lifelong plan to eventually use all of my shares for philanthropic purposes. In my will I've stipulated that the proceeds from all Berkshire shares I still own at death are to be used for philanthropic purposes within ten years after my estate is closed. Because my affairs are not complicated, it should take three years at most for this closing to occur. Adding this 13-year period to my expected lifespan means that proceeds from all of my Berkshire shares will likely be distributed for societal purposes over the next [two decades].

I've set this schedule because I want the money to be spent relatively promptly by people I know to be capable, vigorous and motivated. These managerial attributes sometimes wane as institutions—particularly those that are exempt from market forces—age. Today, there are terrific people in charge at the five foundations. So at my death, why should they not move with dispatch to judiciously spend the money that remains?

Those people favoring perpetual foundations argue that in the future there will most certainly be large and important societal problems that philanthropy will need to address. I agree. But there will then also be many super-rich individuals and families whose wealth will exceed that of today's Americans and to whom philanthropic organizations can make their case for funding.

These funders can then judge first-hand which operations have both the vitality and the focus to best address the major societal problems that then exist. In this way, a market test of ideas and effectiveness can be applied. Some organizations will deserve major support while others will have outlived their usefulness. Even if the people above ground make their decisions imperfectly, they should be able to allocate funds more rationally than a decedent six feet under will have ordained decades earlier. Wills, of course, can always be rewritten, but it's very unlikely that my thinking will change in a material way.

———————

Lest we end on a morbid note, I also want to assure you that I have never felt better. I love running Berkshire, and if enjoying life promotes longevity, Methuselah's record is in jeopardy.[81]

———————

[81] [According to the Bible, Methuselah lived 969 years. *Genesis* 5:27.]

INDEX

Concept Glossary

Cigar Butt Investing. A foolish method of investing akin to taking the last puff on a cigar, it is the purchase of a stock at a sufficiently low price that there will be some short-term profit, though the business' long-term performance is likely to be terrible. *See* Part II.G.

Circle of Competence. The limits of one's ability to judge the economics of businesses, intelligent investors draw a thick boundary and stick with companies they can understand. *See* Part II.F.

Dividend Test. Retention of earnings is only justified if each dollar retained produces at least a one dollar increase in per share market value. *See* Part IV.C.

Double-Barreled Acquisition Style. A sensible acquisition policy of buying either 100% of businesses in negotiated acquisitions or less than 100% in stock market purchases. *See* Prologue.

Institutional Imperative. A pervasive force in organizations that leads to irrational business decisions from resistance to change, absorption of corporate funds in suboptimal projects or acquisitions, indulgence of the cravings of senior executives, and mindless imitation of peer companies. *See* Part II.G.

Intrinsic Value. A hard-to-calculate but crucial measure of business value, it is the discounted present value of the cash that can be taken out of a business during its remaining life. *See* Part VI.B.

Look-through Earnings. An alternative to GAAP rules governing investments in marketable securities of the investee less than 20%, this measures the investor's economic performance based on its percentage interest of the investee's undistributed earnings (after an incremental reduction for income taxes). *See* Part VI.C.

Margin-of-Safety. Probably the single most important principle of sound and successful investing, Ben Graham's principle says not to purchase a security unless the price being paid is substantially lower than the value being delivered. *See* Part II.E.

Mr. Market. Ben Graham's allegory for the overall stock market, a moody manic-depressive where price and value diverge, making superior intelligent investing possible. *See* Part II.B.

Owner Earnings. A better measure of economic performance than cash flow or GAAP earnings, equal to *(a)* operating earnings *plus* *(b)* depreciation and other non-cash charges *minus* *(c)* required reinvestment in a business to maintain present competitive position and unit volume. *See* Part VI.E.

311

Disposition Summary

The disposition table on the opposite page shows where in this collection you may find excerpts from various annual letters. The far columns on the left and right indicate the year of each letter, beginning with *79* for 1979 and going through *14* for 2014. Across the top of the rows the table divides the collection according to its Parts (I through IX) and its sub-headings (such as A through H). Letters excerpted in the opening paragraphs of a Part are reported in the table as being excerpted in Section A of that Part. The Prologue is from 1979 and 1996. This disposition table may be of special interest to those who have read previous editions carefully, to see what is new and some rearrangements that have been made.

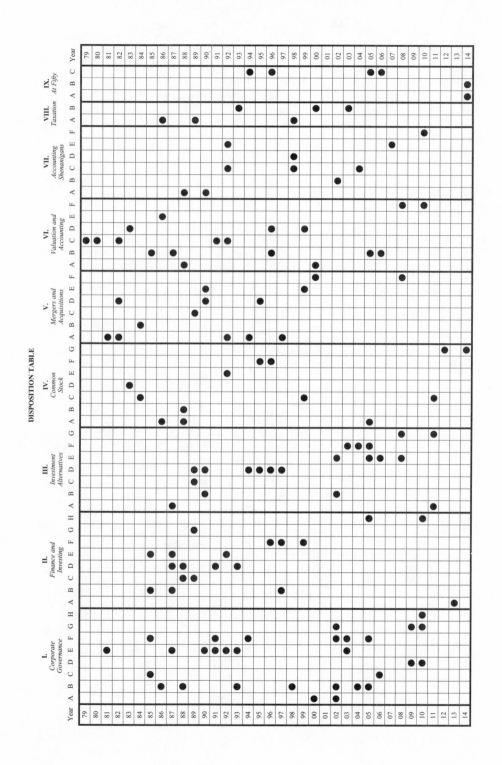